An artist's impression of the action between S.E.5as of No. 24 Squadron, R.A.F. and a Fokker D-VII of Jagdstaffel 15, in which Leutnant Kurt Wüsthoff was shot down to become a prisoner-of-war—painted specially for 'Fighter Aircraft of the 1914–1918 War' by J. D. Carrick.

FIGHTER AIRCRAFT
OF THE 1914-1918 WAR

Compiled by

W. M. LAMBERTON

Edited by

E. F. CHEESMAN

Drawings by

J. D. CARRICK *and* **F. YEOMAN**

Produced by **D. A. RUSSELL,** *M.I.Mech.E.*

First Published Summer 1960

COPYRIGHT © *1964 by*

HARLEYFORD PUBLICATIONS LIMITED
LETCHWORTH, HERTS

Published in the

UNITED STATES OF AMERICA

by

AERO PUBLISHERS, INC.

Library of Congress Card No.

60-11220

MADE AND PRINTED IN THE U.S.A. BY

AERO PUBLISHERS, INC. 329 AVIATION ROAD FALLBROOK, CALIF.

SQUADRON LINE-UPS

The 95th American Aero Squadron—seen here preparatory to a patrol—was formed in February 1918 and like other American units, flew French designed and built aircraft, first the Nieuport 28 and later the Spad 13.

A line-up of S.E.5a aircraft of No. 2 Squadron, Australian Flying Corps in France 1918. The 'Boomerang' marking (seen on the fuselage of the far right aircraft) was used also by No. 4 Squadron, A.F.C. on their Sopwith Camels.

Fokker D-VIIs of Jagdstaffel 11—one of the component units of the famous Jagdgeschwader Frhr. von Richthofen No. 1. Such outstanding pilots as Udet, Lothar von Richthofen, Wolff, Reinhard and Weiss, flew in this squadron.

The year 1960 appears to mark the 'beginning of the end' of manned fighter aircraft. Most of the World's Air Forces, certainly the major ones, now accept the fact that fighter aircraft no longer have a worthwhile future in military operations. These Powers are commencing to run down their programmes of experimentation and development of this type of warplane, as indeed they must do in the face of modern requirement of Air-War.

This book, however, is not concerned with the future, but with that period of some forty to fifty years ago; when the forcing house of a World War produced the first military aircraft, and in a space of only four years developed the designs from mere 'stick-and-string' creations, to the highly specialised types evolved and used at the end of that conflict.

'Air Aces of the 1914–1918 War,' which dealt with the fighter *pilots*, has well satisfied the seekers after facts in that connection. The present volume now completes the picture by describing the *aircraft* in which these Aces flew. Thus it came about that I was asked to co-ordinate the work of four men, who were already well known as enthusiastic researchers of this period. Our directive was, indeed, to compile a companion to the 'Aces' book, and I could hardly have wished for a Team with more application and ability. Such success as this book achieves will be largely due to their whole-hearted efforts through the three-year period of preparation.

After careful consideration it was agreed that eighty-four aircraft would need to be illustrated with text, photographs and 1/72 scale three-view drawings. Consequently a very large amount of material had to be found prior to describing these aircraft, and the search for such data and photographs continued for a number of years through various friends and associates on an International basis. The problem of finding this material can best be likened to the completing of a jig-saw puzzle, the pieces of which had been scattered world-wide!

With the help of these friends at home and abroad we have collected a vast amount of information and numerous photographs, so that Bill Lamberton and Bruce Robertson have had the best available sources from which to compose the descriptive text to illustrate their respective sections. Frank Yeoman and Douglas Carrick have likewise benefited in their preparation of the drawings, some of which appear for the first time ever. My appreciation and thanks are also due to Mrs. Carrick, Miss Yeoman and Bill Hepworth who have so successfully traced the eighty-four drawings with such a high degree of accuracy and consistency. Many other enthusiasts were contributors, to a greater or lesser extent, of valuable material . . . there are too many of them to list fully, but acknowledgement is hereby made of their helpfulness.

However, I take this opportunity of expressing the thanks of the Team to all those who have made our task easier by their help so freely given. Special mention is due to J. M. Bruce and Peter Gray for their assistance (both seen and unseen) and also to Heinz J. Nowarra who has been a constant and willing donor of information and photographs.

The customary complete co-operation of the Imperial War Museum staff in the person of the Deputy-Director, A. J. Charge, Esq., M.B.E., J. L. Golding, Esq., C. V. McCann, Esq., and Miss R. Coombs was received; and their efforts on our behalf are much appreciated. Our thanks are due also to Major Bryant, Director, and Mark Sloan, Associate Director of the Air Force Museum, Wright Patterson Air Force Base, Ohio, U.S.A., for the loan of many useful and interesting documents and photographs.

Finally, I acknowledge the co-operation and skill of P. J. Jago, professional photographer of Letchworth, who so ably copied and enlarged or reduced some hundreds of photographs for use in this book.

Letchworth, 1960   E. F. Cheesman

ACKNOWLEDGEMENTS FOR PHOTOGRAPHS

I wish to acknowledge gratefully the loan of photographs and documents from the following sources: Air Ministry, G. Apostolo, Major K. S. Brown, J. M. Bruce, M.A., Lt.-Col. J. Castle, C. C. H. Cole, G. A. Cull, L. A. Dell, H. W. G. Debenham, Wg.-Cdr. Dimmock, A.F.C., The Director Science Museum, London, Major C. Draper, D.S.C., The Editor of *Flight*, J. Garwood, B. T. Gibbins, D. S. Glover, P. L. Gray, A. B. Guidotti, G. Hardie, Junr., H. D. Hastings, N. H. Hauprich, H. Hugener, Imperial War Museum, G. S. Leslie, Capt. C. J. Marchant, M.C., H. B. Norris, J. B. Petty, W. Pollard, W. R. Puglisi, Real Photographs, Ltd., Rolls-Royce Ltd., and H. H. Russell.

PUBLISHER'S NOTES

Although this volume deals fully in text and drawings with eighty-four Fighter Aircraft, reference to the Index will reveal that over 300 aircraft are mentioned and or illustrated. Additional, the eighty-four aircraft which form the basis of the book are often referred to on numerous occasions apart from their individual descriptions, and it was therefore felt that a special method of indexing would prove convenient and valuable to the reader.

Where an aircraft is specifically dealt with in text and photographs, the page on which this information appears is indicated by HEAVY TYPE. Similarly, where an aircraft is illustrated by a three-view drawing, the page number followed by the letter 'P' appears in heavy type.

Page numbers indexed in standard type indicate further reference in text and photographs. Special sections deal with Armament, Camouflage, and Engines and these are indexed separately. These three Indices, used in conjunction with the rapid-reference Master Tables immediately preceding them, will provide the reader with all the information for which he seeks.

The eighty-four three-view drawings in this book are all drawn to the popular 1/72 scale (one inch = six feet).

Numbering of photographs in the groups facing the drawings is 1–5 from top to bottom. Numbering of photographs in the chapters on Armament, Camouflage, and other groups of photographs is from top to bottom, and where photographs appear side-by-side, it is from left to right. Numbering of photographs where eight, nine or ten are grouped on one page, is from top to bottom, left column first then right column.

About This Book

By **D. A. RUSSELL**, *M.I.Mech.E.*

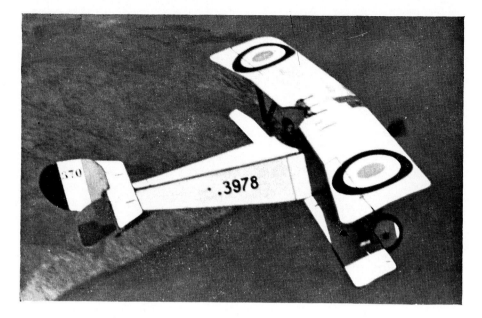

Air-to-air photographs of W.W.1 aircraft are especially rare, but here is an excellent example of one. A Nieuport 11 Scout of No. 2 Wing R.N.A.S., flown by Lieutenant Bettington, is seen over the Gulf of Smyrna in 1916.

The world-wide interest in the many aspects of early military aviation continues to expand, and perhaps to the greatest degree in the complementary subjects of Fighter Aircraft and their Pilots.

Publication of 'von Richthofen and the Flying Circus' in 1958, followed by 'Air Aces of the 1914–1918 War', in 1959, in the steadily expanding series of 'Harborough' Air Historical Books, was the natural result of this interest. Both of these books have had to be reprinted, so great was the enthusiasm with which they were received, supported by the oft-expressed hope that further books on this and similar subjects would be forthcoming as the years went by.

Bearing in mind the success of, and the continuing increasing demand for, the 1945 and 1954 editions of 'Aircraft of the 1914–1918 War' (which went out of print in 1956) it was at that time decided to produce an entirely new book. This would be a companion to 'Air Aces of the 1914–1918 War' in that it was devoted entirely to *Fighter Aircraft* of the 1914–1918 War. Thus it was, that early in 1957 work commenced and continued without interruption into early 1960, and resulted in the publication of this present book.

As is the standard practice with 'Harborough' books, a Team rather than an individual has undertaken this work, an arrangement whereby the specialised knowledge of a number of experts might best be combined in producing a fully authoritative book. Their aim has been primarily to review the operational fighter type of the combatant Nations in a comprehensive manner; from the prototype (and in some instances, forerunners), to the ultimate version of the design as actually used in the 1914–1918 War.

A number of aircraft in the fighter category which due to their later appearance on the scene did not actually see action, have been deemed worthy of inclusion; as also certain experimental types, with the intention of indicating the line of development along which every country proceeded in the matter of fighter aircraft design. Also in the book there appears a large selection of photographs of other aircraft depicting, with brief details, experimental designs or variants of those types which were used at the front.

It will be noted that there are a number of photographs of two-seater aircraft. These were used either by force of circumstances or design. Indeed, perusal of the victory claims by two-seater crews more than justifies the inclusion of these types.

For many years it has been the tradition that 'Harborough' books are well illustrated so as to 'show the story' to the fullest possible extent, and naturally a book such as this demanded a continuation of this policy. Indeed it is quite obvious that justice could only be done to this particular subject by including very many illustrations with which to augment the text.

To this end more than 2,000 photographs were collected from many parts of the world and considered for a final selection of just over 700. Never before has such a complete and varied photographic coverage of aircraft of the 1914–1918 War been achieved in one book. The quality of the prints and their suitability to illustrate certain features has been the guiding factor in the final choice, and the inclusion of the occasional photograph of rather poor quality was considered to be justified where it was either the only one available and/or demonstrated a particular feature of the aircraft type in question. All the photographs are, of course, over forty years old, and

The cockpit of a British Sopwith Camel, the most versatile and highest-scoring of all 1914–1918 fighters.

readers may be interested to know that of the 700 selected for publication, over 400 had to be copied and either reduced or enlarged so that they could be suitably grouped with the remainder. The consequent grouping and mounting alone entailed several hundred man-hours of work.

This vast photographic coverage would not have been possible without the invaluable assistance of numerous individuals who donated photographs or loaned albums, and to whom my sincere thanks are offered. While it has always been my aim to avoid repetition in the use of photographs, adequate coverage in the present book would not have been possible without repetition of a few which have been used before in 'Harborough' books. Nevertheless many of the photographs have never before been published having been copied from personal albums.

In accordance with the well-established policy in previous 'Harborough' publications, as many as eighty-four 1/72 scale three-view general arrangement drawings have been prepared, after extensive research.

The selection of the 420 photographs which illustrate the main section of the book necessitated the inclusion of a number of types which have a considerable resemblance to one another.

It was considered to be wasteful of space and unnecessary duplication to provide drawings of each of these particular types, and in these cases the most representative aircraft have been illustrated. However, no loss of information has been sustained, as each type has been dealt with in the Tables of power units, dimensions, armament and performance data which are at the end of the book.

The Tables of dimensions, armament and performance figures have been compiled after intensive consideration of the various figures quoted by different sources. Those regarded as the most reliable have been used. Performance figures are notoriously variable and range from those supplied by the Constructors (often very optimistic) to those found as a result of evaluating tests made by Technical Departments on a captured aircraft (sometimes quite pessimistic!).

Since a fighter aircraft was essentially a gun platform, information on this all-important feature and its development throughout the 1914–1918 War was essential if this book was to be completely comprehensive. Now for the first time, extensive coverage of this facet of war aviation

Elsewhere in this book will be found details and photographs of the Sopwith Camels modified for night-fighting duties. This photograph depicts such an aircraft of No. 44 (H.D.) Squadron, flown by the Commanding Officer, Major G. W. Murlis-Green.

is provided by text and many photographs which show progress made in the armament field from the days of steel darts up to use of fighters armed with *canon*.

The camouflage and markings used on Military aircraft of the 1914–1918 War has proved to be a source of much interest and enquiry in the past. This subject has been most fully examined in a companion 'Harborough' book 'Aircraft Camouflage and Markings 1907–1954', by Bruce Robertson. However, since it was the aim to combine all relative information of fighter aircraft into this present book, no apologies are offered for inclusion of this section. In fact, collection of later information and further photographs of various examples of markings, has made it essential that this subject be dealt with in order to achieve a completely over-all coverage in 'FIGHTER AIRCRAFT OF THE 1914–1918 WAR'.

Bearing in mind the requirements of the many builders of model aircraft; selections of photographs of engines, airframes, cockpits, machine-gun mountings and other component parts are also included.

Fighter aircraft of the 1914–1918 War are now gone for ever, but to fly in them was to know the thrill of both *flying* as well as combat. Not only did these pilots fight each other, but they fought also against the elements of Nature.

Truly may it be said that these aircraft were flown by men. Men who in open, unheated and unarmoured cockpits, with the minimum of instrumentation, often as not flew 'by the seat of their pants' as well as 'on a wing and a prayer'.

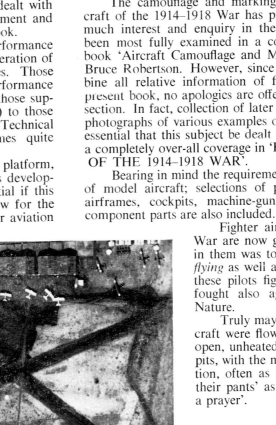

Droglandt aerodrome in early 1917—a photograph to revive nostalgic memories for members of 46 and 21 Squadrons, R.F.C., who flew their Nieuport 12s and R.E.8s respectively from its cinder runways—necessary to combat the mud of a French winter.

CONTENTS

84 AIRCRAFT EACH DESCRIBED WITH A PAGE CONTAINING TEXT AND FIVE PHOTOGRAPHS, OPPOSITE A PAGE OF 1/72 SCALE 3-VIEW DRAWINGS.

LE PÈRE LUSAC 11

The Packard Motor Car Company of Detroit, Michigan, played an important part in the creation of the Liberty 8 and 12 aero engines, their engineer J. G. Vincent, being one of the chief designers. The eight-cylinder version was abandoned in December 1917, and development work was concentrated on the bigger engine, which after a good deal of modification proved to be a first-class power unit.

The company obtained the loan from the French Government of an experienced aeronautical engineer, Capitaine G. Le Père, and began to design aeroplanes. A two-seater fighter biplane of striking appearance and performance, the LUSAC (Le Père U.S. Army Combat) 11, was the first and best of these.

In September 1918 the prototype, probably '42128', was handed over to the U.S. Army Air Service. Its power unit, naturally, was the big 400 h.p. Liberty 12, entirely enclosed in a blunt-nosed metal cowling. Twin exhaust pipes passed rearwards along each side of the fuselage; the radiator was set in the centre section, with its cooling surfaces both above and below the wing. Flat staggered wings of wire-braced wood and fabric were fitted; there were plain ailerons, connected by light struts, on both planes, which were of equal span and chord.

The wooden interplane struts were unique; they were of 'O' shape, flattened at the top and bottom, and required no incidence bracing wires, although the usual flying and landing wires were fitted. The wooden centre-section struts were also of robust construction, and the whole wing cellule was one of great strength. Fuselage construction was of the wooden box-girder type, with a covering of veneered plywood; the pilot sat below the cut-out in the top wing; the observer's gun ring was built up level with the top of the rounded fuselage decking. The small tail-plane, braced from below by a strut on each side, carried large horn-balanced elevators, and the fin and rudder together were of a neat rounded shape. The sturdy undercarriage had a faired axle, supported by three struts at each end.

Twin Marlin synchronised machine-guns, both situated on the starboard side of the fuselage, and fixed to fire through the airscrew arc, were provided for the pilot. The observer had twin Lewis guns, mounted on a Scarff ring.

The LUSAC 11 was strong, manœuvrable, heavily armed and very fast (132·2 m.p.h.), and would have been a useful weapon had the war continued into 1919. By the Armistice the Packard company had supplied thirty machines, two of these, 42130 and 42131, both of greater span than the original model, being in France undergoing official service trials. The consensus of opinion of pilots who test-flew '42131' was that due to cooling and fuel feed imperfections this type, whilst otherwise of considerable promise, would require extensive modifications in these two installations before use in combat. A further 995 LUSAC 11s were on order from Packard, and three other contracts, for no less than 3,495 machines, had been placed.

The LUSAC 21 was similar to the 11, but was powered by the 420 h.p. Bugatti 16 engine. The first of the three examples built of this type was delivered to the Air Service in January 1919. It was a heavier aeroplane and had a poorer performance.

1. 2. and 3. Standard model Le Père LUSAC 11 with 400 h.p. Liberty engine. No. 3 has twin Marlin and twin Lewis guns. 4. and 5. LUSAC 11 on test with the Project No. P.54. The U.S. style of camouflage markings is worthy of note.

LE PÈRE LUSAC 11

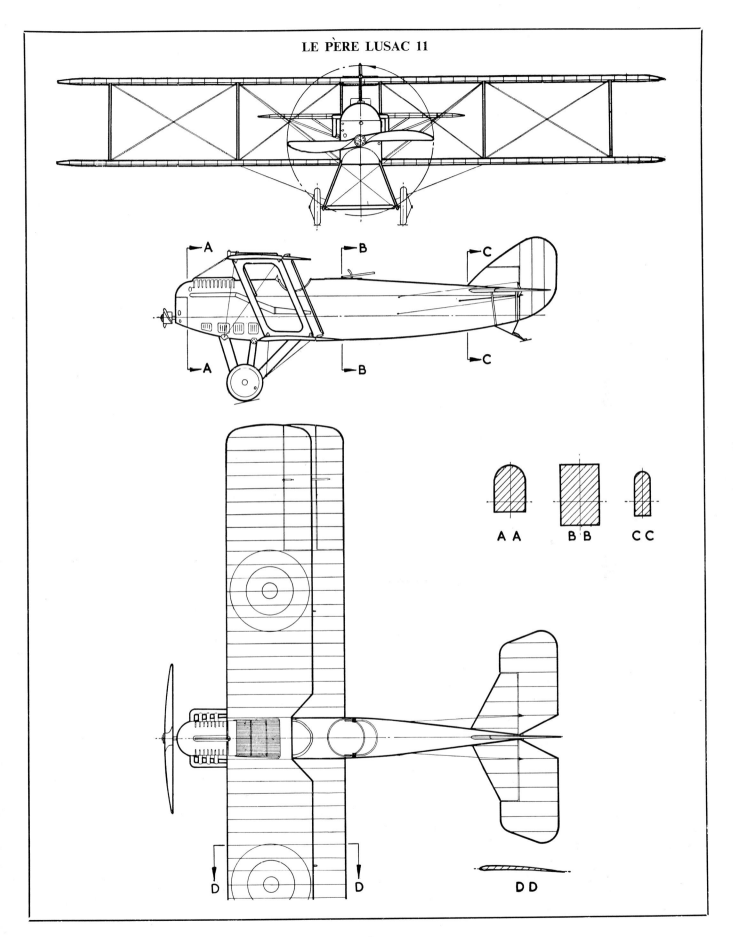

A A   B B   C C

D D

STANDARD E-1

The Standard Aircraft Corporation of Elizabeth, New Jersey, began to supply aeroplanes to the U.S. Signal Corps in 1917, when three Standard H-2 (formerly Sloane H-2) reconnaissance biplanes were delivered. Soon afterwards nine examples of the improved H-3 biplane were procured; some of these saw service on the Mexican border. A third model, the Standard Military Trainer, became the famous SJ-1 primary trainer, which was built in very large numbers after America's entry into the war, sharing with the Curtiss 'Jenny' the task of training the new pilots of the rapidly expanding U.S. Air Service.

By late 1918 the Standard company had risen to be the second largest producer of aeroplanes in the United States. In addition to the manufacture of such well-tried Allied types as the D.H.4, the Handley-Page 0/400 and the Caproni, the firm designed its own types, such as the Twin Hydro, the JR-1 and 1B, and the E-1.

The first two machines of the latter type were delivered in January 1918. A single-seater biplane intended for M-Defence duty, its power unit was the 80 h.p. Le Rhône 9C rotary engine, partly enclosed in a circular open-fronted cowling provided with cooling slots in its lower side. A bowl-shaped spinner was fitted to the airscrew hub. The two-bay wings, of R.A.F. No. 15 section, had both stagger and dihedral, and were of wire-braced wood and fabric construction. There was a small cut-out in the trailing-edge of the centre section and ailerons were carried on both wings. Interplane bracing struts of wood braced with wire were fitted; the centre-section struts were short and splayed outwards in front elevation. The top wing was set low above the top of the fuselage, giving the pilot a good view forwards and upwards. The fuselage, of rectangular wooden box-girder type, was covered from the cowling to just aft of the cockpit with aluminium sheeting; a single portion of the same material covered the top decking and head-rest, while the remainder was covered with doped fabric. The tail surfaces, of welded steel tube on a combination of metal and wood, were fabric-covered; a small fin and horn-balanced rudder were fitted. Conventional wooden vee struts carried the undercarriage wheels, which were sprung with rubber shock-absorbers.

A heavier version of the E-1, intended as an advanced trainer, was supplied from August 1918 onwards. It had a 100 h.p. Gnôme B-9 rotary engine, manufactured by the General Vehicle Company.

The handling characteristics of the type proved to be unsatisfactory, and the empennage underwent some modification; a triangular fin and plain rudder became standard. On later models the nose spinner was removed.

Provision was made for installation of a ·30 Marlin gun on the port side of the fuselage top to fire through the revolving airscrew; a camera gun could be mounted to starboard, parallel to the machine-gun.

In November 1918 a further ninety-eight Le Rhône-powered E-1s were procured by the U.S. Air Service.

A total of 100 Le Rhône-powered E-1s and 30 Gnôme-powered E-1s were supplied; at least one is still regularly flown at U.S.A.F. displays. It carries two Marlin guns and the registration number is N3783C.

1 to 4. Standard E-1 44556 with horn-balanced rudder. The spinner of the earlier models has been abandoned. 5. E-1 of the type with plain fin and rudder, rebuilt by Wesley Tallent of N. Carolina, and currently flown at U.S.A.F. displays by Lt.-Col. K. S. Brown, U.S.A.F.

10

STANDARD E-1

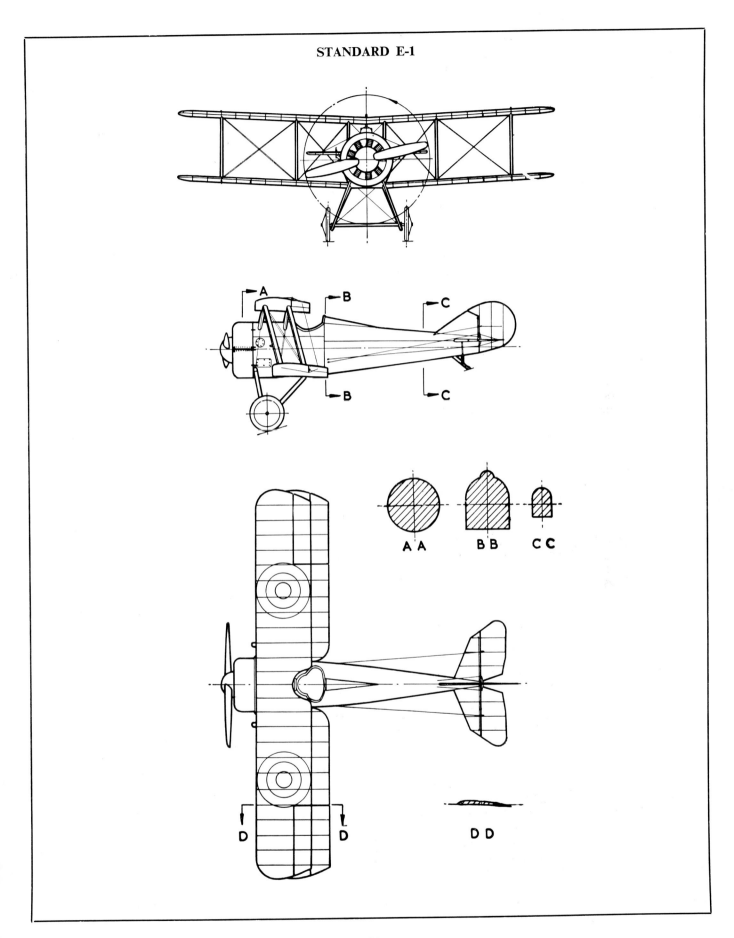

A A   B B   C C

D   D   D D

11

THOMAS-MORSE SCOUTS S-4, S-4B, S-4C, S-4E AND S-5

The Thomas company was founded by a young Englishman, W. T. Thomas, who emigrated to the United States and obtained a position with Glenn Curtiss at Hammondsport, New York. He was later joined by his brother Oliver, and they set up the aircraft firm of Thomas Brothers at Hammondsport, where an experimental pusher biplane was constructed in 1910.

The firm then moved to Bath, New York, where a number of types were built; one of these gained the world's altitude record in 1913. Shortly before the outbreak of war in Europe, B. D. Thomas—no relation—joined the concern; he had worked for both the Vickers and Sopwith companies in England. His first design was the T-2 tractor biplane, twenty-four of which were supplied to the British Admiralty in 1915.

After a second move, to Ithaca, New York, the firm began to produce aero engines, one of which was installed in their next design, the D-2 tractor biplane. During 1915 two seaplanes and the D-5 landplane were built for the U.S. Navy and Signal Corps respectively; further seaplanes and a flying boat appeared in the following year.

In January 1917 the firm merged with the Morse Chain Company of Ithaca, and the concern was reorganised as the Thomas-Morse Corporation. The first Thomas-Morse aeroplane was a trim little single-seater biplane, the S-4. Its 100 h.p. Gnôme Monosoupape 9-B rotary engine was partly enclosed by a circular open-fronted cowling, which was faired into the flat-sided fuselage by triangular fillets. The staggered wings were constructed of wood, wire-braced and fabric-covered; the top plane was flat, the lower plane had slight dihedral. There was a semicircular cut-out in the trailing-edge of the top wing, which carried the ailerons; these were operated by vertical rods. Single-bay wooden interplane struts, braced by wire, were fitted; the centre-section struts were slightly splayed outwards. The fuselage was a wooden wire-braced box girder, with a rounded top decking; the whole structure being covered with fabric. The neatly shaped empennage was of wood and fabric construction. Wooden vee struts formed the undercarriage legs; the wheels were sprung with rubber cord.

As it could be easily converted into a seaplane, the S-4 was offered to both the U.S. Army and Navy. The prototype was tested at Hampton, Virginia, and as a result of these trials fifty modified machines, known as S-4Bs, were ordered shortly after the United States entered the war.

This order was increased to 150 to cope with the increased need for training aeroplanes. Meanwhile a similar model with twin floats, the S-5, was put into production for the Navy Department.

The last fifty machines ordered had shorter-span wings and were designated S-4Cs. Further orders were placed for this version, with the 80 h.p. Le Rhône 9-C rotary, built by the Union Switch and Signal Company of Swissvale, Pennsylvania, in place of the Mono-Gnôme; the fuselage of the Le Rhône 'Tommy' was slightly shorter.

In all 447 Le Rhône versions were delivered, and they were widely used as advanced trainers. The final model in the series was the S-4E aerobatic trainer; it had shorter tapered wings and a mounting for a synchronised gun.

1. Early model Thomas Morse Scout; the upper wing has dihedral. 2, 3 and 4. Thomas Morse S-4Cs, used as pursuit trainers, fitted with synchronised Marlin guns. 5. S-5 twin float training seaplane, supplied to the U.S. Navy Department.

THOMAS-MORSE S-4C

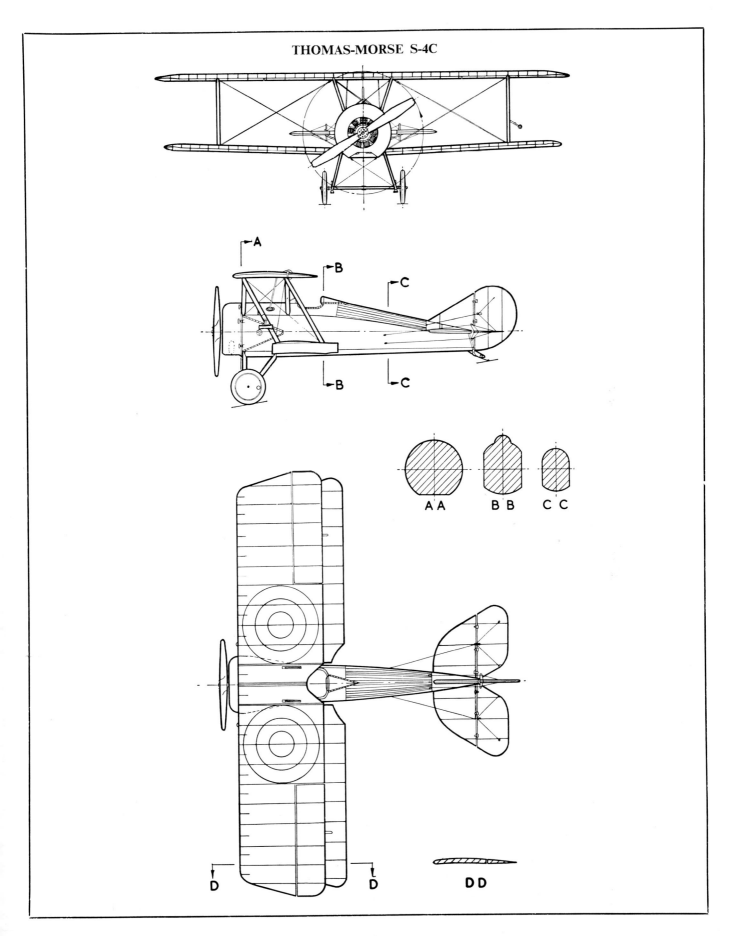

AUSTRIAN-AVIATIK D-I

In the early years of the war the Oesterreichische-Ungarische Flugzeugfabrik Aviatik, the Austro-Hungarian branch of the German Aviatik company, produced B-type biplanes. Early in 1917 the firm's designer, Julius von Berg, brought out two rather similar types, the two-seater C-I and the single-seater D-I. The latter, more frequently referred to as the 'Berg Scout', was the first Austrian-designed fighter.

The early D-Is had the 185 h.p. Austro-Daimler engine; more powerful models of this engine were fitted as they became available. Two side radiators were carried on the first Aviatik-built machines, but as these proved inefficient a large car-type radiator became standard. In order to improve performance, some machines of the later 238. series reverted to side-radiators, but although speedy they tended to overheat. Finally, a box-type wing radiator, similar to that of the Phönix Scout, was installed.

The wings, square-cut and without dihedral, were built up of spruce box spars, and ribs with spruce flanges and poplar webs. The leading-edges were of spruce, the trailing-edges were of wire, and the whole structure was fabric-covered. Ailerons, with considerable wash-out, were fitted to the top wing only. Interplane struts and N-shaped centre-section struts were of steel tubing.

Considerable ingenuity was displayed in the fuselage design; it was deep, with a narrow high turtle-back; the pilot sat high up with his eyes just below the level of the top wing, and had a good view in most directions. Structurally it was a light framework of wood, without bracing wires, covered with plywood. Metal cowling plates enclosed the upper part of the engine. The empennage was framed in steel tubing; the tail-plane was braced to the fin by a strut on each side. A structure of plywood-covered wooden strips supported the tail-skid. The undercarriage was a plain steel-tube affair. Early machines had a single Schwarzlose gun mounted in front of the cockpit, to fire forwards above the airscrew arc; twin synchronised guns were next mounted on either side of the engine. Finally the standard arrangement consisted of twin guns above the instrument panel; extension tubes prolonged their barrels to the front of the engine to prevent the flashes from igniting petrol fumes. Some D-Is had four-bladed 70°/110° airscrews of Jaray design; according to one source to facilitate gun synchronisation. Five firms manufactured the D-I in no less than eleven series, and the type was in use until the Armistice.

The Berg Scout had excellent flying characteristics and a fine rate of climb. The early models, however, were weakly built with unusually thin wings which became deformed or broke even during normal flights. Later versions were strengthened and proved very satisfactory. Manufacturers of the type were as follows: Austrian-Aviatik (Av)—series 38, 138, 238, 338; Vienna Carriage Works (WKF)—series 84, 184, 284 and 384; Hungarian Engineering Works (MAG)—series 92; Thöne and Fiala (Th)—series 101; and Jakob Lohner (Lo)—series 115.

The D-I was to be replaced with the Austrian-Aviatik D-II, a biplane with a cantilever lower wing, but the war finished before the first production machines became available for service.

1. An Aviatik-built D-I with side radiators. 2. 38.63, with frontal radiator. 3. D-I of series 138, with four-bladed airscrew. 4. A 238 series machine with side-radiators. 5. The final version with radiator in front of the centre section.

14

AUSTRIAN-AVIATIK D-I

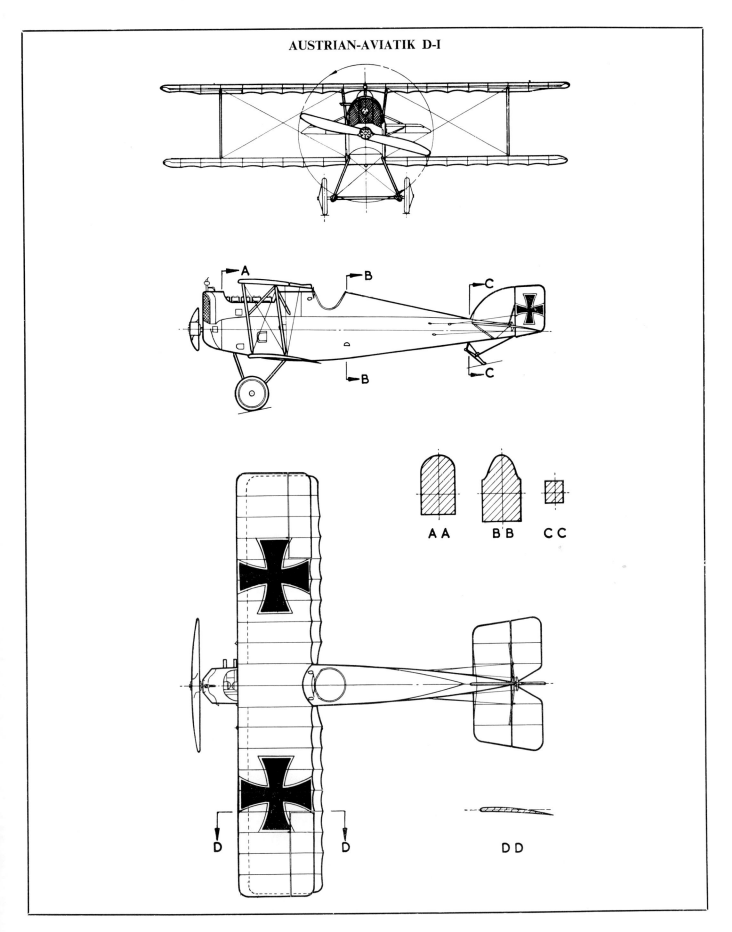

A A B B C C

D D D D

HANSA-BRANDENBURG CC FLYING BOAT

A small single-seater fighter flying boat was developed by Ernst Heinkel, the Hansa-Brandenburg designer, early in 1916; out of gratitude to the proprietor of the firm, Camillo Castiglione, he christened it the CC.

The first CC boat to be supplied to the German Navy, No. 946, was ordered in May 1916, but was not delivered until the following February. Like all German-built CCs, it was powered by the 150 h.p. Benz engine mounted close under the top wing on steel-tube struts streamlined with laminated wooden coverings, and driving a two-bladed pusher propeller. The radiator was directly in front of the engine. Its wing structure much resembled that of the D-I landplane; square-cut planes with ailerons incorporating wash-out, and the same 'star-strut' interplane bracing. Below and in front of the engine was the pilot's cockpit. The wooden hull, of well-streamlined shape, was provided with a step underneath. Wing-tip floats of streamlined section with flat sides were attached to the planes by means of one forward strut and two rear struts, with cross-wire bracing in between. A low aspect-ratio fin of thin laminated wood carried the rather square tail-plane, which was braced from below by two struts on each side; the rudder was horn-balanced.

The armament consisted of a single Spandau gun, which protruded through a windshield of large proportions.

Although the German Navy had no love for flying boats, the CC was evidently considered satisfactory; for two further series, 1137–1146 and 1327–1351, were built during 1917. The later machines were somewhat modified, having longer hulls, radiators in the top wings, and twin guns. On some, the engine was enclosed in an egg-shaped cowling and a pointed spinner was fitted to the propeller; others had extra interplane bracing struts. The operational history of these flying boats is obscure.

The Austro-Hungarian Navy, however, were well aware of the value of flying boats, and found the CC to be a useful weapon. Known as the KDW (*Kampf Doppeldecker Wasser*—Fighter Biplane, Water) it was employed in defence of the Adriatic ports. The KDW had either the 185 h.p. Austro-Daimler or the 200 h.p. Hiero, in place of the Benz engine. In performance it compared favourably with the opposing Italian Nieuport 11; although less manoeuvrable the flying boat was faster.

Austro-Hungarian fighter flying boats were designated the 'A' class; A.24 was flown by the well-known Austrian naval pilot, Gottfried Banfield.

In 1918 an experimental triplane version of the KDW appeared, numbered A.45; it was not put into production.

The Phönix company developed an improved fighter flying boat based on the Hansa-Brandenburg CC design in the last year of the war; it was powered by the 185 h.p. Austro-Daimler engine, had a hull of simpler cross-section, orthodox interplane struts and twin Schwarzlose guns mounted on a transverse steel tube inside the front portion of the cockpit.

However, in the last few months of the war the single-seat flying boats were unable to deal with the ever-increasing Italian air raids. Production figures for the 'A' class were: 1916 6; 1917 64; 1918 65; a total of 135 boats.

1. CC prototype. 2. No. 946, the first production CC flying boat. 3. Austro-Hungarian Brandenburg KDW A.24. 4. Late model CC, with wing radiator, additional wing bracing, longer hull and twin guns. 5. A.50, an Austro-Hungarian Phönix flying boat.

HANSA-BRANDENBURG CC FLYING BOAT

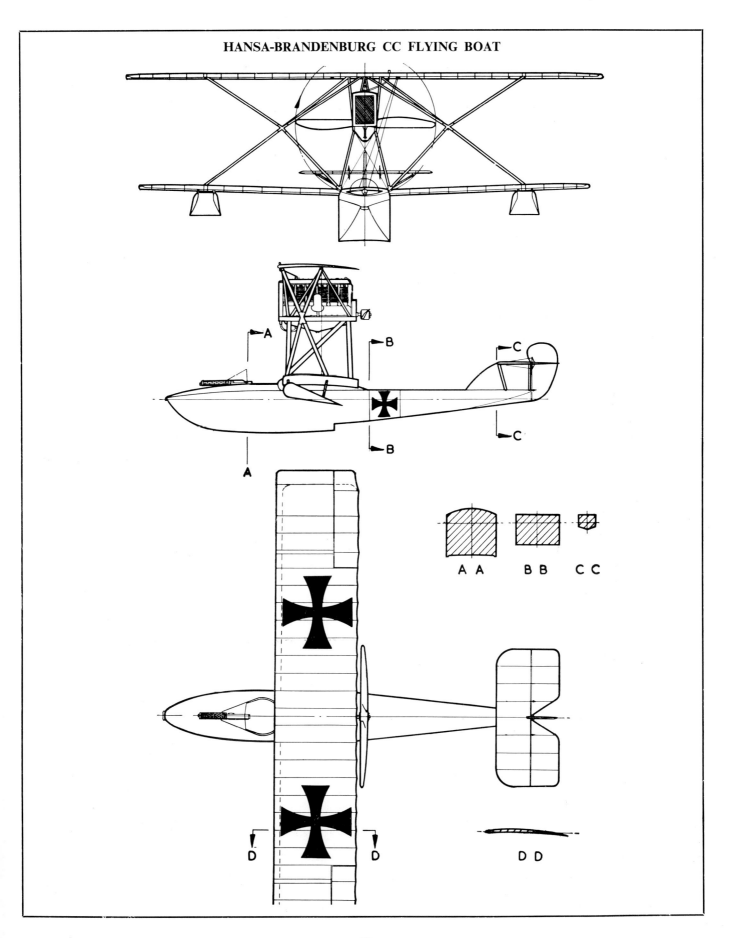

A A   B B   C C

D D

HANSA-BRANDENBURG D-I

Camillo Castiglione, the owner of the Hansa und Brandenburgische Flugzeugwerke, was an Austrian citizen, and consequently a number of aeroplanes designed by his protégé, Ernst Heinkel, were manufactured under licence in Austro-Hungary. Of these, the C-I reconnaissance two-seater, built in seventeen series, and the KD *Kampf Doppel-decker* (Fighter Biplane) were the most successful.

A small single-seater of bizarre appearance, the KD's interplane bracing consisted of twin 'stars', each made up of eight short struts, which met at a point midway between the top and bottom wings; no bracing wires were, therefore, necessary.

The prototype appeared early in 1916 and was promptly nicknamed the *'Spinne'* (Spider). It had an orthodox plywood fuselage, a small triangular fin and a feeble-looking rudder; its radiator was mounted above the nose.

An improved version (military designation D-I) was put into production in Austro-Hungary by the Phönix (series 28.) and Ufag (series 65.) firms. Phönix-built machines had the 160 h.p. Austro-Daimler engine; those built by Ufag the 185 h.p. model. The exhaust manifold was fixed along the starboard side of the nose, the cowling panels of which were of metal. Square-cut wings constructed of fabric-covered wooden spars and ribs were fitted; ailerons with some wash-out of incidence were carried on the top plane, as was the radiator which was offset to starboard. The interplane struts were of steel tubing with fairings of laminated wood; the top inner pair of each 'star' sloped up to meet the top of the steel-tube cabane trestle; the front lower inner struts were connected to the tops of the front undercarriage legs. Longerons and formers covered with three-ply made up the fuselage; in section the top decking followed the shape of the pilot's head and shoulders, thereby providing him with a good view fore and aft. No windshield was fitted. Behind the cockpit the decking tapered in plan but not in elevation, to finish in a vertical knife-edge which compensated for the lack of a fin. The rudder was small and horn-balanced; two struts above and below braced the large fish-like tail. Laminated wood covered the steel-tube undercarriage vees.

As there was no synchronising gear available, a stripped Schwarzlose gun, enclosed in a light casing, was fixed on the top of the cabane, to fire above the revolving airscrew. This was an unsatisfactory mounting, for the casing increased 'drag' and stoppages could not be cleared during flight.

In its early form the KD had poor lateral control, and involuntary swings could only be checked by putting the nose down sharply. Accidents were common, and the type was christened the 'Sarg' (Coffin). In order to counteract this tendency, the later Phönix-built examples were given low aspect-ratio fins and rudders. Occasionally a small faired head-rest was provided. Late production machines built by Ufag had frontal radiators; it would seem that these aircraft had Hiero engines, for the exhaust stubs discharged to port.

The KD was the standard Austro-Hungarian single-seat fighter from autumn 1916 until mid-1917, and was flown by most of the aces of these countries in that period.

1. The Hansa-Brandenburg KD prototype. 2 The first Phönix-built production machine, 28.01. 3. and 4. Standard D-Is with wing-mounted Schwarzlose guns. 5. 65.71, an Ufag-built Hansa-Brandenburg D-I with car-type radiator. Behind is Fokker 03.63.

18

HANSA-BRANDENBURG D-I

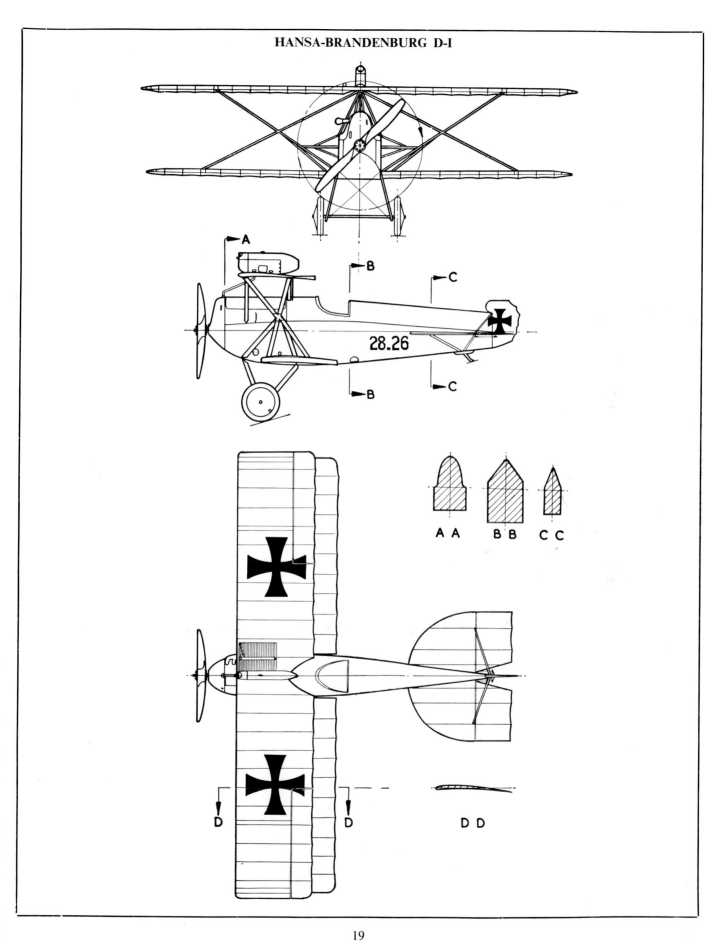

28.26

A A   B B   C C

D   D   D D

FOKKER B-II (AUSTRIAN)

In addition to building aeroplanes for the German Government, the Fokker Aeroplanbau supplied a number of types to Austro-Hungary. The early Austrian Fokkers were unarmed two-seater reconnaissance monoplanes; they were followed by the M.10E training biplane, which had the military designation B-I.

In 1916 the Fokker company brought out two M.16 biplanes, each with a deep fuselage which entirely filled the gap between the wings. The first was an experimental single-seater, nicknamed the 'Karausche' (Carp); the second was a two-seater, used in small numbers by Austro-Hungary with the military designation B-III. A rotary-engined version of the 'Carp', the M.17E, failed to gain a production order; it was followed by a small single-seater of more orthodox appearance, believed to have been called the M.17K (K = *Kurze Fläche* or Short Wings). It was powered by an 80 h.p. Oberursel rotary, installed in an aluminium 'horseshoe' cowling; the wire-braced wood and fabric wings were staggered. Lateral control was effected by wing-warping, the control wires passing over twin pulleys attached to the trailing-edge of the centre section. Both wings had wash-out of incidence; the trailing-edges were of wire, which was distorted by the doped fabric covering and presented a scalloped appearance. The centre section, placed fairly close to the fuselage top, was supported by steel-tube struts; the front pair being of inverted vee shape.

In typical Fokker fashion the fuselage was framed in welded steel tubing and covered with fabric. The fairings to the circular cowling and the top decking and side panels in front of the cockpit were of aluminium. Apart from a small rounded turtle-back behind the pilot the fuselage was rectangular in section and tapered to a horizontal knife-edge to which was attached the balanced elevator. The prototype had a small rectangular balanced rudder, which was later replaced by a comma-shaped rudder. A synchronised Spandau gun was fitted.

The German Inspectorate of Flying Troops (*Idflieg*) was unimpressed by the performance of the little biplane, but a development with longer two-bay wings, the M.17Z, was later put into production as the Fokker D II.

Fifty machines (03.60 to 04.10) were supplied to Austro-Hungary; the type was designated the B-II; it should not be confused with the two-seater Fokker B-II trainer used in Germany.

The 'Baby Fokker', as it was called, was employed as a light scouting aeroplane, but with little success. It had a limited radius of action and its ceiling of about 8,500 feet was inferior to that of the earlier Fokker E-I which had the same engine. Some B-IIs were experimentally fitted with machine guns; one example had a stripped Schwarzlose gun mounted about the centre section to fire above the airscrew arc; hardly a satisfactory arrangement, for the slipstream must have interfered with the belt feed. After a brief operational career, the type was relegated to the training schools.

Castor oil was essential for the rotary engine, and as supplies were restricted in Austro-Hungary, an aeroplane with that type of power unit had little chance of coming into general use there.

1. The Fokker M.17E. 2. The prototype M.17K, with Spandau gun. 3. M.17K in its final form. 4. One of the fifty production machines supplied to Austro-Hungary. 5. B-II with Schwarzlose gun on an experimental mounting.

FOKKER B-II (AUSTRIAN)

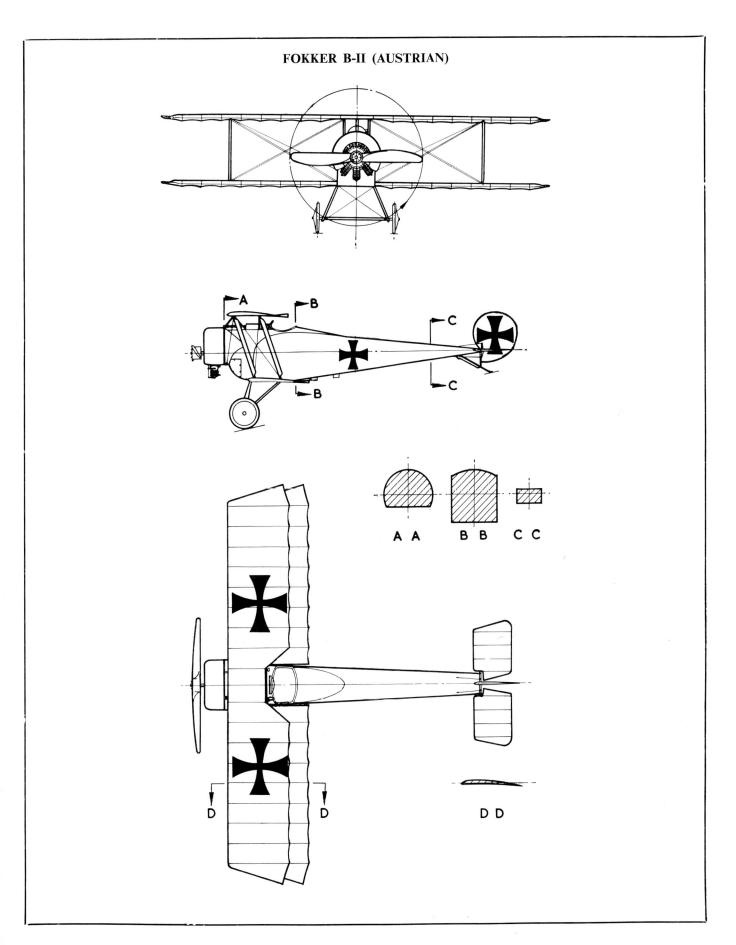

A A   B B   C C

D   D   D D

PHÖNIX D-I, D-II AND D-III

The Phönix Aeroplane Works of Vienna manufactured the Hansa-Brandenburg D-I single-seater fighter from the autumn of 1916 until early in 1917. It then became evident that the type was incapable of further development, for its airframe could not accommodate a more powerful engine than the 185 h.p. Austro-Daimler. Work therefore began on a design which, it was hoped, would permit the installation of a larger power unit which could provide a much-improved performance.

The new machine, 20.15, had the 200 h.p. Austro-Daimler engine; its exhaust system consisted of six stubs which discharged on the starboard side. The radiator was situated in the top wing, to starboard of the centre section. Square-cut staggered wings with fabric-covered wooden spars and ribs were fitted; the ailerons, carried on the top wing only, had a good deal of wash-out. In place of the Hansa-Brandenburg 'star-strut' interplane bracing were orthodox wooden struts, slightly splayed inwards; there were additional steel-tube centre-section struts. Fuselage, empennage and undercarriage were apparently identical to those of late-production Phönix-built Hansa-Brandenburg D-Is. A Schwarzlose gun, enclosed in a casing, was mounted above the centre section to fire above the revolving airscrew.

Later in the year a second aeroplane, 20.16, appeared, which became the prototype Phönix D-I. (An earlier Phönix experimental fighter with Nieuport-type sesquiplane wings also had the serial 20.16; probably the same fuselage was used for both machines.) The prototype Phönix D-I differed from 20.15 in having rounded wing-tips, modified centre section bracing and a box-type radiator above the top plane.

The production D-I had the 200 h.p. Hiero engine (developed by Eissler, Warschalowski & Co. of Vienna), N-shaped centre-section struts and sometimes a small head-rest. Its armament consisted of twin synchronised Schwarzlose guns, mounted either on each side of the engine or inside the fuselage with their breeches above the instrument panel. The former had hollow-cone flash eliminators to prevent blast damage; the latter had long extension tubes from their barrels to the front of the engine, to prevent the muzzle flashes from igniting petrol fumes. Three series were built, 128., 228. and 328. The Phönix D-II, which differed only in having balanced elevators, was also manufactured in three series (122., 222. and 322.).

Both versions served with the *Fliegerkompagnien* during 1918, and a few, designated class 'J', were supplied to the land-based Austro-Hungarian Naval fighter units. Phönix Scouts equipped with cameras were flown by the *Fotoeinsitzer* (single-seater photographic) units, the forerunners of the single-seat P.R.U. squadrons of 1939–45.

The type has been described as being fast but rather stable and with a slow rate of climb. The early models were of dangerously weak construction; this fault was later rectified. In Spring, 1918, both services received the D-III (Series 422). It had the 230 h.p. Hiero engine and ailerons on both wings. The Swedish Army Air Service used a number of D-IIIs after the war; these machines to some extent influenced the trend of Swedish fighter design.

1. Phönix experimental fighter 20.15. 2. The prototype Phönix D-I, 20.16. 3. Production Phönix D-I, series 228. 4. Naval D-I, forced down at Marcon airfield, July 19th, 1918. 5. Phönix D-III J.41 with 230 h.p. Hiero engine, built for the Navy.

PHÖNIX D-III

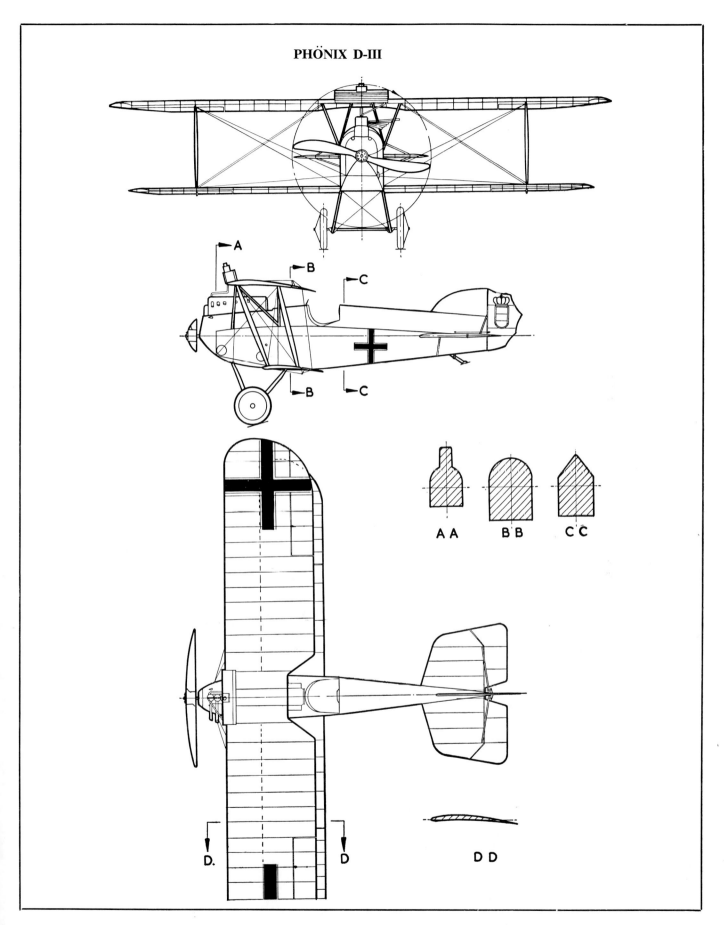

A A   B B   C C

D D

AUSTIN-BALL A.F.B.1

In early April 1916, while serving in France with No. 13 Squadron, R.F.C., Second Lieutenant Albert Ball was sent the plans of a new single-seater fighter biplane. Although at that time a relatively inexperienced pilot, Ball at once realised the possibilities of the design, and obtained permission from his commanding officer 'to fly it if I can get one out'.

During the ensuing months, as Ball's fame as a fighter pilot grew, there is no doubt that he corresponded with the designer and supplied him with ideas and advice.

Ball went on leave in October 1916 and tried to arrange for the construction of the aeroplane. The authorities, however, would not grant a contract or licence to build it, until Ball personally interviewed the Director of Air Organisation, Brigadier-General Sefton Brancker. It was then agreed that two prototypes would be manufactured by the Austin Motor Company.

The Austin-Ball had the 200 h.p. Hispano-Suiza engine, which was enclosed in a metal cowling; below the front pair of centre-section struts were fitted two box-like side radiators. The machine's general structure was of wood with a fabric covering; the wings, without either dihedral or stagger, were slightly swept back and had raked tips. An unusually deep fuselage almost filled the gap between the mainplanes. The pilot, therefore, sat with his eyes level with the top wing and had an excellent view forwards and upwards. A large triangular tail-plane was fitted; the rudder was balanced and small in area; presumably the large side area of the fuselage made a fin unnecessary.

The A.F.B.1's armament was unique: two Lewis guns were carried; the position of the first, mounted on the top wing, was probably suggested by Ball, who had scored many successes with a Lewis gun in a similar position on his Nieuport Scout. The second was fixed behind the engine, with its breech below the instrument panel, and fired through the airscrew shaft, which was hollow. This mounting was not the first of its kind, for a patent had been taken out for a similar arrangement by Franz Schneider, the L.V.G. designer, as early as 1912.

Not until July 1917 was the A.F.B.1 completed; two months after Captain Ball, V.C., D.S.O., M.C., had fallen in action. It was in many ways a first-rate aeroplane, being pleasant to fly and as fast as the S.E.5a with at the same time a better rate of climb. However, both the S.E.5a and the Sopwith Camel were being built in large numbers, and it was not considered wise to interfere with the construction programme.

The Austin-Ball Scout was an aeroplane which incorporated many of the ideas of an experienced fighter pilot; had it appeared a few months earlier it would have probably been manufactured in quantity.

An A.F.B.1 which differed considerably from the original machine was tested at Martlesham Heath. It had straight square-tipped wings, fitted with additional light struts at the intersections of the interplane bracing wires, after the manner of the French Spad. Whether this was a modified version of the first Austin-Ball, or the second aircraft, is uncertain.

1 to 4. The Austin-Ball Scout in its original form with single bays of struts. 5. Modified version of the Austin-Ball, at Martlesham, with wings and interplane strutting resembling those of the Spad fighter of the same period; possibly they were in fact, Spad wings.

AUSTIN-BALL A.F.B.1

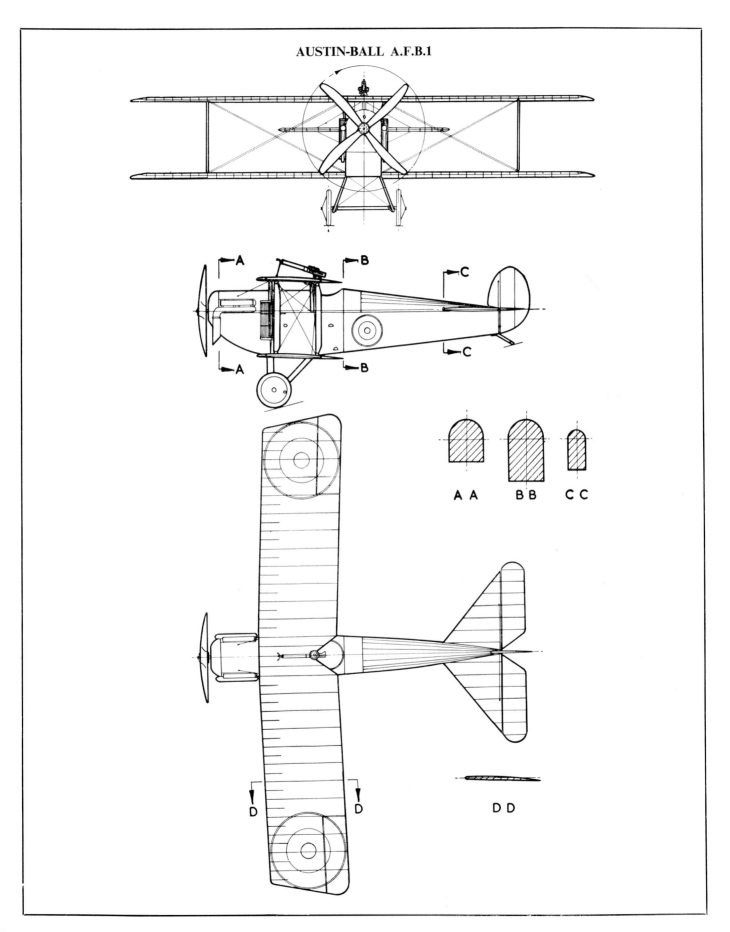

A A   B B   C C

D D

25

AVRO 504K (NIGHT-FIGHTER)

The Avro 504 two-seater biplane made the first organised bombing raid in history, on November 21st, 1914, when three R.N.A.S. machines, Nos. 873, 874 and 875, attacked the airship sheds at Friedrichshafen. The 504 later became an outstandingly successful trainer and was manufactured in large numbers.

It is less well known that three single-seater fighter versions of the 504 were constructed, one of which equipped operational squadrons as late as 1918.

The Avro 504C was built for the R.N.A.S. for anti-Zeppelin and long-distance reconnaissance duties. Based very closely on the two-seater 504B naval trainer, it had an 80 h.p. Gnôme rotary engine enclosed in a swollen-sided cowling. The standard 504 wings had two main spars and ribs of spruce, and were wire-braced and fabric-covered. Long-span ailerons were fitted and there were semi-circular cut-outs in the lower wing-roots. The fuselage had ash longerons and stringers braced by wire, and was fabric-covered except for plywood decking round the cockpit, which was cut below the level of the top longerons. The space occupied by the front cockpit on the 504B was faired over and carried a large petrol tank with a fuel capacity for eight hours' flying. The usual Avro undercarriage with faired-in rubber shock-absorbers and central wooden skid was fitted; the tail-skid was of the pylon variety. The 504C had the same plain rudder and long fin as the 504B; all the later naval Avros could be distinguished by their vertical tail surfaces—those of the R.F.C. having the original comma-shaped balanced rudder. The anti-airship 504C carried a Lewis gun fixed to fire upwards through a centre-section cut-out at an angle of 45 degrees. About eighty 504Cs were manufactured.

A very similar single-seater, the 504D, was built for the R.F.C. Designed for precisely the same duties, it was, however, based on the 504A, and had short-span ailerons and a comma-shaped rudder. The engine was the usual 80 h.p. Gnôme rotary. Six of this type were built.

When Major Smith-Barry founded the School of Special Flying at Gosport in August 1917 with the object of training flying instructors, he chose the 100 h.p. Gnôme Monosoupape Avro 504J as the best available type for the purpose. Consequently the 504J was selected as the standard R.F.C. trainer and was built in large numbers. A shortage of the necessary Mono-Gnôme engines led to the development at Gosport of the 504K, a model with a universal engine mounting capable of taking any of the available rotaries. The old bulbous enclosed cowling was replaced by a larger open-fronted type. The K supplanted the J as the standard trainer and was eventually used all over the world.

Early in 1918 a single-seater version of the K, powered with the 110 h.p. Le Rhône rotary, was supplied to five Home Defence squadrons based on the north side of London. The pilot sat in what was normally the rear cockpit, the front seat being covered in. Some of these Ks had a vee-type undercarriage. A Lewis gun was carried on a Foster mounting above the centre section, the central gravity tank being moved to port to accommodate it. During the year the type was supplied to other H.D. units outside the London area.

1. Avro 504C 1488, built by the Brush Electrical Engineering Co. 2. 504C with Lewis gun. 3. A standard two-seater 504K, built by the Eastbourne Aviation Co. 4. 504K single-seater night-fighter, 77 Squadron, Penston, Scotland. 5. 504K single-seater night-fighter.

26

AVRO 504K (NIGHT-FIGHTER)

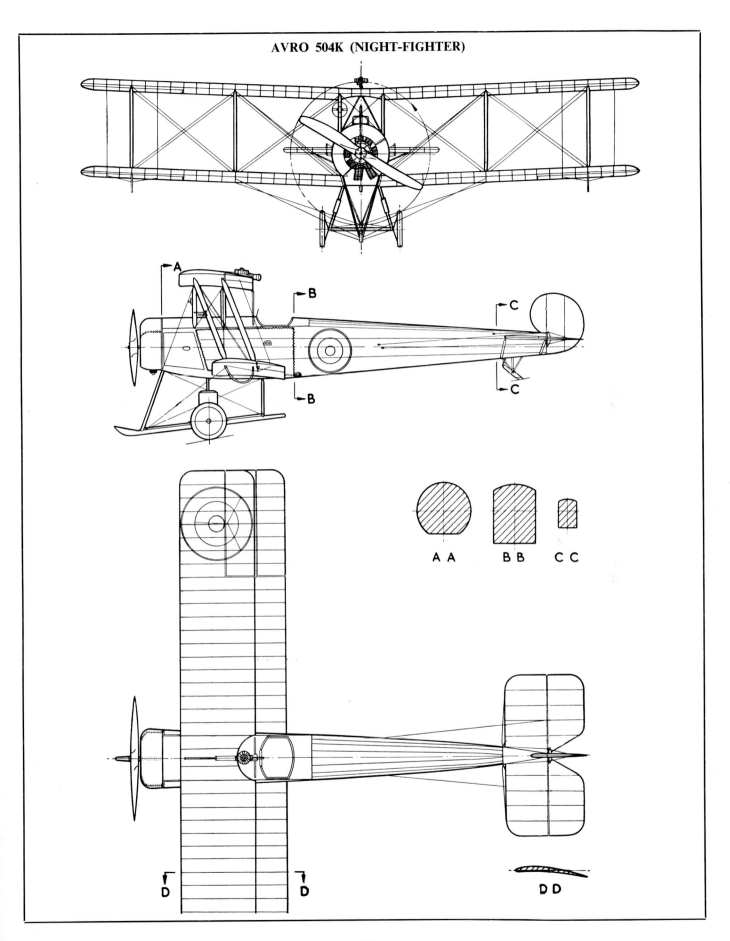

A A   B B   C C

D D

27

B.A.T. BANTAM Mk.I

In 1917 the Dutch aircraft designer Frederick Koolhoven left the firm of Sir W. G. Armstrong, Whitworth & Co. Ltd., and joined the newly formed British Aerial Transport Company. His first design for B.A.T., the F.K.22, was a small single-seater fighter biplane with two-bay wings and a wooden monocoque fuselage. The centre section was joined to the fuselage, so that the pilot's head protruded through a circular hole in the top wing. Ailerons were carried on both planes; the fin was small, the rudder horn-balanced. A peculiar wide-track undercarriage with independently sprung wheels was fitted. It had been intended to install the 120 h.p. A.B.C. Mosquito radial engine, but this power unit proved to be a complete failure. The 100 h.p. Gnôme Monosoupape or 110 h.p. Le Rhône rotary was therefore experimentally fitted.

A second single-seater, the F.K.23, was a smaller edition of the F.K.22, and had the new 170 h.p. A.B.C. Wasp radial; the lower wing only had dihedral, and a low aspect-ratio fin and plain rudder was fitted. Its armament consisted of twin synchronised Vickers guns, mounted low on each side of the nose. The F.K.23 prototype (B9947) was named the Bantam Mark I; the earlier F.K.22 (B9945) was retrospectively designated the Bantam Mark II.

The Mark I was test-flown early in 1918; it was found to behave very dangerously when in a spin, for its speed of rotation increased rapidly and recovery was difficult. After two spinning accidents, investigations were made which proved that the trouble was due to the centre of gravity being too far aft; other contributory factors were the type's small ratio of gap to chord and lack of stagger.

Modifications were carried out and a small batch of machines (F1653–F1661) were ordered. These production Bantams had larger wings, both with dihedral, steel-tube interplane struts, larger rudders and smaller fins. One aircraft is believed to have been sent to France for operational trials. The new version was fast (128 m.p.h. at 6,500 feet) and very manœuvrable, and but for the unreliable behaviour of the A.B.C. Wasp radial would have been a success. So undependable was this power unit that it was eventually decided to abandon its production; automatically this decision meant the end of the Bantam production programme.

One of the later production Bantams had the 200 h.p. A.B.C. Wasp II radial; the more powerful engine improved its rate of climb and gave it a speed of 146 m.p.h. at 10,000 feet. By this time, however, the war was over and the B.A.T. company had practically disappeared, having been merged with the Alliance Aeroplane Co. Ltd., and the British Nieuport and General Aircraft Co. Ltd. One Bantam went to the U.S.A. for evaluation; it was flown at Wright Field, in American markings with the serial number A.S.94111. The Bantams K.123 (later G-EACN) and K.125 (later G-EACP) were flown in the 1919 Aerial Derby by Clifford Prodger and Major C. Draper, D.S.C. The former aeroplane is now in the Shuttleworth Collection.

Frederick Koolhoven purchased G-EAYA (formerly F1661) in 1924 and took it with him to Holland. Fitted with a 200 h.p. Armstrong-Siddeley Lynx radial engine it is said to have reached a speed of 154 m.p.h.

1 and 2. The Le Rhône and Monosoupape-engined Mark II appeared before the Mark I. 3. B.9947, the first Mark I without top-wing dihedral. 4 and 5. Production Bantam Mark Is. One Mark I is reported to have gone to France for service trials.

B.A.T. BANTAM Mk.I

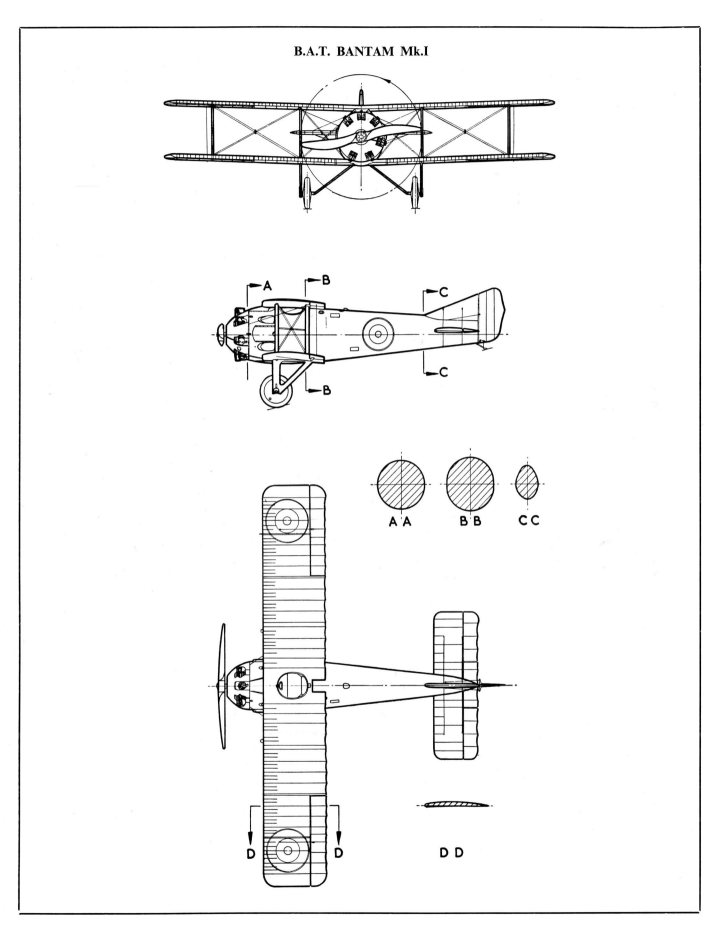

A A   B B   C C

D D

B.E.12, 12a AND 12b

The B.E.12 was designed by the Royal Aircraft Factory in response to an urgent appeal for a single-seater fighter to combat the growing menace of the Fokker Monoplane.

To save time a standard B.E.2c two-seater (No. 1697) was adapted by fairing over the front cockpit and installing a 150 h.p. R.A.F. 4a engine in place of the 90 h.p. R.A.F. 1a. On the prototype a small air-scoop was fitted to the engine and the exhaust stacks were connected to form a peculiar inverted fork. The rest of the machine's construction was of course identical to the B.E.2c; the two-bay wings had wooden main spars and ribs, wire-braced and fabric-covered; the fuselage was a wire-braced box girder, fabric-covered except for plywood top decking in front of the cockpit. The fin and rudder were of fabric-covered steel tubing; the tail and elevators were square cut.

The production version had twin exhaust stacks and a large air-scoop, and the upper longerons in front of the cockpit were altered to make room for a large petrol tank, the top of which was wedge-shaped to make a neat joint with the rear end of the scoop. A gravity tank was fitted to the underside of the port upper wing. Early production models had the triangular B.E.2c fin; later aircraft had the rounded outline type, and a tail-plane with raked tips.

A Vickers gun with Vickers interrupter gear was carried on the port side of the fuselage; some B.E.12s had in addition one or two Lewis guns on Strange-type mountings, firing forwards and outwards beyond the arc of the airscrew or a single rearward-firing Lewis.

In August 1916 the B.E.12 was supplied to Nos. 19 and 21 Squadrons on the Western Front. As might have been expected, it shared the inherent stability of the B.E.2c and was a complete failure as a fighter. After a few weeks it was relegated to bombing duties.

A few B.E.12s were used in the Near East and in Macedonia, where Captain G. W. Murlis-Green was unusually successful with the type, shooting down several German aeroplanes. Lieutenant L. P. Watkins of No. 37 (Home Defence) Squadron, flying a B.E.12 (No. 6610) shot down the Zeppelin L.48 on June 17th, 1917.

The B.E.12a was a similar makeshift fighter, with the same engine, but derived from the B.E.2e. The prototype had large horn balances to the ailerons, which were carried on the upper wing only. The production version, named the B.E.12Ae, resembled the B.E.2e more closely with ailerons on both wings which had raked tips. The designation 'B.E.12Ae' was soon discarded in favour of 'B.E.12a'.

The Home Defence variant, the B.E.12b, appeared in 1917, with the 200 h.p. Hispano-Suiza engine, a frontal radiator and large head-rest. It was armed with twin Lewis guns on a special mounting, which enabled the pilot to fire upwards or forwards over the top wing. The more powerful engine gave the B.E.12b quite a good performance. Some machines were fitted with bomb-racks; German night bombing raids on Britain ceased in the early summer of 1918, and it is possible that these machines carried out anti-submarine patrol work.

About 600 B.E.12s, 12as and 12bs were constructed; some 150 of this total were B.E.12bs.

1. The prototype B.E.12, No. 1697. 2. Daimler-built B.E.12, with enlarged fin. 3. A.6303, a standard B.E.12a. 4 and 5. B.E.12b night-fighters. No. 77 Squadron, Penston, near Edinburgh. Note the 112 lb. bombs slung underneath the wings.

B.E.12

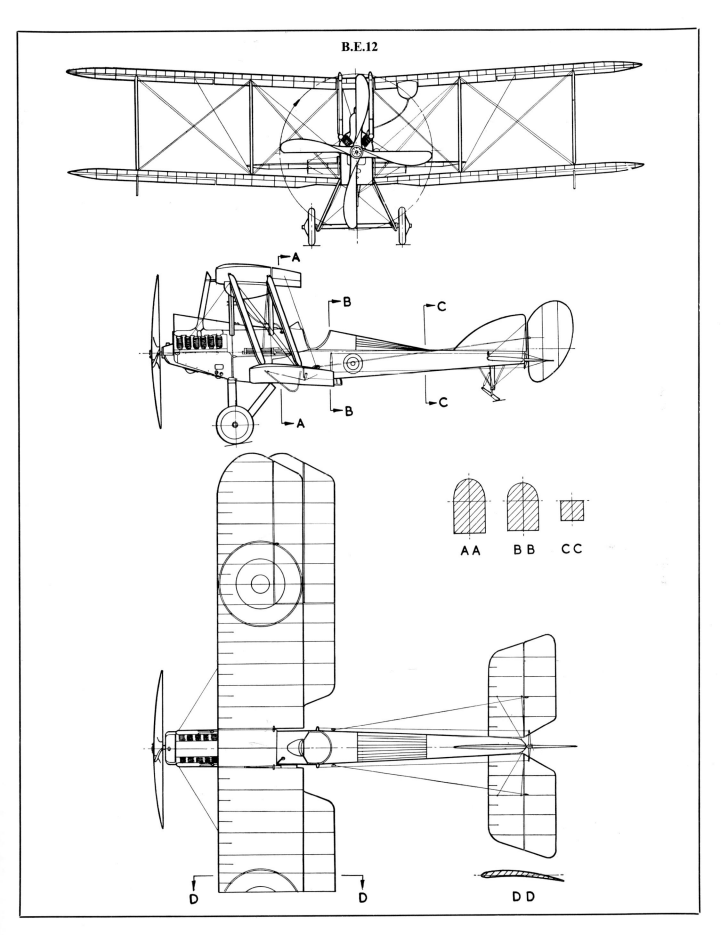

A A   B B   C C

D D

BRISTOL F.2A AND F.2B FIGHTER

The first prototype Bristol F.2A Fighter, A3303, was completed in the autumn of 1916. Designed by Captain F. Barnwell, it had the new 190 h.p. Rolls-Royce engine (later known as the Falcon I) enclosed in a neat cowling, and narrow vertical radiators fitted to the fuselage sides. The wings were of wood braced by wire, the wing-tips resembled those of the B.E.2c, and the uncovered lower centre section was connected by struts to the fuselage. End-plates were fixed to the lower wing-roots.

The fuselage was wooden-framed and wire-braced and sloped down to a horizontal knife-edge at the tail. The pilot sat with his eyes on a level with the top plane and had a good view forwards and upwards; the cockpits were close together, making communication easy.

It was soon found that the radiators obscured the pilot's view when landing, so a frontal radiator was fitted. The second prototype, A3304, also had a frontal radiator, but its engine was the 150 h.p. Hispano-Suiza.

Fifty production machines (A3305–A3354) based on A3303 were constructed; they had frontal radiators, blunt wing-tips and open lower-wing centre sections. The lower wings had no end-plates. A synchronised Vickers gun fixed under the cowling fired through a hole in the radiator. The observer had one, and later, two Lewis guns mounted on a Scarff ring.

The operational career of the Bristol Fighter began very badly; four out of six F.2As of No. 48 Squadron failed to return after an encounter with Manfred von Richthofen and his pilots on April 5th, 1917. The serious mistake had been made of staying rigidly in formation and relying on the observers to deal with the attacking fighters.

After a time pilots began to realise that the 'Brisfit' was strong, fast and manœuvrable, with the advantage of a 'sting in the tail', and they started to use their machines aggressively, like single-seaters.

These tactics were immediately successful and many pilots and observers ran up impressive scores of enemy aeroplanes destroyed.

In the early summer of 1917, a modified version, the F.2B, appeared. The pilot's forward view was further improved by sloping the upper longerons downward and fitting a narrower top to the cowling. The petrol tank was increased in capacity, and the lower-wing centre section was covered in. Except for the first few, all the F.2Bs had radiator shutters.

Captain A. E. McKeever, a Canadian ace of 11 Squadron, scored most of his thirty victories on the type.

The first 150 F.2Bs had the 190 h.p. Rolls-Royce Falcon I engine, the next fifty the 220 h.p. Falcon II. Thereafter it was hoped to fit the 275 h.p. Falcon III to all F.2Bs, but there was eventually a shortage of this superlative engine. Various substitutes, the Hispano-Suiza, the Sunbeam Arab, the R.A.F. 4d and the Siddeley Puma were tried, with little success.

A modified version of the Bristol Fighter served with the R.A.F. until 1932—a striking proof of its excellent qualities. Three thousand one hundred and one of the type were built up to the end of 1918.

1. First prototype Bristol F2A, A.3303, with 190 h.p. Rolls-Royce engine. 2. A.3343, a production F.2A of No. 48 Squadron R.F.C. 3 and 4. Standard F.2B with 275 h.p. Rolls-Royce Falcon III engine. 5. F.2B with the third and final Sunbeam Arab engine installation.

BRISTOL F2B

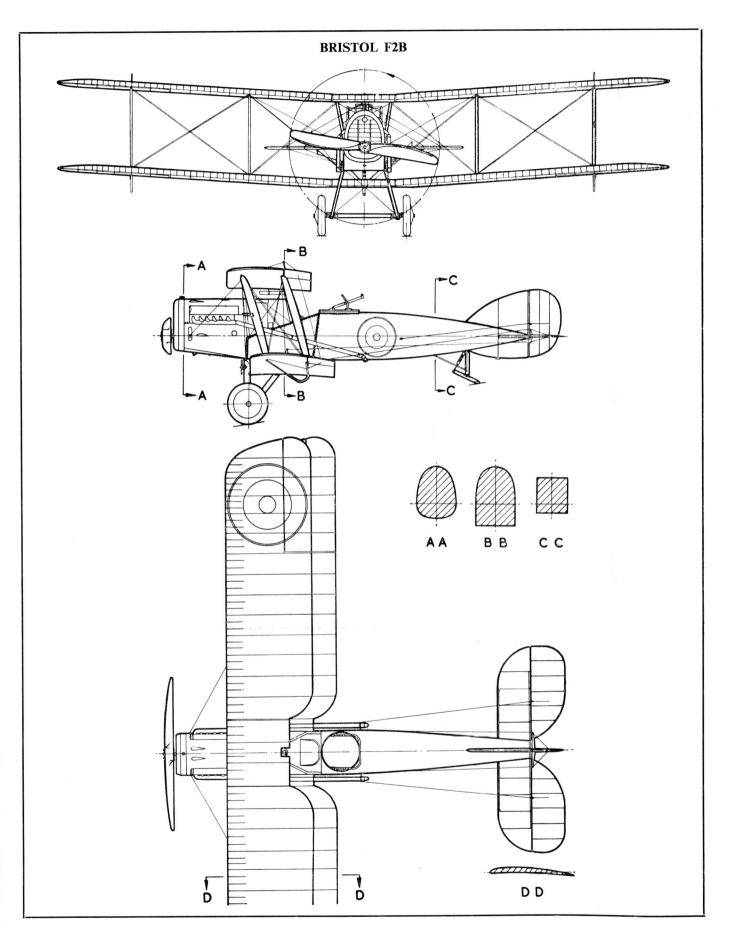

A A   B B   C C

D D

BRISTOL M.1A, B AND C

In early October 1912 a committee was formed to investigate three fatal crashes, all involving monoplanes of the Military Wing, Royal Flying Corps. Although the 'Monoplane Committee' found no reason to ban the type, a strong feeling that the monoplane was fundamentally dangerous remained. This feeling was mainly responsible for the R.F.C.'s failure to use the Bristol M.1C monoplane on the Western Front.

The prototype, A5138, was built in the late summer of 1916 to the designs of Captain F. Barnwell. The M.1A, as it was called, had a 110 h.p. Clerget rotary engine with a large rounded spinner, in the centre of which was a small cooling aperture. The fuselage, basically the usual wire-braced box-girder construction of the time, was faired by means of formers and stringers to a circular cross-section. The wooden fabric-covered wings had swept-back leading-edges and joined the fuselage at the upper longerons. From the upper surface of the wings the landing wires were brought up to an unusual cabane consisting of two half-loops of steel tubing; the flying wires were attached to the lower longerons. The pilot sat directly over the wings and had a good view in all directions except downwards. Two wires on each side braced the large fin to the tailplane. On trial the M.1A reached the high speed, for that time, of 132 m.p.h., and proved very manœuvrable.

Four modified machines (A5139–A5142), designated M.1Bs, came out in early 1917. The M.1B's cabane was of a more normal pyramid shape, a cut-out was provided in the starboard wing-root to improve downward vision, and a synchronised Vickers gun was mounted on the port side of the cowling. One of these aeroplanes was experimentally fitted with a 150 h.p. A.R. (Admiralty Rotary—later Bentley Rotary) engine, but the result was disappointing.

It was at this stage that the decision was made not to use the Bristol Monoplane on the Western Front; the official reason being that the landing speed of 49 m.p.h. was too high. R.F.C. squadrons in France who had been hoping to be re-equipped with the type were greatly disappointed; there is no doubt that it would have given them command of the air.

The production model, the M.1C, had a 110 h.p. Le Rhône rotary and a larger cooling hole in the spinner. Cut-outs were made in both wing-roots and the Vickers gun was positioned directly in front of the pilot.

One hundred and twenty-five were constructed (C4901–C5025), but only the thirty-five that were sent to Macedonia and the Middle East saw any operational service, mainly in attacks on ground targets. The rest were used at training schools, where they were particularly popular with the instructors.

Six M.1Cs went to Chile in 1917, and one of them, piloted by a Chilean Air Force officer, Lieutenant Godoy, made the first air crossing of the Andes on December 12th, 1918. A Bristol Monoplane (ex-C4964) took part in the 1921 Aerial Derby. Another aircraft of the type, G-AUCH, later became VH-UQI, the D.H. Gipsy-engined M.1C which won the 1932 Australian Aerial Derby.

The Bristol Monoplane could have been one of the outstanding aeroplanes of its time, but for official prejudice.

*1. A.5138, the Bristol M.1A, with steel-hoop cabane.
2. M.1B, with re-designed cabane and single Vickers gun offset to port. 3, 4 and 5. Standard production M.1Cs with centrally mounted Vickers guns. 6. C.4965, a training machine flown at Hounslow.*

BRISTOL M.1C

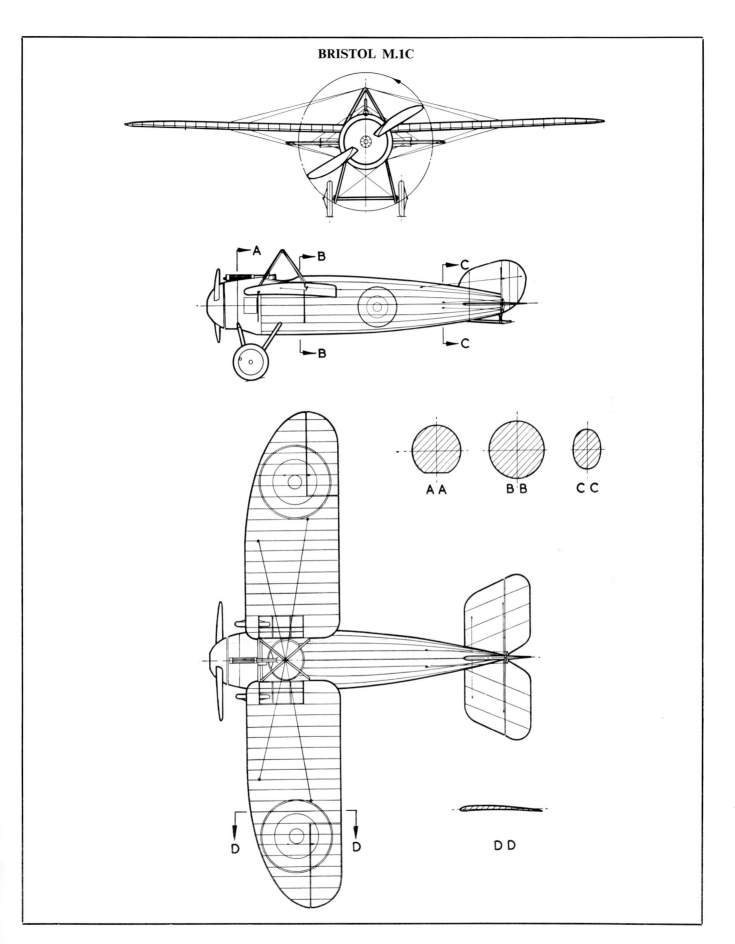

A A   B B   C C

D D

BRISTOL SCOUTS B, C AND D

The Bristol Baby Biplane or Scout, designed by F. Barnwell, first appeared in February 1914. It was a neat single-seater powered by the 80 h.p. Gnôme engine, which gave it the high maximum speed of 97 m.p.h. The wings had fabric-covered wooden main spars and ribs; the fuselage was wooden-framed and fabric-covered. The engine had a semi-enclosed cowling.

In May larger wings and a circular open cowling were fitted, and it was hoped that the Scout would do well in the summer air racing season. Bad weather and mishaps, however, robbed the little aeroplane of success. Finally, in July 1914, with its owner Lord Carbery at the controls, it came down in the Channel during the London–Paris–London air race and could not be salvaged.

Two more Scouts were completed in August 1914 and were sent to France in September. These aeroplanes were designated the Scout 'B'; two further developments, the Scouts 'C' and 'D', appeared in November 1914 and December 1915.

The power units and distinguishing features of the Scouts can be summarised as follows: 'B' 80 h.p. Gnôme. External stiffeners on cowling; wing-tip skids under interplane struts. 'C' 80 h.p. Gnôme; 80 h.p. Le Rhône; 80 h.p. Clerget; 110 h.p. Clerget. No external stiffeners on cowling. 'D' 80 h.p. Le Rhône; 100 h.p. Gnôme Monosoupape; 80 h.p. Gnôme. Shorter ailerons; increased dihedral; wing-tip skids nearer wing-tips.

The early models were unarmed, although some pilots carried a rifle or a pistol. A few machines had a Lewis gun fitted to fire forwards and outwards beyond the airscrew arc; others had a Lewis mounted on the top wing to fire over the airscrew. Some R.N.A.S. pilots fired their Lewis guns through the revolving airscrew without the benefit of any interrupter gear. The occasional holes were plugged and then bound with tape! The Vickers-Challenger synchronising gear was first tried out on a Bristol Scout. Later machines were equipped with a Vickers gun synchronised by this system.

No squadron was ever completely equipped with the type, but in early 1916 nearly every unit in the R.F.C. had two or three on its strength.

They were gradually withdrawn during that year, and by late summer had passed on to the training units, with the exception of a few kept by officers for their own use.

The Victoria Cross was won by Captain L. G. Hawker flying a Bristol Scout armed with a Lewis gun. On July 25th, 1915, he attacked three enemy two-seaters, destroying one and damaging the others.

The Scout was used in the Aegean, in Macedonia, Palestine and Mesopotamia, and operated from the aircraft carrier *Vindex* as early as November 1915. In order to provide a rapid means of putting a single-seater within attacking distance of Zeppelins, a Scout 'C' (No. 3028) was accommodated on the top wing of a Porte Baby flying boat. On May 17th, 1916, the pair took off successfully, and the Scout released itself at 1,000 feet and flew away.

Pilots have described the type as being light on the controls and a pleasure to fly; properly armed, it could have greatly influenced the course of aerial warfare.

1. The second version of the Scout A, when flown in races by Lord Carbery, pre-war. 2 and 3. R.N.A.S. Scout Cs. 4. R.F.C. Scout C with synchronised gun. 5. R.F.C. Scout D of the series A.1742–1791, which had 80 h.p. Le Rhône engines.

BRISTOL SCOUT D

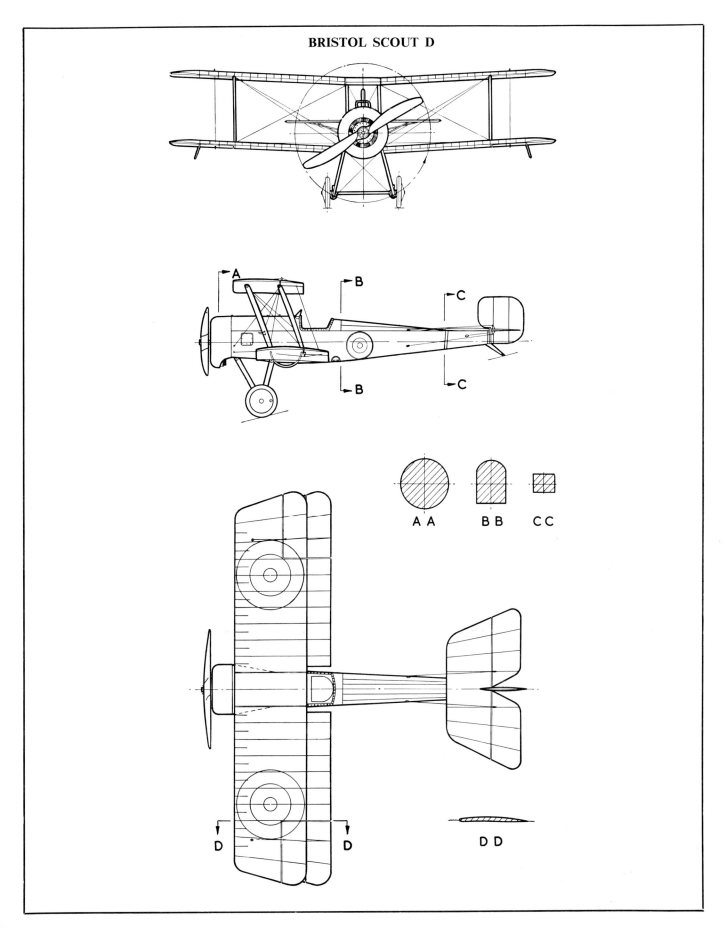

A A   B B   C C

D D

37

BRITISH NIEUPORT NIGHTHAWK

The British Nieuport and General Aircraft Co. Ltd. of Cricklewood, London, at first built Nieuport designs under licence, and later undertook the construction of Sopwith Camels. In 1917 the firm began to develop its own types, the first of these being the B.N.1, designed by H. P. Folland, who had previously worked at the Royal Aircraft Factory. The B.N.1's power unit was the 230 h.p. Bentley B.R.2 rotary, enclosed partially in a circular open-fronted cowling; a large domed, open-ended spinner fitted to the airscrew was soon discarded. The unstaggered wings had blunt tips, and ailerons were carried on the top plane only, which was of much broader chord. Two bays of I-struts formed the unusual interplane bracing. Side fairings streamlined the cowling into the square-sided fuselage, which had a rounded top decking and a small fairing behind the cockpit. The lower tail-fin and -skid were identical to those of the S.E.5.

Twin Vickers guns were fixed to fire through the airscrew arc by means of the Constantinesco gear, and a Lewis gun was mounted above the centre section. The B.N.1 had a first-class performance, but it was passed over in favour of the Sopwith Snipe.

Work commenced in the summer of 1918 on a second Folland-designed single-seater named the Nighthawk, which had the new 320 h.p. A.B.C. Dragonfly radial. Great things were expected of this engine, which had an excellent power-weight ratio and was designed for easy production. The Nighthawk's wings were staggered, with double bays of interplane struts and double ailerons. Light wooden stringers fixed to the box-girder fuselage gave it a circular cross-section. The empennage resembled that of the B.N.1, and several S.E.5 parts were incorporated, with a view to ease of construction; these included the lower tail-fin and -skid, the axle and wheels, the control stick and rudder bar, and some internal cockpit fittings. Two synchronised Vickers guns were mounted in front of the cockpit and fired through the revolving airscrew.

The Nighthawk was a fine aerobatic aeroplane with the remarkably high ground-level speed of 151 m.p.h., and consequently it was put into production. However, it became apparent after a few months that the Dragonfly engine was totally unreliable, as it vibrated excessively and frequently failed after a few hours' running. This was likely to be disastrous, for 11,050 had been ordered from thirteen sub-contractors; it was intended to install the engine in many of the new aircraft types. Luckily for the R.A.F., the Armistice was signed before the Dragonfly had to be used on operations. The failure of the engine meant the cancellation of the Nighthawk production programme. Those aircraft which had been completed saw service in Britain and India during the immediate post-war years; some were powered by the Bristol Jupiter radial engine. Mr. Folland became chief designer to the Gloucester (later Gloster) Aircraft Co. Ltd. in 1920, and a number of Nighthawk variants were turned out by the firm. These included the Nightjar, designed for use on aircraft carriers, and the Gloucester Mars series. Fifty Mars IV machines, known as Sparrowhawks, were purchased by Japan in 1922.

1. Prototype Nieuport Nighthawk. 2. Early Nighthawk, actually the 3rd prototype. 3. Production machine. 4. Nighthawk with heating muffs on its exhaust pipes. 5. H.8535, a Nieuport "Nightjar" with 230 h.p. B.R.2 rotary engine.

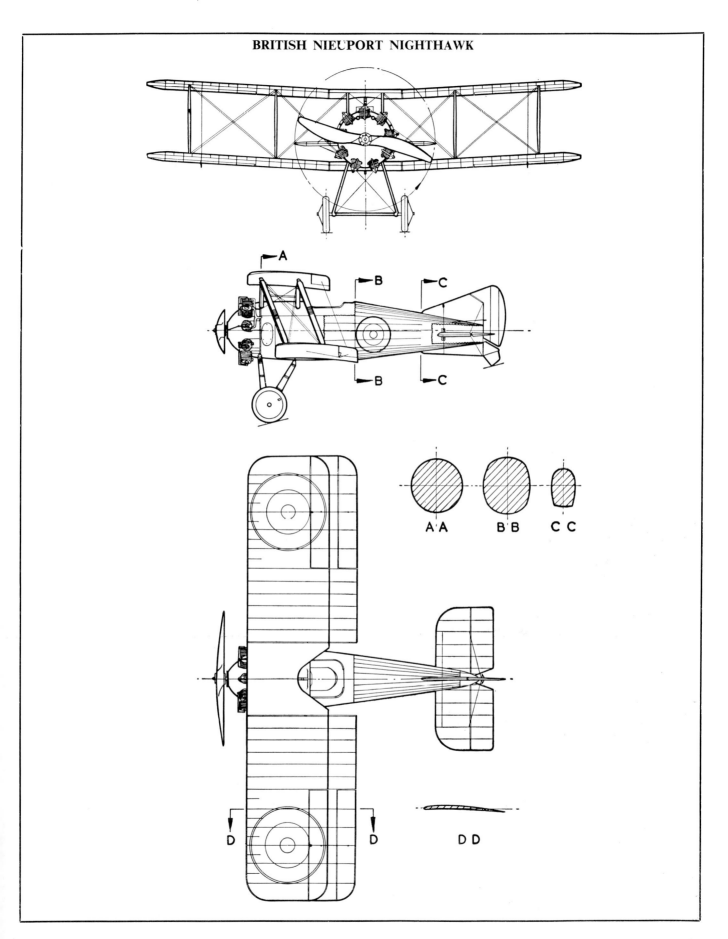

BRITISH NIEUPORT NIGHTHAWK

A A   B B   C C

D D

D.H.2

The De Havilland 2 was the second type designed by Geoffrey de Havilland for the Aircraft Manufacturing Company ('Airco'). It was a pusher aeroplane because it was intended to carry a forward-firing machine-gun, and in early 1915 no British interrupter gear was available.

The prototype appeared in July 1915 and was powered by the 100 h.p. Gnôme Monosoupape rotary, which remained the standard engine, although a few D.H.2s had the 110 h.p. Le Rhône.

The wings had wooden main spars and ribs, fabric-covered; there were two bays of interplane struts. The wooden tail-booms were wire-braced and met at the tail to form a vee in plan-view. The nacelle was wooden-framed with fabric-covered sides and plywood-covered nose and top decking. The elevator control wires passed by way of the junction of the tail-booms and wings to external rocking-levers on the nacelle sides. A sturdy vee-type undercarriage was fitted.

Brackets for a movable Lewis gun were fixed to each side of the prototype's cockpit, but it was soon evident that a fixed gun gave better results, and the nacelles of the production machines were modified accordingly. Racks for ammunition drums were provided on each side of the cockpit. A gravity tank was fitted on production models, either above or below the centre section or under the port upper wing.

No. 24 Squadron, commanded by Major L. G. Hawker, V.C., the first single-seat fighter squadron ever to be formed, went to France equipped with D.H.2s in February 1916. Some spinning accidents occurred in the early stages of the little pusher's career, but as soon as pilots became accustomed to the sensitive controls, they realised that the D.H.2 was strong and easy to fly.

Although not specifically designed for the purpose, the D.H.2 played a big part in clearing the skies of the dangerous Fokker Monoplane, with the result that the R.F.C. had complete air superiority when the Battle of the Somme began on July 1st, 1916. On that day a D.H.2 pilot, Major L. W. B. Rees, C.O. of 32 Squadron, won the Victoria Cross for a single-handed attack on a formation of ten German two-seaters. Although wounded, he forced down two and dispersed the remainder.

The rotary engine was liable to be dangerous; two experienced pilots were killed when the cylinders blew out and severed the tail-booms of their machines. It was also a very cold little aeroplane! McCudden, who flew the type during the winter of 1916–17, wrote of one patrol '. . . I did not care whether I was shot down or not. I was so utterly frozen.'

The new German Halberstadt and Albatros D types which appeared in the autumn of 1916 were much superior to the D.H.2. Replacements, however, were not forthcoming in sufficient quantity and the pushers had to battle on until the early summer of 1917, suffering heavy casualties. A few D.H.2s were supplied to Home Defence units; one flown by Captain Saundby assisted in the destruction of the Zeppelin L.48. The type also served in Macedonia and Palestine. A total of 400 machines were supplied to the R.F.C.

1. The prototype D.H.2 with movable side-brackets for a Lewis gun. 2. 5923, an early production machine with a four-bladed propeller. 3. 4. and 5. Standard production D.H.2s. No. 4 and 5 have gravity fuel tanks below their top wings.

D.H.2

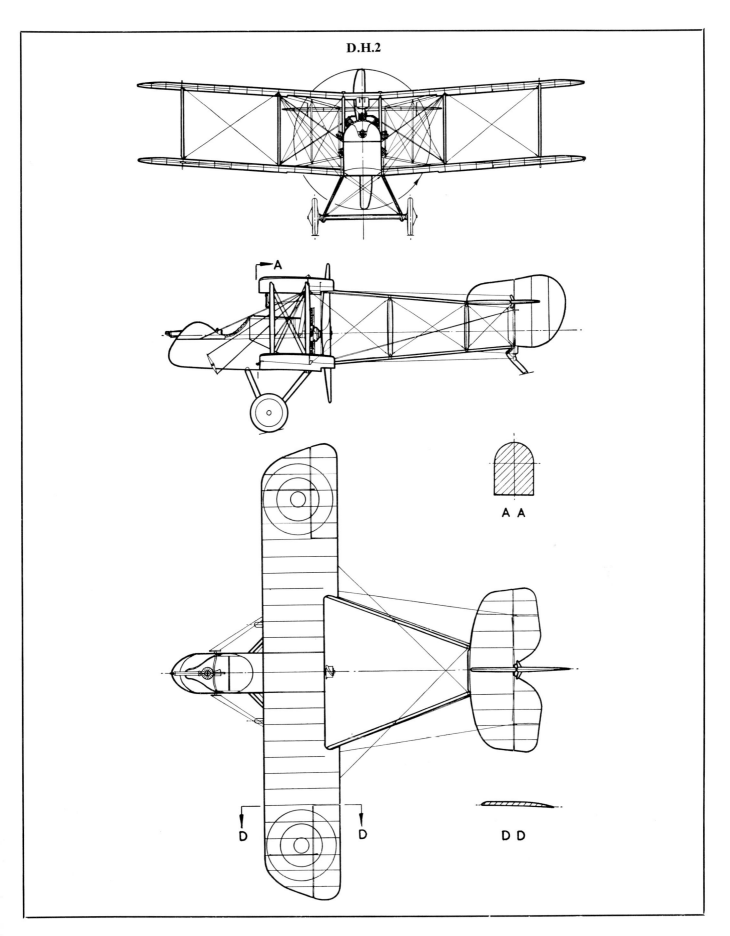

A

A A

D   D   D D

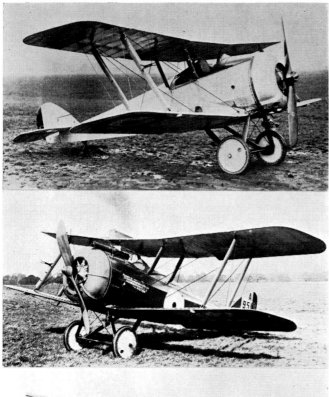

D.H.5

The unconventional D.H.5 biplane was built in late 1916 to the design of Geoffrey de Havilland. The wings were given twenty-seven inches of 'backward stagger' in order to provide a first-class view forwards and upwards. The leading-edge of the top plane was immediately above the pilot's head.

The prototype, A5172, had a 110 h.p. Le Rhône rotary engine, installed in a plain open-fronted cowling, which was faired into a flat-sided box-girder fuselage. The top decking around the cockpit was of plywood. The wings had two wooden main spars and steel-tube compression struts, and were wire-braced and fabric-covered. Large ailerons were fitted to both planes. The rudder was horn-balanced; the main fuel tank was behind the cockpit and a gravity tank was carried on the starboard upper wing. The vee-shaped undercarriage had steel-tube spreader bars and was sprung with rubber cord.

Later the prototype was modified by fitting a rudder similar in shape to those of the production machines, but horn-balanced, and a Vickers gun fixed to fire upwards at several degrees angle. A second machine, A9186, had the same armament; both were probably used in Home Defence experiments.

On the production D.H.5 the fuselage was modified by means of formers and stringers to an octagonal cross-section. The rudder was more pointed in shape and had no horn balance, and the cowling was strengthened with six external ribs. A Vickers gun synchronised by the Constantinesco interrupter gear was mounted on the cowling slightly to port.

In May 1917, as had been intended, the type replaced the D.H.2s of Nos. 24 and 32 Squadrons, R.F.C., and in July No. 41 Squadron received the D.H.5 in exchange for their F.E.8 pusher scouts. Two new squadrons, No. 68 (Australian) and No. 64, arrived in France equipped with the type in September and October 1917.

The D.H.5 never became popular; it was rumoured that it stalled viciously at 80 m.p.h. This was quite untrue, but it was certainly difficult to land, and there were many accidents at training units. More serious defects were the D.H.5's poor performance above 10,000 feet and its tendency to lose height rapidly in combat. At lower altitudes it was a good aeroplane, easy to fly and able to take plenty of punishment.

From August 1917 onwards the type was mainly used for ground attack duty, for which it was well suited with its good forward view and great strength. Four 25 lb. Cooper bombs were carried in racks under the fuselage for this work.

The last D.H.5s disappeared from the Western Front in January 1918, when sufficient S.E.5as became available. Probably the least successful aeroplane designed by de Havilland during the war period, it had a very short operational career.

At least one D.H.5 was experimentally fitted with a 110 h.p. Clerget rotary engine. After its withdrawal from the front, the type was used at training units, where it was thoroughly unpopular. The surviving machines were soon destroyed in accidents. Nevertheless, a total of approximately 550 D.H.5s were constructed.

1. Prototype D.H.5 A5172. 2. Production type, A9513 'Benin', built by Darracq. 3. B371 'Solanki', built by the British Caudron Company. 4. Airco-built version A9340, 'C' of No. 32 Squadron. 5. B7775, a D.H.5 re-built by No. 1 (Southern) Aeroplane Repair Depot.

D.H.5

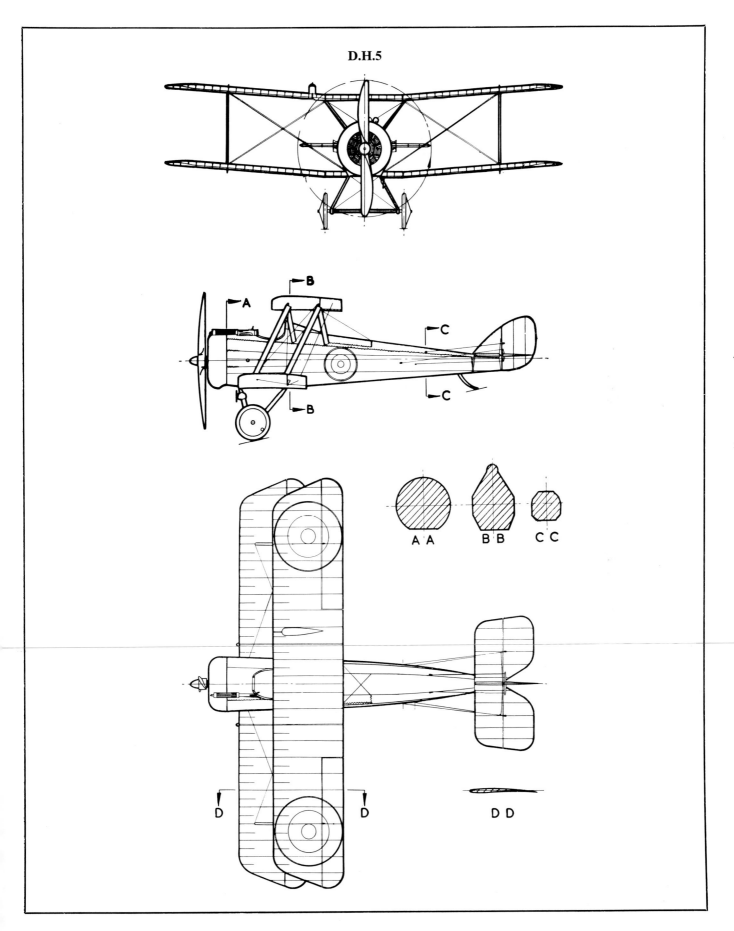

A A   B B   C C

D D

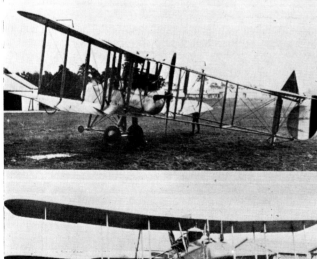

F.E.2a, 2b AND 2d

In 1911 and 1913 two separate pusher biplanes were built at the Royal Aircraft Factory with the designation F.E.2. The F.E.2a, however, which appeared a year later, 1914, was an entirely new type, specifically designed as a fighting aeroplane.

The power unit was the 100 h.p. Green engine; the unstaggered wings had fabric-covered wooden spars and ribs; the outer panels were identical to those of the B.E.2c and could be interchanged if necessary. The rear portion of the upper centre section was hinged and could be lowered to form an air brake. The nacelle was a wooden structure, plywood- and fabric-covered, with metal panels almost enclosing the engine. The wooden tail-booms were wire-braced; the rudder was balanced and a small triangular fin was mounted on the tail-plane. The oleo-sprung undercarriage had a nose-wheel to prevent the machine turning over in a bad landing.

When war began twelve F.E.2as were ordered from the Factory. The Green engine was unsatisfactory; it was replaced by the 120 h.p. and later by the 160 h.p. Beardmore. The centre-section air brake and the engine cowlings were discarded. This modified version was named the F.E.2b.

At first a Lewis gun was carried on a bracket in front of the observer's cockpit; later a second Lewis on a telescopic mounting was fitted to fire backwards over the top plane. The observer, without a parachute, had to stand with only his feet inside his cockpit to do this. Both guns had leather bags to catch the ejected cartridge cases, which otherwise would have smashed the propeller.

The first units completely equipped with F.E.2bs, Nos. 20, 25, 23 and 22 Squadrons, went to France in the early months of 1916. The type was found to be capable of dealing with the Fokker Monoplane. On June 18th, 1916, Max Immelmann, the most famous of the Fokker pilots, was shot down by Corporal Waller and Second Lieutenant McCubbin, flying a 2b of No. 25 Squadron.

An improved model, the F.E.2d, with the 250 h.p. Rolls-Royce engine, appeared in July 1916. It could be distinguished from the F.E.2b by its larger radiator and bulkier engine. The Rolls-Royce gave the 2d a better performance, and it was possible to fix one or two extra Lewis guns to fire forwards, for the pilot's use.

The nose-wheels on both versions were often removed to improve their performance.

The F.E.s were easily outclassed by the new German fighters of 1916–17, but they were not withdrawn from the front until the autumn of 1917. When attacked, their crews learned to form a 'defensive circle' and thus protected the 'blind spot' under their tails. The 'Fees' could put up a hard fight; in combat with them Manfred von Richthofen was badly wounded and Karl Schaefer (thirty victories) was killed.

During the last eighteen months of the war the F.E.2b equipped several night-bomber units. A few F.E.2bs were equipped with one-pounder guns which were used by night against ground targets. 2bs and 2ds supplied to Home Defence units were unsatisfactory because of their poor 'ceiling'. Some 2,190 F.E.2bs and 2ds were built.

1. F.E.2a. 2. Early production F.E.2b, 'Baroda'. 3. F.E.2b with vee undercarriage. 4. Prototype F.E.2d, with four-bladed propeller and stack-type exhausts. 5. F.E.2d night-fighter, 78 Squadron, Sutton's Farm, 1917. Note the large radiator, a characteristic of the type.

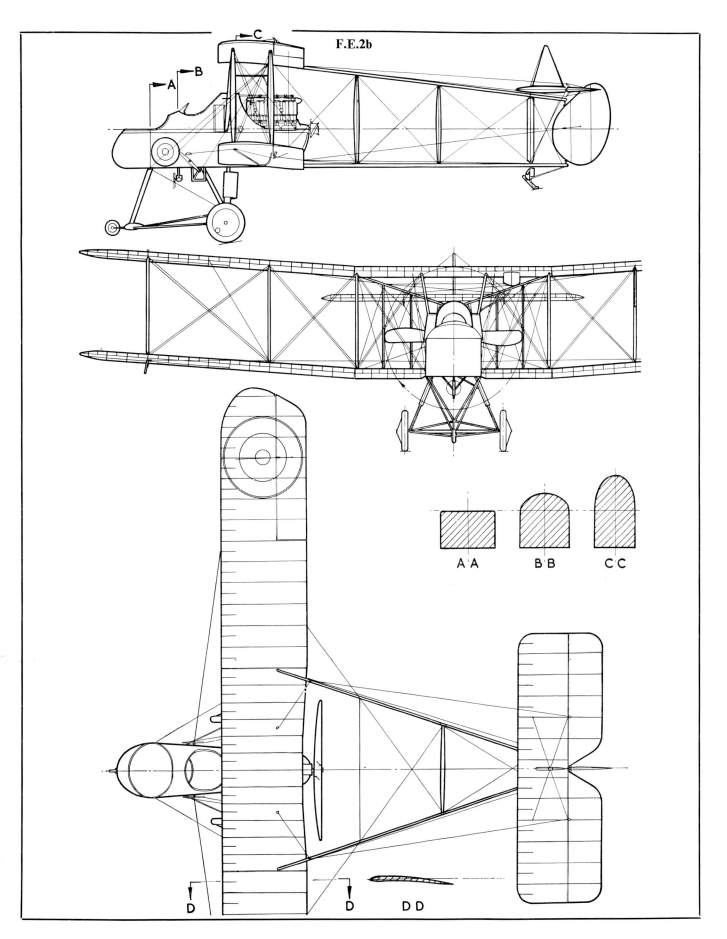

F.E.2b

A'A   B'B   C'C

D   D   D D

45

F.E.8

In early 1915 the British had not developed an interrupter gear which would allow a machine-gun to fire safely
through the revolving blades of an airscrew. Consequently
the F.E.8 was a 'pusher' type, providing the pilot with an
unrestricted field of fire in a forward direction, but without the performance of a tractor aeroplane.

Designed by J. Kenworthy of the Royal Aircraft
Factory, the F.E.8 prototype was completed in October
1915. It was an angular little machine, powered by a
Gnôme Monosoupape rotary engine which drove a four-
bladed propeller provided with a large spinner. Narrow-
chord wings of the usual fabric-covered, wire-braced construction were fitted. The centre section was wide, stretching between the inner bays of the interplane struts; long-
span ailerons were carried. The wooden wire-braced
tail-booms converged at the tail-plane to form vees in side
elevation. The fin was bisected by the horizontal tail surfaces, and the tail-skid was attached directly to the bottom
of the rudder. Sheet aluminium covered the pointed
wooden-framed nacelle, which was connected to the middle
of the centre section by inverted vee struts. A streamlined
head-rest was fixed behind the cockpit.

The prototype had a stripped Lewis gun, which protruded from the lower part of the nacelle; it was fired by
remote control and could not be reached by the pilot
during flight.

In November 1915 this machine was completely destroyed in a crash. A second prototype, built from spare
parts, passed its service trials in France in December, and
the design was put into production.

The production model was somewhat modified; there
was no spinner, the Lewis gun was mounted more conveniently in front of the cockpit, and racks for spare
ammunition drums were fixed on each side of the nacelle.
The 110 h.p. Le Rhône and 110 h.p. Clerget rotaries were
fitted experimentally, but the Mono-Gnôme remained the
standard engine.

Like the D.H.2, the F.E.8 was at first involved in
several spinning fatalities. Major Goodden, the Factory test
pilot, therefore demonstrated how to bring an F.E.8 out of
a spin, and thereafter the machine became popular.

As a result of manufacturing delays, the first squadron
to be entirely equipped with the type, No. 40, did not reach
the Western Front until August 1916. A second F.E.8
unit, No. 41 Squadron, followed in October. The type
began its operational career, therefore, at the time when
the much superior Albatros D-I and D-II were coming into
use, and had little chance of success.

No. 40 Squadron's unequal struggle culminated on
March 9th, 1917, in a thirty-minute contest with the
Albatros D-IIIs of von Richthofen's *Jagdstaffel* 11. All
nine F.E.8s were forced down, five being completely destroyed. Luckily it became possible to re-equip the
squadron with French Nieuport 17s soon afterwards. No.
41 Squadron had to wait until July 1917, when D.H.5s
were supplied.

The F.E.8 was a good design which unfortunately was
already obsolete when it started its fighting career. Just
under 300 of the type were built.

*1. Unarmed prototype F.E.8. 2. Prototype with re-
motely controlled Lewis gun. 3. 7624, a production
machine in German hands; the serial number is painted
on the nacelle above the lower wing. 4 and 5. Production F.E.8s with standard Lewis gun mountings.*

F.E.8

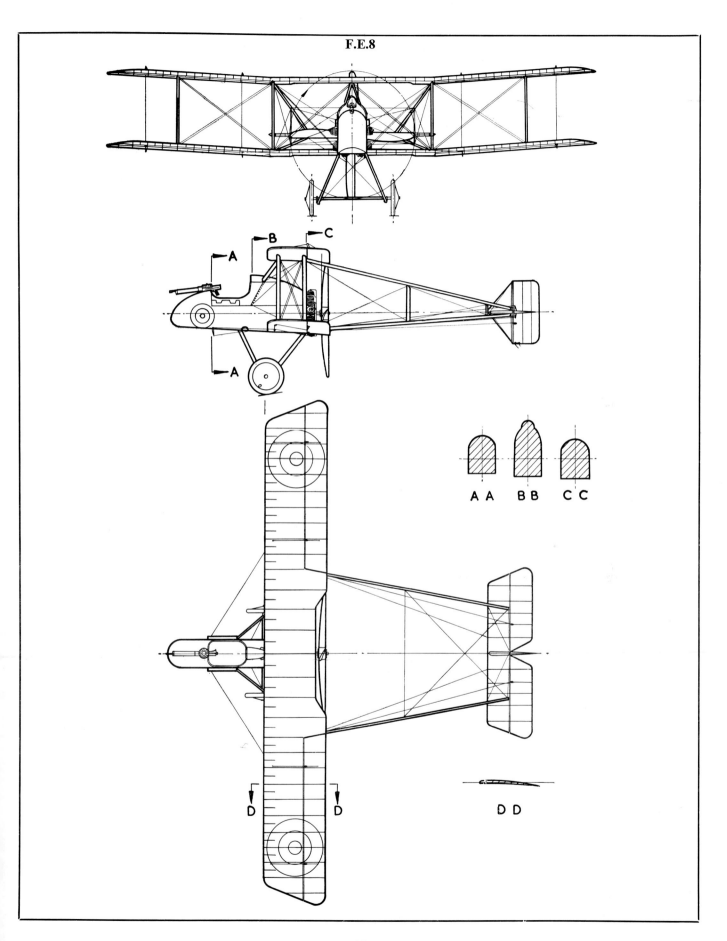

A A B B C C

D D

MARTINSYDE S.1

The Martinsyde S.1., a small single-seater tractor biplane greatly resembling the successful Sopwith Tabloid, appeared in 1914.

It had a 80 h.p. Gnôme rotary engine, almost enclosed in a metal cowling; a horizontal slot in the front provided ventilation. The wings had fabric-covered wooden spars and ribs; there was no dihedral and ailerons were fitted to both planes. The fuselage was a wire-braced wooden box girder, plywood-covered from behind the cowling to the rear of the cockpit, and fabric-covered from there to the tail. The general trim appearance was spoiled by a clumsy and complicated undercarriage; twin skids fitted with small wheels were intended to prevent the machine nosing over in a rough landing. When at rest the weight of the aeroplane was carried on the rear extensions of the skids, the tail being off the ground. A small skid was fixed under the tail to prevent damage to the rudder.

Later S.1s had neat vee-shaped undercarriages and the usual sprung tail-skids.

Small numbers of Martinsyde S.1s were delivered to some of the units on the Western Front in late 1914. Like the Bristol Scouts and Sopwith Tabloids they were used for fast scouting duties, and no squadron had more than one or two. Some had a Lewis gun mounted on the top plane to fire forwards and upwards. Captain L. A. Strange of No. 6 Squadron had a narrow escape when attacking a German two-seater in one of these armed S.1s. After firing the contents of his first ammunition drum (at this period forty-seven rounds) he attempted to replace it with a full one. It refused to come off, and he stood up in the cockpit to wrestle with it; whereupon the machine stalled and turned over, leaving Strange hanging from the jammed drum! Luckily he was able to catch one of the centre-section struts, and swinging his legs up into the cockpit, managed to right the aeroplane before it struck the ground. His return flight was rather difficult, for he had smashed all the instruments with his feet, and his cushion having fallen out he found himself sitting on the control cables!

The S.1 was inferior to both the Bristol Scout and the Sopwith Tabloid. It was unstable both fore and aft and laterally, and its top speed was only 87 m.p.h., very little better than that of the Avro two-seater biplane of the same period. Machines were attached to Nos. 1, 4, 5, 6, 12 and 16 Squadrons, R.F.C., but by the summer of 1915 the last S.1 had been withdrawn from the Western Front.

Four Martinsydes were sent to Mesopotamia in the summer of 1915 as part of the equipment collected for Major-General Townshend's proposed advance on Baghdad. The Gnôme rotary proved unsuitable for operations in the desert, but one machine, flown by Major Reilly, carried out a useful reconnaissance which greatly helped in the capture of Kut. The remaining three aeroplanes were either shot down or damaged in accidents.

Most of the S.1s supplied to the R.F.C. were used for training purposes, four machines being delivered to training establishments in 1914, and over forty in 1915. It is believed that about sixty of the type were built, but it is impossible to make an accurate estimate, for the official figures group the S.1 with the G.100/102.

1. and 2. 2831, a Martinsyde S.1 with the early type of undercarriage. 3. S.1 with vee-type undercarriage and tail-skid. The rudder marking is that in use very early in the war. 4. and 5. Late production machines 4241 and 4243, at training units.

MARTINSYDE S.1

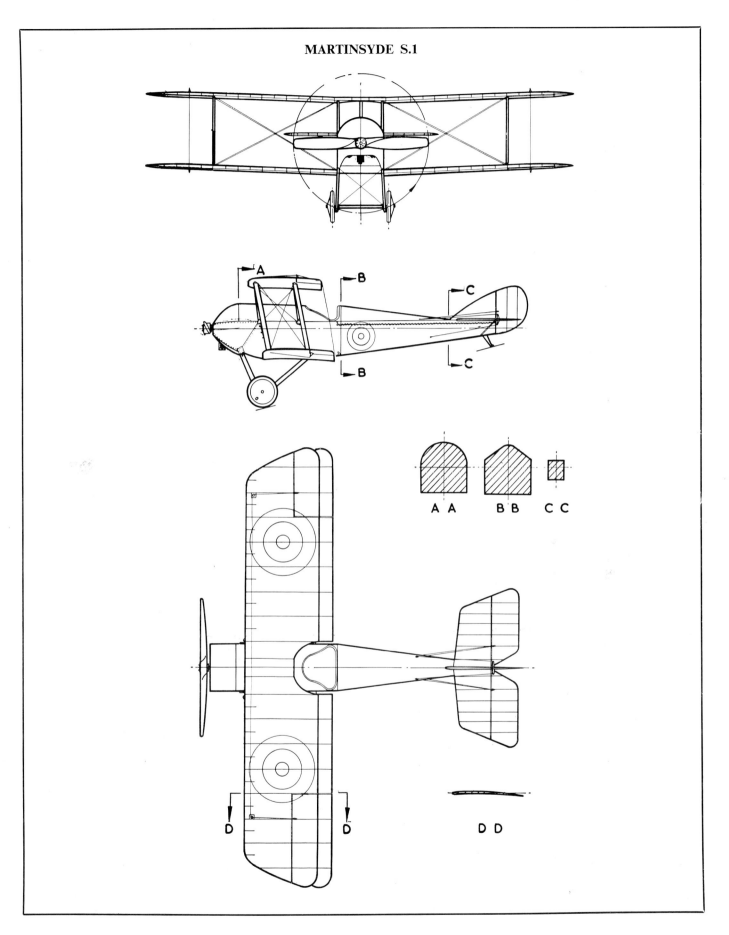

A A   B B   C C

D D

MARTINSYDE G.100 AND G.102 ELEPHANT

The Martinsyde G.100, built to the designs of A. A. Fletcher in the summer of 1915, was intended to be a long-range escort fighter. A large aeroplane for a single-seater, it was capable of carrying enough fuel for five and a half hours' flying.

The prototype, No. 4735, had a 120 h.p. Beardmore engine enclosed in a clumsy open-fronted cowling; each cylinder had its own exhaust stub. The radiator was behind the engine, and a three-bladed airscrew was fitted. The staggered wings had fabric-covered wooden main spars and ribs; the centre-section struts were attached to the fuselage by metal fishplates.

The fuselage was the usual wooden structure, wire-braced and fabric-covered, except for plywood side sections between the mainplanes and plywood top decking around the cockpit. The fin and rudder were similar to those of the Martinsyde S.1, and a large plain tail-skid was fitted.

The production model had a neater cowling, single exhaust manifold and a normal two-bladed airscrew. The flying wires were doubled and a new pylon-type tail-skid was substituted for the original one.

A Lewis gun was carried above the centre section on a complicated mounting, no British interrupter gear being available at this time. A second Lewis gun was fixed to the port side of the fuselage behind the cockpit, and could be fired *backwards*, but without much chance of hitting the enemy!

The first G.100s went to France in early 1916, and were attached in small numbers to two-seater reconnaissance and bombing squadrons. They were expected to provide protection for these slower machines. The only squadron to be completely equipped with the type, No. 27, arrived at the front on March 1st, 1916.

It soon became obvious that the Martinsyde was too big and awkward for fighting duties; it turned too slowly, and the pilot's view was obscured by the broad-chord wings. Its excellent lift, however, made it a satisfactory bomber, and it was used for this work from mid-1916 until November 1917.

The performance was improved by the installation of the 160 h.p. Beardmore engine. This modified version was designated the G.102, and could be distinguished by its three stub exhausts in place of the manifold of the production G.100. It soon received the nickname 'Elephant', which was subsequently applied to both versions.

The G.102 could carry a bomb load of up to 260 lb., and No. 27 Squadron did good work with it until they were supplied with D.H.4s in November 1917.

Martinsydes undertook both fighting and bombing duties in Palestine and Mesopotamia, and two reached Baku on the Caspian Sea, where they did excellent work against the Bolsheviks. Eventually the machines were burned, when the British force withdrew from the area.

The 'Elephant' had great strength and lifting power. It was, however, rather stiff on the controls, and its clean design made it liable to 'float' when landing. Its name is perpetuated in the elephant crest of No. 27 Squadron, Royal Air Force.

1. 4735, the prototype Martinsyde G.100, with three-bladed airscrew. 2. Early production G.100. 3. A No. 27 Squadron machine at Dover en route for France. 4. G.100 with 112 lb. bombs, in the Middle East. 5. A G.102 presented by Rhodesia. Note the bomb-racks.

MARTINSYDE G.100

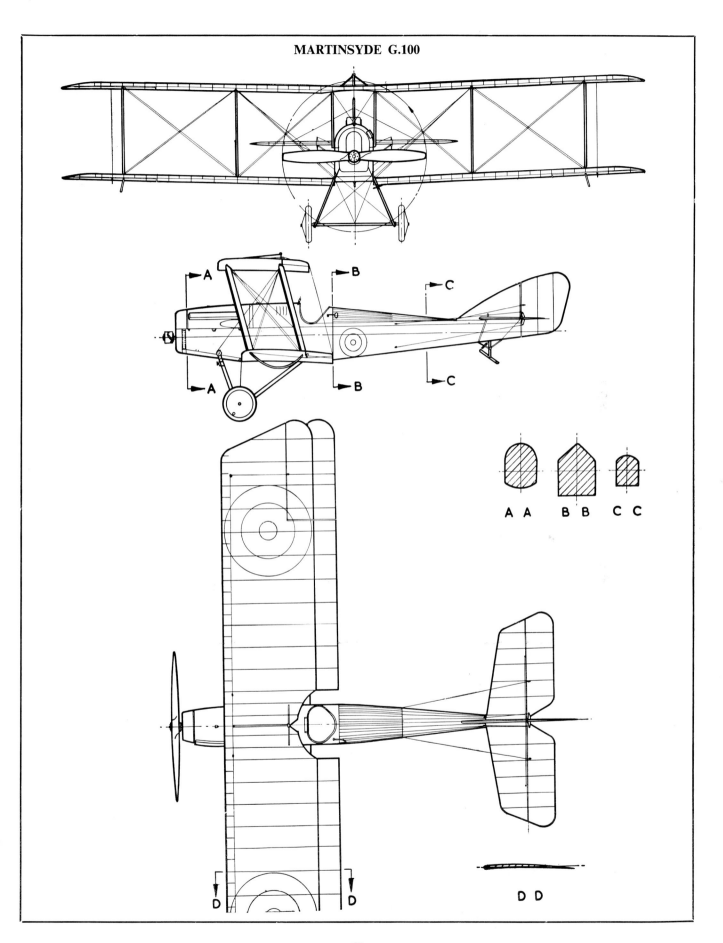

A A   B B   C C

D D

MARTINSYDE F.3 AND F.4 BUZZARD

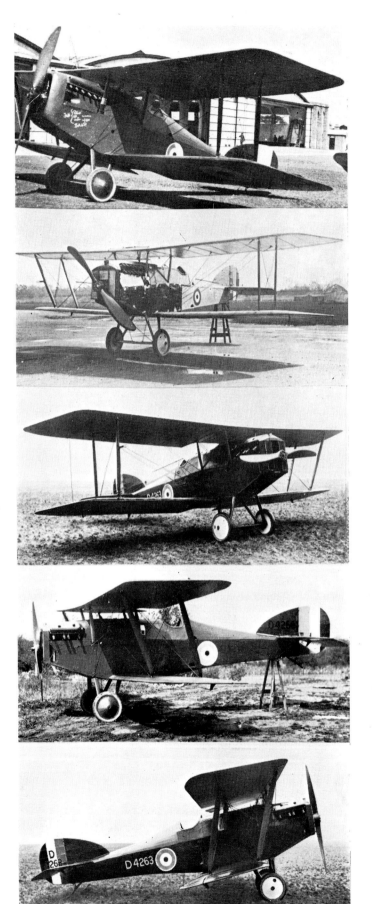

A new Martinsyde single-seater fighter biplane, the R.G., was tested at Farnborough in February 1917. In appearance it was a smaller and neater G.100. Both the 190 h.p. Rolls-Royce Falcon I and the 275 h.p. Falcon III were fitted at different times, and even with the former its performance was extremely good. Unfortunately the decision had already been made to manufacture the S.E.5 and Sopwith Camel, and the R.G. was not developed.

The Martinsyde F.3, which was brought out in the autumn of 1917, bore a resemblance to both the R.G. and the unsuccessful F.2 two-seater. On its first test in November the experimental 285 h.p. Rolls-Royce Falcon was installed—later the Falcon III became the standard power unit. A frontal radiator, without shutters, was fitted; the exhaust gases discharged through six stubs on each side of the nose. Broad-chord staggered wings of the usual fabric-covered wire-braced wooden construction were fitted; the lower wing-roots were faired into the side of the fuselage, and ailerons were carried on both planes. The fuselage, a wooden box girder covered with three-ply and fabric, was very deep, and the pilot sat high up with his eyes on a level with the trailing-edge of the top wing. Fin and rudder were typically Martinsyde; two struts braced the tail-plane from below. The short undercarriage vees seemed out of proportion to the thick fuselage. Under the cowling were mounted twin synchronised Vickers guns.

The F.3 did well in its tests and was ordered into production; but there was such a shortage of Falcon engines that it was decided to fit the 300 h.p. Hispano-Suiza. Modifications were necessary, and the redesigned aeroplane was named the F.4. Four of the six F.3s ordered went to Home Defence units in 1918; engine shutters were added to the radiators of the machines with the Falcon III engine.

The dimensions of the F.4 varied slightly from those of the F.3, but the most obvious difference was the position of the cockpit, which was moved farther aft to improve the pilot's view. The type was named the Buzzard; two versions were manufactured, the Mark I or standard model, and the Mark Ia, a long-range fighter probably intended for escort duty with the day bombers of the Independent Force. In addition to the extensive British building programme, 1,500 Buzzards were to have been constructed in the U.S.A. When the war finished, however, less than fifty machines had been delivered to the R.A.F., and no squadron was ever equipped with the type.

The Sopwith Snipe, a slower type, had been chosen as the standard British post-war fighter, so there was no place for the Buzzard in the R.A.F. One went to Japan, and a few were used by Spain and by the Irish Air Corps. After the closing down of the Martinsyde firm, a number of Buzzards were purchased by the Aircraft Disposals Company. Some of these machines went to Finland in 1924, and the type was still in use there as late as 1935 as a gunnery trainer.

A variety of engines were installed in privately owned Buzzards; they included the Rolls-Royce Falcon III, the Armstrong Siddeley Jaguar radial, and the 230 h.p. Siddeley Puma. One machine was fitted with floats.

1. Martinsyde F.3. This type was evaluated as a possible night-fighter at Biggin Hill in 1918. 2. Prototype Martinsyde F.4 in clear dope finish at Brooklands early in 1918. 3, 4 and 5. Three views of the standard production version.

MARTINSYDE F.4 BUZZARD

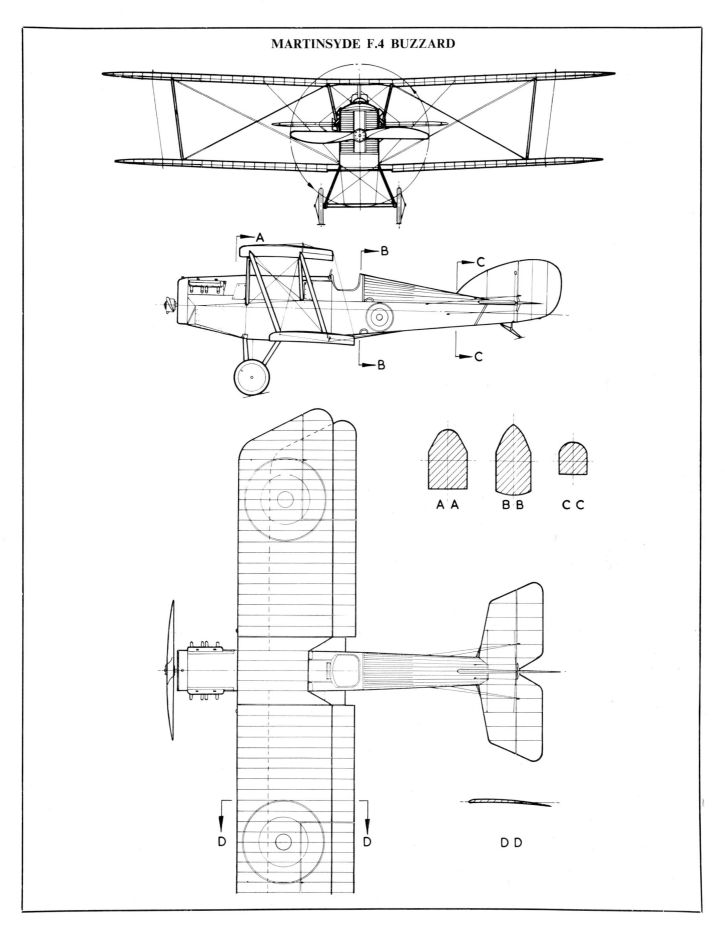

A A   B B   C C

D D

S.E.2a

The S.E.1 was a box-like 'canard' or tail-first aeroplane, constructed in 1911 at H.M. Balloon Factory, Farnborough, from the parts of a Blériot monoplane. S.E. signified 'Santos Experimental'—the Brazilian pioneer Santos-Dumont being associated with the canard type of aeroplane. The machine crashed in August 1911, killing the assistant director of the Factory, Lieutenant Ridge.

In the following year the same establishment, renamed the Royal Aircraft Factory, constructed a small single-seater tractor biplane, the first true high-performance scout. Named the B.S.1 (B.S. stood for Blériot Scout—'Blériot' denoting a tractor aeroplane), it was mainly designed and flown by Lieutenant Geoffrey de Havilland. Both in appearance and performance the B.S.1 was far ahead of its time. The power unit was a twin-row 100 h.p. Gnôme rotary engine, fitted with a neat metal cowling. The staggered wings had wooden spars and ribs, covered with fabric; the tips were rounded. Lateral control was by means of wing warping. The fuselage was a streamlined wooden monocoque; the tail unit had a large one-piece elevator, and a small balanced rudder. The general trim appearance was spoiled by a clumsy twin-skid undercarriage.

The balanced rudder proved to be inadequate, and caused the B.S.1 to crash in March 1913, shortly after it had flown at the remarkable speed of 90 m.p.h.

The rebuilt machine was renamed the B.S.2. It was given divided elevators, a larger rudder with fins both above and below the fuselage, and the engine was replaced by a Gnôme rotary of 80 h.p. Soon the designation B.S.2 was changed to S.E.2; this time the initials S.E. meant 'Scouting Experimental'.

Further modifications took place later in 1913. The monocoque fuselage was replaced by a fabric-covered wooden-framed structure of circular cross-section. Fin and rudder were increased in area, and a pointed spinner was fitted, which gave the nose a fairly clean entry. This modified machine was named the S.E.2a.

With the serial number 609, the S.E.2a joined No. 5 Squadron, Royal Flying Corps, early in 1914. The average pilot of the time looked on it as a dangerously fast aeroplane, and consequently it was rarely flown. For some ten months it was stationed at Netheravon.

In October 1914 No. 609 was sent to join No. 3 Squadron, R.F.C., in France. Like the contemporary Bristol, Sopwith and Martinsyde Scouts it was intended to protect the slower two-seater reconnaissance machines. At first its only armament consisted of a service revolver, but later two rifles were experimentally fixed on each side of the fuselage to fire forwards and outwards to clear the revolving airscrew. It proved to be much faster than any of the opposing German aeroplanes, and would have been a useful weapon had it been possible to fit a forward-firing machine-gun. The S.E.2a did not go into production, for the remarkable S.E.4 biplane was undergoing development. The latter type was for a time the fastest machine in the world, with a top speed of 135 m.p.h.

The S.E.2a was withdrawn from front-line service in March 1915.

1. The world's first single-seat high-speed scout, the B.S.1. 2 and 3. The B.S.2 (S.E.2). 4 and 5. The S.E.2a, serial 609, which saw service on the Western Front. It was flown by Lieutenant Shekleton of No. 3 Squadron, R.F.C.

S.E.2a

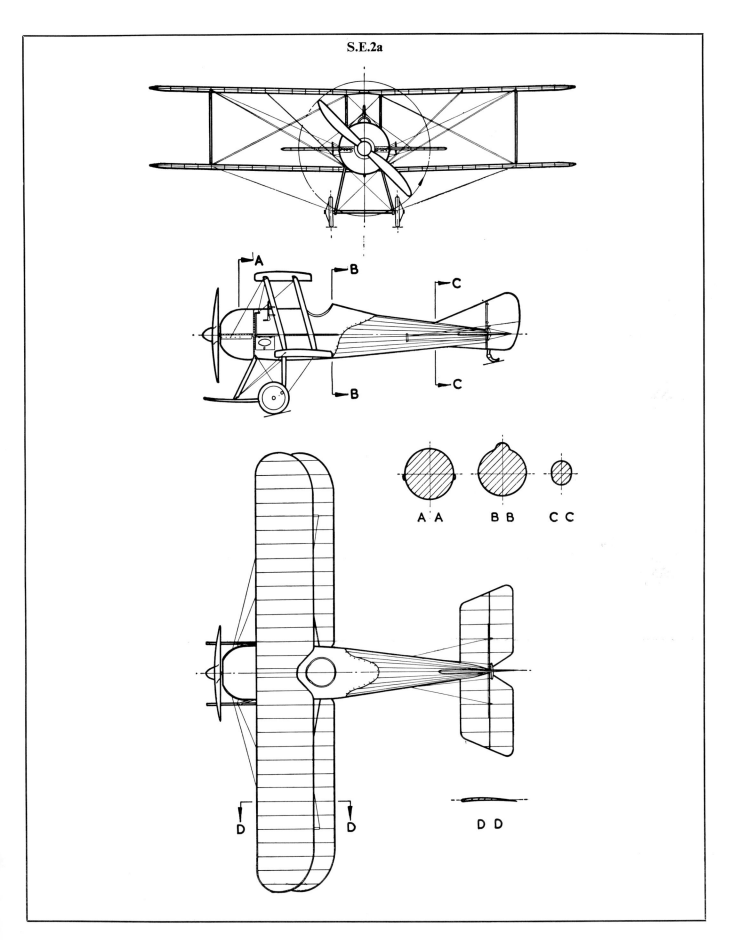

A A   B B   C C

D D

S.E.5 AND S.E.5a

The S.E.5/5a, rival of the Camel for the title of the most successful British fighter of the First World War, was designed by H. P. Folland, J. Kenworthy and Major F. W. Goodden of the Royal Aircraft Factory.

The prototype S.E.5, A4561, appeared in December 1916; it had the new 150 h.p. Hispano-Suiza engine with a car-type radiator and short exhaust manifolds. The wings had wire-braced spruce spars; in place of compression struts, some ribs were of solid construction. The tail-plane incidence could be changed in flight. A wire-braced wooden box girder, the fuselage was fabric-covered except for plywood sides from the nose to the front spar of the lower wing, with plywood round the cockpit. The main fuel tank was behind the engine, and there was a gravity tank to port of the centre section.

In January 1917 the wings of the prototype collapsed in flight, and Major Goodden was killed. The main planes of subsequent machines were strengthened, their span was reduced and blunter tips were fitted. A few of the early production aircraft, however, retained the wing plan of the first two prototypes.

A Vickers gun, fixed on the port side of the fuselage with its breech inside the cockpit, fired through the air-screw by means of the Constantinesco synchronising gear. A Lewis gun on a Foster mounting could be fired ahead over the top wing or directly upwards.

The type first went to France on April 7th, 1917, with No. 56 Squadron. The early machines had celluloid 'green-houses' over the cockpits; these were liable to be dangerous in a crash, so Major Blomfield, the C.O., had them replaced by flat Triplex windscreens. The gravity tank was soon moved from the top of the wing to a position inside the centre section. A few S.E.5s had faired head-rests.

A modified version, the S.E.5a, powered by the 200 h.p. geared Hispano-Suiza engine, was introduced in June 1917. It had a rather deeper nose than that of the S.E.5, radiator shutters and long exhaust pipes. The standard faired head-rest was frequently removed to improve the rearward view. From December 1917, the front struts of the undercarriage vees were strengthened.

The geared 200 h.p. engine suffered from manufacturing faults, and there were frequent failures; in addition, engine construction lagged behind airframe manufacture, and the S.E.5a was not available in quantity until well into 1918. Eventually the Wolseley W.4a Viper 200 h.p. engine, based on the Hispano-Suiza, became standard and there were no more engine difficulties. The Viper's radiator was square and bulky, with short horizontal shutters.

Both friend and foe recognised the S.E. as a formidable fighting machine; it was fast, extremely strong and easy to fly. Superior to the Albatros D-III and D-V, the Pfalz D-III and the Fokker Dr-I, it was not outclassed when the excellent Fokker D-VII appeared in May 1918. It is significant that the S.E.5a was the mount of Mannock (seventy-three victories), Bishop (seventy-two), McCudden (fifty-seven) and Beauchamp-Proctor (fifty-four).

Some machines of No. 24 Squadron were rigged with reduced dihedral to improve their manœuvrability.

A total of 5,205 S.E.5s and 5as was constructed.

1. Prototype S.E.5, with Major Goodden in the cockpit. 2. Early S.E.5 with 'greenhouse' windshield. 3. S.E.5a with 200 h.p. Hispano-Suiza engine and strengthened undercarriage. 4. Viper-powered late production S.E.5a. 5. S.E.5a of No. 24 Squadron, with reduced dihedral.

S.E.5a

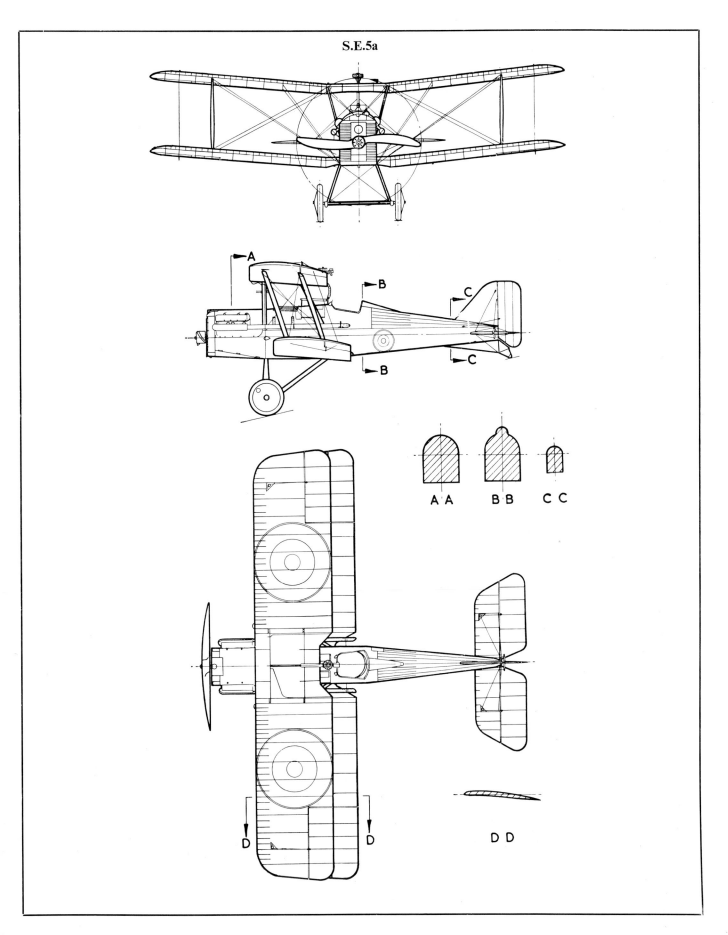

A A   B B   C C

D D

SOPWITH SCHNEIDER AND BABY

The 1914 Schneider Trophy race was won by a seaplane version of the Sopwith Tabloid, piloted by Howard Pixton. Soon after the outbreak of war, the British Navy felt the need for a fast scouting seaplane, and the Schneider machine was ordered into production in November 1914.

The production aircraft was similar to Pixton's seaplane, with the same 100 h.p. Gnôme Monosoupape rotary engine; there were, however, extra float bracing struts and the fin and rudder were slightly larger. A stripped Lewis gun was mounted to fire through a rectangular aperture in the centre section. Later models had ailerons instead of wing warping and even larger fins.

From early 1915 onwards the 'Schneider' seaplanes, as they were called, undertook anti-submarine and anti-airship patrols. Operations from early seaplane carriers were unsuccessful, for the Schneider's floats too often collapsed as soon as it was lowered into a choppy sea. Experiments were carried out to overcome this difficulty, and on August 6th, 1915, a Schneider mounted on a special wheeled trolley took off from the flight deck of the seaplane carrier *Campania*. The little seaplane operated not only from bases in the British Isles, but also in the Aegean, the Mediterranean and the Red Sea.

In order to improve the performance, the 110 h.p. Clerget rotary was installed; the 'bull-nose' cowling gave place to an open-fronted 'horseshoe' type. Although various gun mountings continued to be fitted, a synchronised Lewis gun, mounted centrally in front of the cockpit, became common. This version became known as the 'Baby', but the name 'Schneider' was loosely used for both types.

By 1917 operational needs frequently required the Baby to carry two 65 lb. bombs, a machine-gun and ammunition, a pigeon, drinking water and a sea-anchor, so that it was dangerously overloaded. Steps were taken to improve the machine's lift; not, strangely enough, by the Sopwith company, which was busy producing Camels, but by the Blackburn Aeroplane and Motor Company and by the Fairey Aviation Company of Hayes and Hamble. The former concern built ten Babies with modified wings, and installed 130 h.p. Clerget engines in their later production machines. The Fairey company fitted their 'Hamble Baby' with a new set of thicker wings, incorporating the Fairey Patent Camber Gear, a type of trailing-edge flap, which increased the wing-lift. Its main floats and tail float were redesigned, and the fin and rudder were almost square in outline. Most of the Fairey Hamble Babies, however, were built by Parnall & Sons of Bristol, and retained the Sopwith-type main floats, fins and rudders. Both the 110 h.p. and 130 h.p. Clergets were installed. The last seventy-four Parnall-built machines, known as Hamble Baby Converts, were intended for carrier use and had enormously wide wheeled undercarriages. Yet another variant was developed by the R.N.A.S. Experimental Construction Depot, Isle of Grain; the Port Victoria P.V.1, as it was called, had high-lift section wings.

The Blackburn and Hamble Babies were just as widely used as their predecessors. In all, 136 Schneider and 286 Baby seaplanes were constructed.

1. 3726, an early production Schneider with warping wings and triangular fin. 2. Later production Schneider with ailerons and larger fin. 3. Standard Blackburn-built Baby. 4. Baby with synchronised Lewis gun. 5. Fairey Hamble Baby with synchronised Lewis gun.

SOPWITH BABY

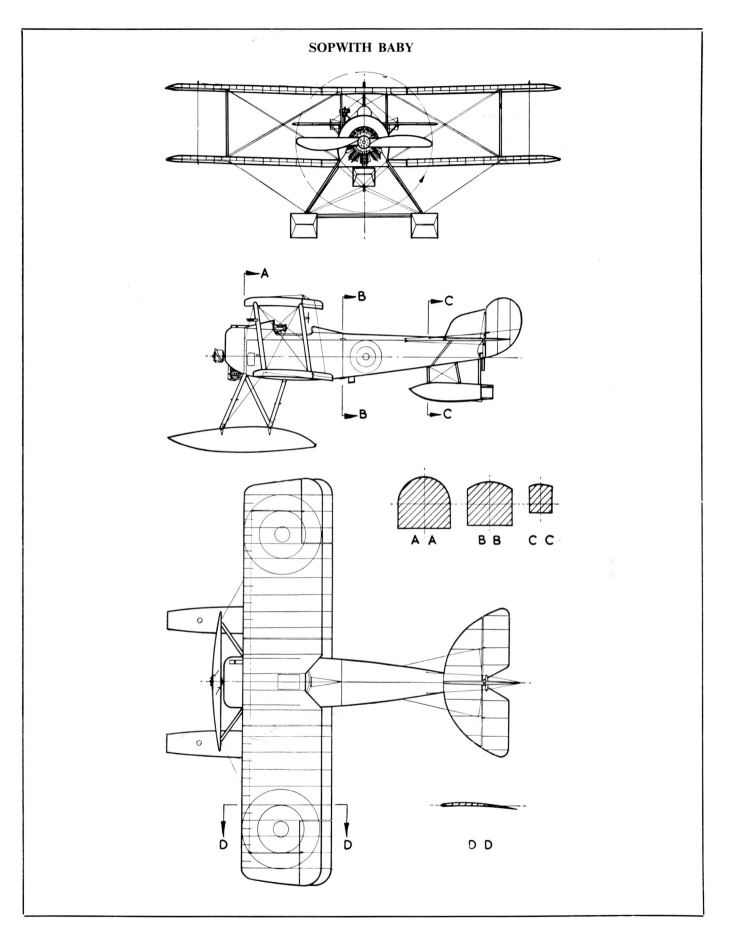

A A   B B   C C

D D

SOPWITH F.1 AND 2F.1 CAMEL

As the successor to the Pup, the Sopwith Aviation Company produced a fiery, temperamental little biplane, the famous, and notorious, Sopwith F.1 Camel.

The prototype F.1 had the 110 h.p. Clerget rotary engine; the first production machines, however, had the 130 h.p. Clerget. Many F.1s were powered with the 110 h.p. Le Rhône, the 150 h.p. B.R.1, or the 100 h.p. Gnôme Monosoupape. The fabric-covered wings had wire-braced wooden spars and ribs and steel-tube wing-tips and trailing-edges; the lower wing only had dihedral. The centre section was wide, so that the centre-section struts were splayed outwards. To improve the pilot's view there was a 'skylight' in the top wing. Tail, rudder and fin were outlined in steel tubing.

The fuselage was a wire-braced wooden box girder; apart from aluminium panels behind the cowling and plywood cockpit sides and top decking, the covering was of fabric. The undercarriage was of the split-axle type; the steel-tube vees were relatively short, the wheels relatively large.

It was the first British type to carry twin Vickers guns; their breeches were enclosed in a 'hump', which gave the Camel its name.

In the hands of an experienced pilot the Camel could outmanœuvre any contemporary aeroplane, with the possible exception of the Fokker Triplane. From July 1917, when it reached the Front, until the Armistice, the Camel accounted for no less than 1,294 enemy machines.

To the beginner the Camel too often displayed the unpleasant side of its character. Its amazing agility was partly due to the torque effect of its rotary engine; on right-hand turns the nose tended to drop; on left-hand turns to rise. A tight turn, uncorrected, was liable to finish in a fatal spin.

The Clerget rotary would choke if the mixture were not weakened just after take-off; the machine would then stall and spin into the ground. The casualty rate among Camel pupils was very high.

Units using night-flying Camels found that the flashes from the twin Vickers guns blinded their pilots. A special version was therefore devised; the pilot sat farther aft. Twin Lewis guns on a double Foster mounting were fitted above the centre section. These could be pulled down to reload or to fire upwards. The cockpit had a faired headrest; there was a large centre-section cut-out, and occasionally cut-outs in the lower wing-roots.

The Sopwith 2F.1 Camel was designed for use on ships; it had a shorter wing-span and the rear fuselage could be detached. The main distinguishing points were the thin steel-tube centre-section struts, the external rocking levers on the fuselage, and the armament—one Vickers gun on the port side of the cowling and a Lewis gun above the centre section.

2F.1s operated successfully from both aircraft carriers and lighters towed by destroyers.

The Camel was either loved or detested; no pilot who flew the stocky little fighter could afford to treat it with indifference.

A total of 5,490 Camels was built.

1. Prototype Camel. 2. Production machine, built by Boulton and Paul. 3. Standard F.1, used by 44 Home Defence Squadron, Hainault Farm. 4. Modified F.1 night-fighter, No. 44 H.D. Squadron. 5. 2F.1 Camel of No. 212 Squadron, R.A.F., Great Yarmouth.

SOPWITH F.1 CAMEL

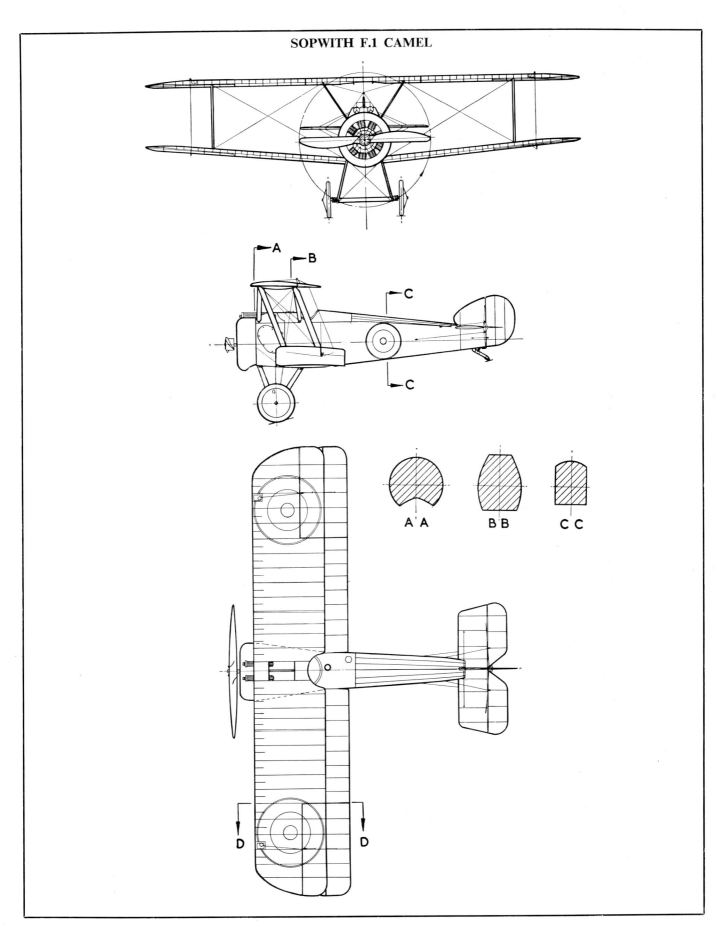

A A   B B   C C

SOPWITH DOLPHIN 5F.1

In May 1917 the Sopwith Aviation Company produced a new single-seater fighter biplane, the 5F.1 Dolphin, powered by the 200 h.p. geared Hispano-Suiza engine. The wings were rather surprisingly given 'backward stagger' with the object of affording the best possible upward view. The top wing was fixed just above the cockpit so that the pilot sat with his head through the open centre section, a frame of steel tubing.

A bulky car-type radiator was fitted; the rest of the aeroplane was of normal wood-framed and wire-braced construction covered with fabric except for the plywood top decking and cockpit sides. The original rudder and fin resembled those of the Camel.

The view forwards and downwards was soon found to be unsatisfactory, so the frontal radiator was replaced by two side radiators with adjustable flaps, the engine was given a rounded cowling and cut-outs were made in both wing-roots. An enlarged horn-balanced rudder was fitted.

The production model appeared with much lower sides to the cockpit, no cut-outs, and an enlarged fin which gave the vertical tail surfaces a more rounded shape.

To the standard armament of two Vickers guns were added a pair of Lewis guns, mounted on the front of the centre section at an angle of 45 degrees. These could be swung upwards to fire almost vertically. On operations, however, the Lewis guns were usually removed. No. 87 squadron transferred theirs to the lower wings, to fire outside the airscrew arc.

Initially the Dolphin was not received by the R.F.C. with much enthusiasm, one of the more obvious reasons being the likelihood of a broken neck if the machine turned over when landing! As a safety measure some units fitted crash pylons over the centre sections, while modifications were made to the centre-section bracing wires to enable the pilot to escape after a crash. The night-flying version was provided with steel half-hoops above the top wing over each inner bay of struts.

In January 1918 No. 19 Squadron on the Western Front replaced their Spads with Dolphins, and in March a new squadron, No. 79, arrived in France equipped with the type. Both units were active during the fierce fighting that followed the start of the German offensive of March 21st. The other Spad squadron, No. 23, received Dolphins in April, and the fourth squadron to use the machine operationally, No. 87, reached the front in the same month.

All four Dolphin squadrons played a useful if not outstanding part in the summer and autumn battles, mainly on escort and ground-attack duty. The type proved to be fast, manœuvrable and easy to fly; the geared Hispano-Suiza engine, however, gave a good deal of trouble.

A few Dolphins were used by No. 141 (Home Defence) Squadron, but were considered unsuitable, due to the lengthy warming-up period required by their liquid-cooled engines.

The Mark II Dolphin with the 300 h.p. Hispano-Suiza was in production in France late in 1918, with apparently the object of equipping both French and American units. The increased power gave this model an excellent performance.

1. Prototype Dolphin. 2. Pre-production Dolphin with deep top-decking to the fuselage. 3. Standard production machine. 4. Night-flying version with steel-tube crash pylons. 5. Dolphin Mk. II with 300 h.p. Hispano-Suiza engine. This model did not see active service.

SOPWITH 5F.1 DOLPHIN

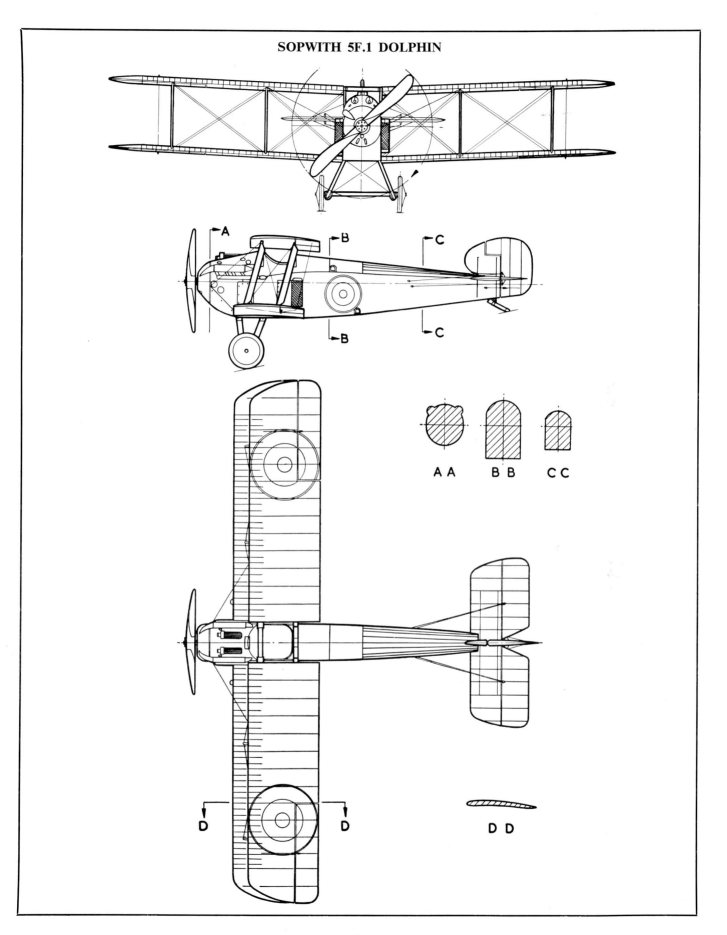

A A   B B   C C

D D

SOPWITH PUP

The neat little biplane, known officially to the R.N.A.S. as Sopwith Type 9901 and to the R.F.C. as the Sopwith Scout, first appeared in February 1916. It was similar in layout to the Sopwith SL.T.B.P., the personal aeroplane of Harry Hawker, the firm's test pilot. Pilots regarded the new scout as the 'pup' of the Sopwith 1½-Strutter, and 'Pup' it became, in spite of official discouragement.

The standard engine was the 80 h.p. Le Rhône rotary, installed in a circular open-fronted cowling. Other engines sometimes fitted were the 80 h.p. Gnôme or the 80 h.p. Clerget, while many of the Home Defence Pups had the 100 h.p. Gnôme Monosoupape with a horseshoe-shaped cowling. The wings had wire-braced wooden spars and ribs; the raked-back wing-tips and trailing-edges were of steel tubing. The centre section was wide, so that the centre-section struts were splayed outwards. The tail-plane was of wooden and steel-tube construction, fabric-covered. The elevators, fin and rudder were of steel tubing. The fuselage, a wire-braced box girder, was fabric-covered except for aluminium sheeting behind the cowling and plywood around the cockpit. The undercarriage was of the Sopwith split-axle type.

The usual armament was a Vickers gun mounted centrally in front of the cockpit, synchronised by means of the Sopwith-Kauper gear. It was fired by depressing a lever that projected backwards from the gun. Pups built for ship use had a tripod-mounted Lewis gun, which fired forwards and upwards through an aperture in the centre section.

As early as May 1916 one of the prototypes was in France, and by September a number were in use with No. 1 Wing, R.N.A.S. The first real successes, however, were obtained by No. 8 (Naval) Squadron, which operated from November 1916 in support of the R.F.C.; in less than two months twenty German machines were shot down. No. 54 Squadron arrived with Pups in December; No. 3 (Naval) Squadron relieved No. 8 in February 1917, and No. 66 Squadron R.F.C. reached the front in March. The only other unit to fly the type, No. 46 Squadron, was re-equipped with it in April 1917. In spite of having exactly half its horse-power, the Pup was superior to the opposing Albatros D-III at high altitudes, because of its lighter wing-loading. McCudden wrote: '... at 16,000 feet the Albatros Scout began to find its ceiling just where the Pup was still speedy and controllable.' There were not, however, enough Pups available to overcome the general German superiority.

Throughout the summer and autumn of 1917 the little biplane gave splendid service on the Western Front.

The R.N.A.S. Pups did much pioneer work on the early aircraft carriers. To facilitate deck landings, the later ship-borne machines were fitted with skid undercarriages; these were designated the Type 9901a. William Beardmore & Co., Dalmuir, developed a modified version specially for carrier work, the W.B.III. It had folding wings and a retractable undercarriage, to save stowage space; about sixty were built.

The Pup was almost unanimously agreed to be the most pleasant to fly of all British aeroplanes of the 1914–18 period. A total of 1,770 was manufactured.

1. Prototype Pup. 2. The first carrier-landing—Squadron Commander E. H. Dunning landing his Pup on H.M.S. 'Furious', 2.8.17. Note rope toggles used to pull the machine down. 3. Whitehead-built Pup. 4. and 5. 100 h.p. Gnôme Monosoupape and 80 h.p. Le Rhône versions.

SOPWITH PUP

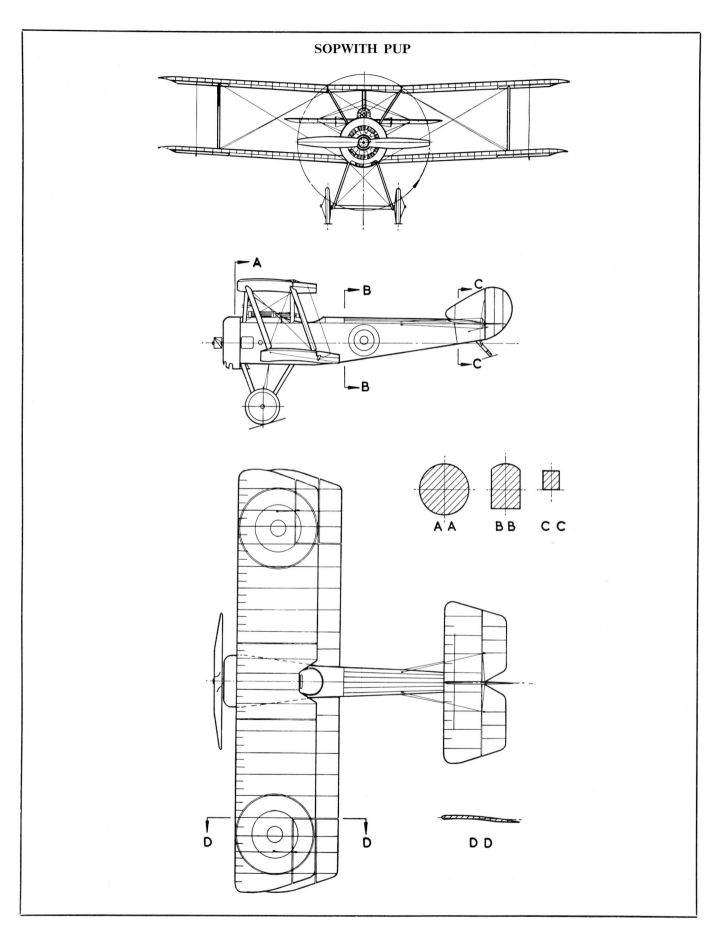

A A   B B   C C

D D

SOPWITH TF.2 SALAMANDER

By late 1917 both sides were using large numbers of aircraft for ground-attack duty. The British employed their ordinary squadron machines on this dangerous work, and their casualty rate was often as high as 30 per cent. There was, therefore, a real need for an armoured machine which would be capable of taking plenty of punishment.

The first British aeroplane to be adapted for 'ground strafing was the Sopwith F.1 Camel B9278. Armour plate was fitted round the pilot's seat; the standard twin Vickers guns were replaced by two Lewis guns which fired downwards through the cockpit floor, and a third Lewis was mounted above the centre section. This version of the Camel was designated the Sopwith TF.1 (TF. meaning 'Trench Fighter'). It was flown experimentally, but did not go into production.

In April 1918 the appropriately named Sopwith TF.2 Salamander* was brought out. From its general appearance it was obviously a development of the Snipe; it had the same 230 h.p. B.R.2 engine.

The first prototype, E5429, had similar equal-span wings to those of the two-bay Snipe, and plain ailerons with single control horns. The front part of the flat-sided fuselage, from the engine to behind the cockpit, was virtually a 650 lb. armour-plated box, containing pilot and fuel tanks. The rear fuselage was a fabric-covered wire-braced wooden box girder; the forward ends of the longerons were attached to the armoured portion. The engine cowling was cut away underneath to provide additional cooling for low-altitude work. A faired head-rest was fitted. The rudder and fin were similar to those of the first two-bay Snipe, but the front struts of the undercarriage were longer.

Twin Vickers guns, synchronised to fire through the revolving airscrew by means of the Constantinesco gear, were the standard armament; 2,000 rounds of ammunition were carried. One Salamander was experimentally fitted with no less than eight machine-guns, which fired downwards through the cockpit floor.

E5431, the third prototype, had two control horns to each aileron and duplicated aileron connecting cables, for added safety when under fire from the ground.

In May 1918 the first prototype successfully underwent service trials in France, and it was decided to build the Salamander in quantity.

The production version had longer-span ailerons and a modified fin and rudder resembling those of the production Snipe. The later Salamanders were given the horn-balanced upper ailerons and larger rounded fins that became standard for late-production Snipes.

Although the type was manufactured from the summer of 1918 onwards, only two of the thirty-seven Salamanders attached to the R.A.F. at the end of October were in France. Most of the rest had only reached aircraft acceptance parks. One Salamander, F6533, was sent to America, and was stationed for a time at McCook field.

With its heavy armour, manoeuvrability and top speed of 125 m.p.h., the Salamander would have been a formidable low-patrol aeroplane; unfortunately for the R.A.F., it was not available in time.

* A lizard-like animal by legend believed to live in fire.

1. Sopwith T.F.1 Camel. The twin downward-firing Lewis guns can be seen between the undercarriage struts. 2, 3 and 4. Three views of E.5429, the first prototype Salamander at Brooklands aerodrome. 5. Production Salamander with a rudder of larger area.

66

SOPWITH TF.2 SALAMANDER

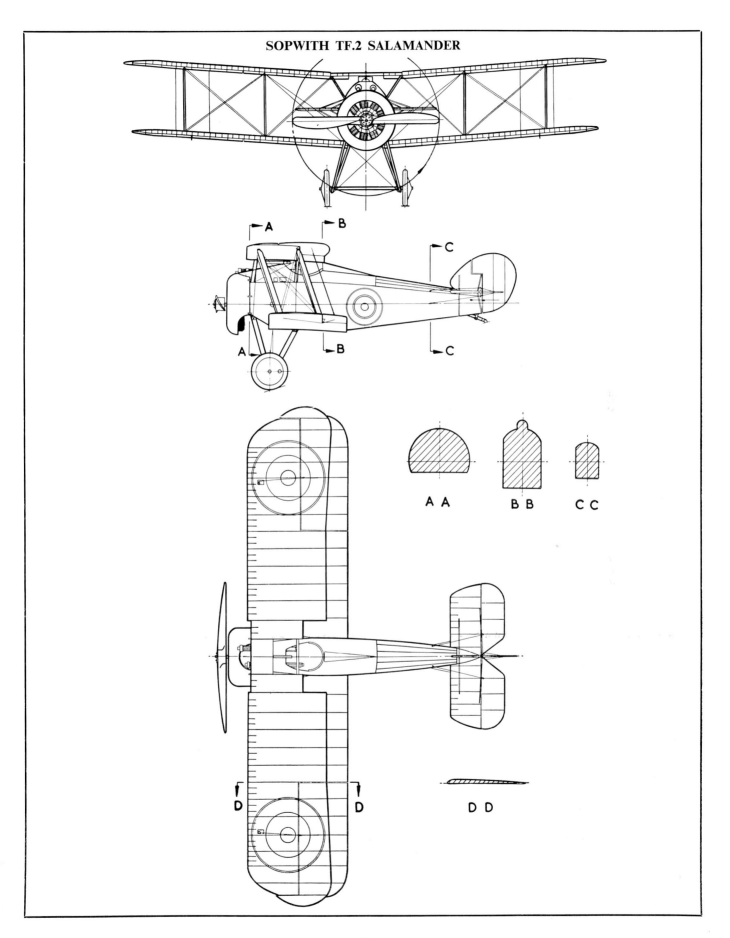

A A   B B   C C

D D

THE SOPWITH 7F.1 SNIPE

The Sopwith 7F.1 Snipe was specially designed to take the new 230 h.p. Bentley rotary engine (B.R.2), an enlarged edition of the 150 h.p. B.R.1, which had been the power unit of many of the Sopwith Camels.

The first prototype had single-bay bracing and dihedral on both wings, which were the usual fabric-covered wire-braced wooden structures. The centre section, just above the level of the pilot's eyes, had a large cut-out, and the trailing-edges of the upper wing-roots were also cut away. Ailerons were fitted to both wings. The flat-sided fuselage, with curved aluminium panels behind the cowling and plywood cockpit sides, resembled that of the Camel, but was deeper, in order to accommodate the larger engine. The steel-tube, fabric-covered empennage was similar to the Camel's. Twin Vickers guns, almost enclosed in a faired 'hump', were mounted in front of the pilot. This machine was first flown with a 150 h.p. B.R.1 engine, there being no B.R.2 available at the time.

The Snipe was much modified before going into production. The various alterations may be summarised as follows: *Second prototype:* Wider centre section, with splayed-out struts; smaller circular cut-out; fuselage faired to better streamlined shape; horn-balanced rudder with rectangular fin. *Third prototype:* Wing-span increased by 4 feet 3 inches; two bays of interplane struts, the inner bays being thicker in section than the outer; temporary mounting of a Lewis gun on the top wing. *Fifth prototype:* B9966. Enlarged rudder, with rounded top to the horn balance. *Early production model:* Similar to B9966, but with large centre-section cut-out and broader rudder with longer horn balance. Both fin and horn balance had rounded leading-edges.

The decision to manufacture the Snipe in quantity was made early in 1918; 1,900 were ordered from six contractors. Even after production had started, experiments to improve performance continued. B9966 was given horn-balanced ailerons on the upper wing, a new tapering tail-plane with horn-balanced, inversely tapering elevators, and an enlarged, rounded rudder and fin. The new ailerons and rounded rudder and fin became standard on the later machines, and many of the earlier Snipes were retrospectively modified.

Only three units, Nos. 43 and 208 Squadrons, R.A.F., and No. 4 Squadron, Australian Flying Corps, had been re-equipped with the Snipe by the end of the war. The type will chiefly be remembered as the aeroplane on which Major W. G. Barker, the Canadian ace, put up his magnificent battle against odds on October 27th, 1918; for this action he was awarded the Victoria Cross. No. 201 Squadron, R.A.F., to which Barker was attached at the time, was equipped with Camels, so it would seem that his Snipe was issued for his personal use.

The Snipe was recognised as the best all-round Allied fighter in use at the time of the Armistice. It was not particularly fast, but its strength and excellent climb and manœuvrability made up for this. The type became the standard R.A.F. post-war fighter, and continued in service until 1927. A total of 497 Snipes had been constructed by the end of 1918.

1. First prototype. 2. Second prototype. 3. Production Snipe with plain ailerons to upper wing. 4. Production Snipe with horn-balanced ailerons to upper wing. (The latter two machines belonged to No. 208 Squadron R.A.F.) 5. Night fighter version used by No. 78 Squadron.

SOPWITH 7F.1 SNIPE

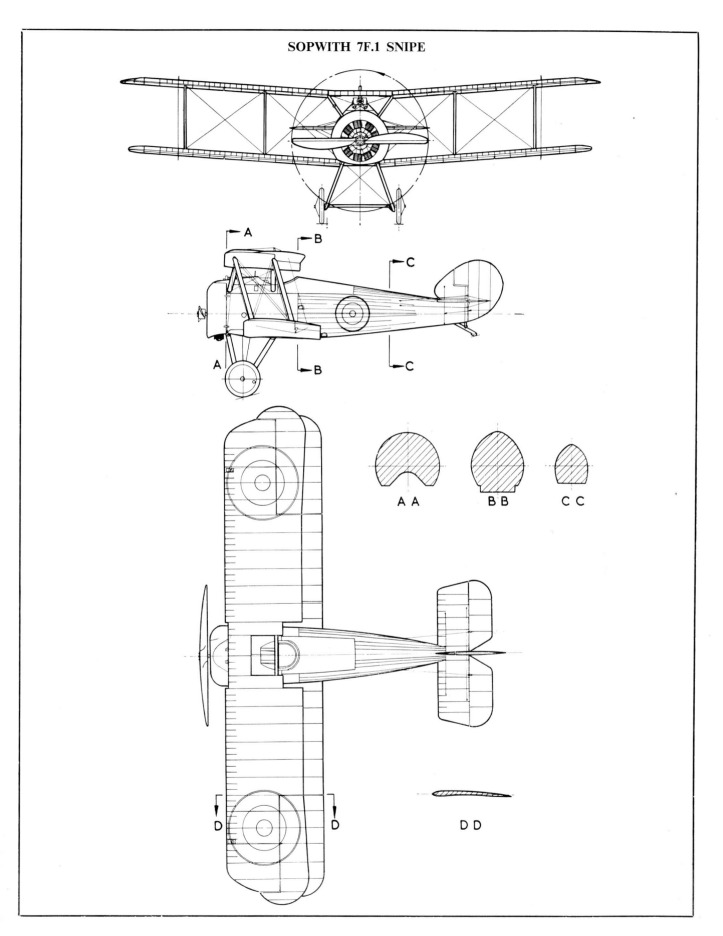

A A   B B   C C

D D

SOPWITH 1½-STRUTTER

The Sopwith Two-Seater (R.F.C. designation), or Sopwith Type 9400 (R.N.A.S. designation), made its appearance in December 1915; a trim biplane with single-bay, equal-span wings.

The power unit was the 110 h.p. Clerget 9Z rotary; the 130 h.p. Clerget 9Bc, 135 h.p. Clerget 9Ba, 110 h.p. Le Rhône 9J, 130 h.p. Le Rhône 9Jby and 80 h.p. Le Rhône 9C were also fitted. The wings were wooden wire-braced fabric-covered structures; an unusual feature was the provision of air brakes, two square portions in the trailing-edges of the lower wing-roots which could be raised at right angles to the slipstream. It is doubtful whether they were much used. The centre-section struts consisted of steel tube 'Ws', which gave rise to the nickname '1½-Strutter'. Another innovation permitted the incidence of the tail-plane to be altered in flight. The fuselage was the usual wooden fabric-covered box girder, with plywood top decking round the cockpits. A Sopwith split-axle-type undercarriage was fitted.

The 1½-Strutter was the first British aeroplane to go into action with a synchronised Vickers gun for the pilot. On machines built for the R.N.A.S., the Scarff-Dibovski interrupter gear was fitted; on those built for the R.F.C. the Vickers-Challenger gear. Later models had the Ross or Sopwith-Kauper systems. The observer's Lewis gun was at first carried on a Scarff pillar mounting; then the Nieuport ring mounting was fitted, and finally the excellent Scarff ring, which became standard on Allied two-seaters.

The first unit to operate with the type was No. 5 Wing, R.N.A.S., in April 1916. Delivery of the machines on order for the R.F.C. did not begin until May. So short of aeroplanes was the Flying Corps at this period that the first squadron to be equipped with the 1½-Strutter, No. 70, proceeded to the front by Flights as soon as machines became available.

To relieve the situation, the Navy generously transferred many 1½-Strutters; the first of these equipped 'C' Flight, 70 Squadron, in July 1916.

The type did useful work during 1916, but was outclassed by the new German Albatros Scouts, which began to appear in late September.

The 1½-Strutter was also built as a single-seater bomber. A single-seater fighter conversion, flown from the rear cockpit, was used by No. 78 (Home Defence) Squadron. It had twin Lewis guns mounted to fire upwards at an angle of 70 degrees. Fitted with wheels or skids, the type operated from ships. No less than 4,500 were built in France, in three different versions: Sop. 1.A.2 (reconnaissance two-seater), Sop. B.1 (single-seater bomber) and Sop. 1.B.2 (two-seater bomber). 1½-Strutters were used by Belgium, Russia, the U.S.A. and Roumania.

The American Expeditionary Force purchased 514 French-built machines, and a total of 1,520 1½-Strutters were built in Britain. A clean design which tended to 'float' on landing, the Sopwith 1½-Strutter was too stable and stiff on the controls to make a good fighter. It was successful mainly on account of its excellent armament, and can justifiably claim to be the first tractor two-seater fighter aircraft to come into use.

1. Production 1½ Strutter. 2. R.N.A.S. machine at Dunkirk. 3. A Mann, Egerton & Co. built machine. 4. 1½ Strutter at Isle of Grain. Note twin 'skylights'. 5. Single-seat conversion carried out by Capt. Honnett of No. 78 H.D. Squadron, Sutton's Farm, 1917.

SOPWITH 1½-STRUTTER

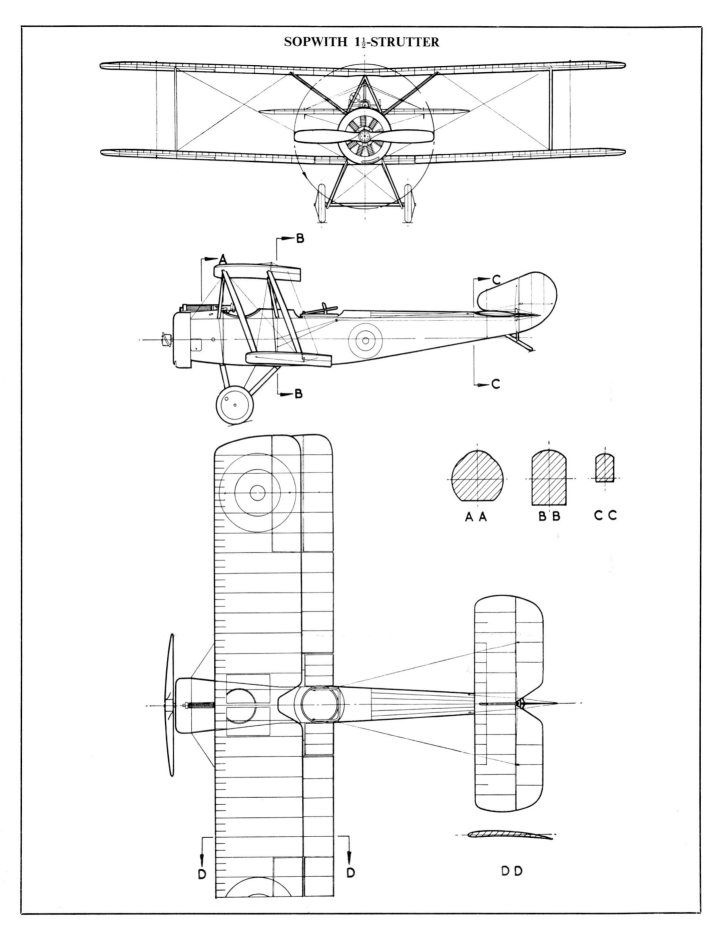

A A   B B   C C

D   D   D D

SOPWITH TABLOID

The Sopwith Tabloid was constructed in 1913 as a two-seater racing aeroplane. The design was one of extreme simplicity. The engine was the popular 80 h.p. Gnôme rotary enclosed in a peculiar metal cowling, with two small cooling slots in front. The fuselage, a wire-braced wooden box girder, was rather broad, for the pilot and passenger sat side by side in the one cockpit. The wings were of the usual fabric-covered wooden construction, with raked tips. Wing warping was used for lateral control. The undercarriage was equipped with twin skids.

Flown by Harry Hawker, the Tabloid performed excellently on test at Farnborough, reaching a speed of 92 m.p.h. and climbing to 1,200 feet in one minute, with pilot, passenger and fuel for two and a half hours' flying. Its first public appearance at Hendon was sensational; it easily outclassed the monoplane, which had hitherto been supreme.

The original machine was taken by Hawker to Australia; he returned in June 1914; by then the aeroplane had a plain vee undercarriage and the fabric had been removed from the rear end of the fuselage.

On April 20th, 1914, Howard Pixton, who had taken over Hawker's duties, piloted a seaplane version of the Tabloid to victory in the Schneider Trophy race. This model had the 100 h.p. Gnôme Monosoupape engine and a plain rudder and fin.

Production commenced in the spring of 1914 for both the R.F.C. and R.N.A.S. The service machines were single-seaters, had rudders and fins resembling those of the Schneider seaplane, and twin-skid undercarriages. A few had extra bracing struts to each skid.

Four Tabloids went to France shortly after the outbreak of war, and were eventually attached to squadrons for fast scouting duties. An early success was obtained by Lieutenant Norman Spratt, who forced down a German machine by circling his Tabloid around it; his only 'armament' at the time being a bundle of steel darts! Some R.N.A.S. machines had Lewis guns fitted on their top wings to fire above the revolving airscrew. One naval Tabloid had a Lewis gun fixed on the starboard side of its fuselage to fire through the airscrew arc; deflector plates protected the blades from damage—a device invented by the French engineer Saulnier and used on the single-seater Morane-Saulnier monoplane.

The type scored its greatest success in the light bomber role. On October 8th, 1914, the first two R.N.A.S. Tabloids to reach the front, Nos. 167 and 168, took off from beleaguered Antwerp to raid the Zeppelin sheds at Cologne and Düsseldorf. Squadron Commander Spenser Grey, flying 167, was unable to find his target, and bombed the railway station at Cologne. Flight Lieutenant Marix dropped his 20 lb. bombs on the airship shed at Düsseldorf and destroyed the new Zeppelin Z.IX. Both aeroplanes were forced to land, but the pilots reached Antwerp before the town was evacuated by the Allies.

Tabloids also saw service at the Dardanelles and in the Aegean, but proved to be of little use.

Later machines had ailerons for lateral control, in place of wing warping. It is believed that about forty of the type were built.

1. Sopwith Tabloid prototype with side-by-side seating. 2. Prototype Tabloid with T. O. M. Sopwith and H. Hawker. 3. and 4. Standard production single-seat Tabloid. 5. Production machine with additional struts in the undercarriage.

SOPWITH TABLOID

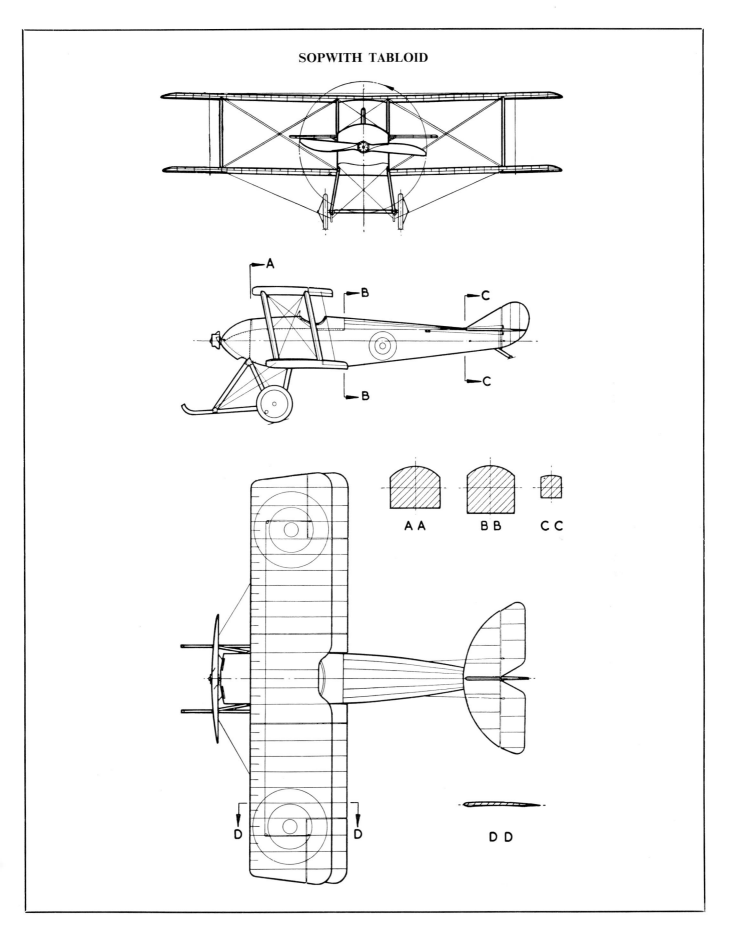

A A B B C C

D D

73

SOPWITH TRIPLANE

In their search for an outstanding fighting aeroplane the Sopwith experimental department decided in early 1916 to build an entirely new design—a triplane. The completed machine had narrow-chord wings, affording the pilot a good all-round view; at the same time, the combined wing area of the three mainplanes gave plenty of lift. Ailerons were fitted to all three wings; the interplane struts were plain but strong and few bracing wires were needed. The fuselage was a typical Sopwith wooden box girder. Tail-plane, elevators, rudder and fin resembled those of the Pup, but later production models had a tail-plane of reduced area.

The power unit, a 110 h.p. Clerget rotary, was eventually replaced by the 130 h.p. Clerget. The standard armament consisted of a fixed Vickers gun, synchronised to fire through the revolving airscrew; six Triplanes, however, were fitted with twin guns.

In June 1916 the prototype, N500, went to Naval 'A' Fighting Squadron at Furnes in France for service trials. The Triplane was a success from the start and was ordered by both the R.F.C. and R.N.A.S. It was destined to be flown operationally by naval units only; the R.F.C., who had already received a present of the first sixty R.N.A.S. Spad S.7s, decided in February 1917 to accept the remaining sixty in exchange for the Sopwith Triplanes on order for the Corps.

No. 1 (Naval) Squadron, 'Naval One', went into action with the type in April 1917, in support of the hard-pressed R.F.C. The hitherto very successful Albatros D-III was completely outclassed, and *IdFlieg*, the German Inspectorate of Flying Troops, received a severe shock. The 'Tripehound' could out-climb and out-turn the Albatros, and was 15 m.p.h faster. Naval Eight and Naval Ten, equipped in April and May, also made their presence felt. Proof of the Triplane's worth was soon to hand. In April 1917 Flight Commander R. S. Dallas and Flight Sub-Lieutenant T. G. Culling attacked a formation of fourteen German aircraft. After forty-five minutes they had shot down three of the enemy and driven the remainder into retreat.

Other famous R.N.A.S. pilots who scored heavily with the type were Collishaw, Little, Booker, Reid, Sharman, Nash and Alexander.

One 'Tripe', N5431, reached Macedonia and eventually operated from Mudros in the Aegean Sea. Another, No. N5486, went to Russia and was eventually provided with skis for operating in the snow.

Some difficulty was found in obtaining spares for the Triplane during the summer of 1917, and one unit, Naval One, had to reduce its establishment from eighteen to fifteen aeroplanes. By the autumn the type had passed its zenith and the rate of casualties in Triplane squadrons rose.

The last operational Triplanes were exchanged for Camels in November 1917. When it is realised that only about 150 were built, it is surprising how much they influenced the trend of design. A host of triplanes and quadruplanes were built by the leading German and Austro-Hungarian aircraft manufacturers in efforts to match the performance of the remarkable Sopwith Triplane.

1. Prototype Triplane N.500 at Chingford. 2. Clayton and Shuttleworth-built Triplane flown by No. 1 Squadron, R.N.A.S. 3. Twin gun version. 4. N.5431, at Mudros in the Aegean. 5. N.5486 serving with the Imperial Russian Air Service.

SOPWITH TRIPLANE

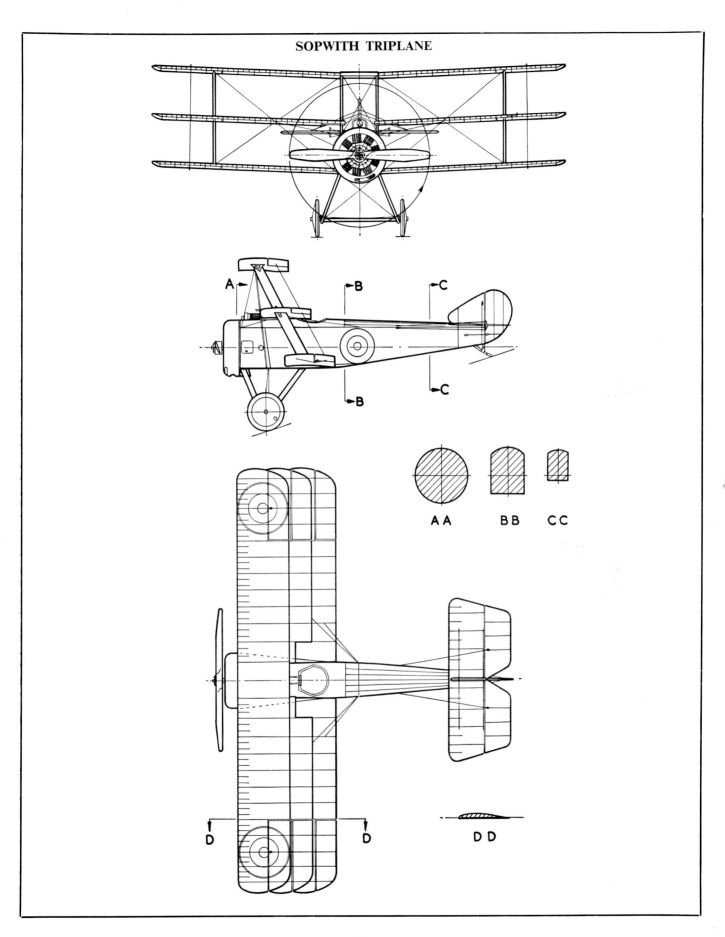

A A   B B   C C

D D

VICKERS F.B.5 AND 9

As early as 1912 the firm of Vickers Ltd. was far-seeing enough to experiment with a machine-gun-carrying aeroplane. At the 1913 Aero Show a Vickers two-seater pusher biplane was exhibited, which had a Maxim gun in the nose of its nacelle. A number of versions of this machine were brought out during 1913 and early 1914. The belt-fed gun was heavy and difficult to aim, and the ammunition was difficult to stow. Consequently the F.B.4 (Fighting Biplane No. 4) which appeared in 1914 had the lighter and more manageable drum-fed Lewis gun.

The F.B.5, a development of the F.B.4, was powered by the 100 h.p. Gnôme Monosoupape rotary engine. The unstaggered, equal-span wings were square-cut and fitted with ailerons. The tail-booms, of steel tubing, had four vertical wooden struts. The large square-cut tail-plane was attached to the upper booms. At first the rudder had a straight trailing-edge; later models had a rounded rudder. The nacelle had a blunt aluminium nose, on top of which was carried an unstripped Lewis gun on a pillar mounting. At least one F.B.5 had a pointed nacelle. The undercarriage had two large wooden skids.

The Company were of the opinion that war was certain, and without waiting for a Government order, commenced the manufacture of fifty F.B.5s. The type successfully passed the official tests at Farnborough in July 1914, and a small number were ordered by the R.F.C. and R.N.A.S.

The 'Gun Bus', as it was called, did not reach France until February 1915. No squadron was at first fully equipped with the type; one or two only being attached to a unit to provide protection for the reconnaissance machines. Forced landings were common until ground crews became used to the vagaries of the Monosoupape engine.

In July 1915 the first two-seater fighter squadron formed, No. 11 Squadron, R.F.C., arrived in France equipped with F.B.5s. Throughout the summer 11 Squadron did good work with their pushers, shooting down a considerable number of German aircraft. By November 1915, however, it could no longer be classed as a first-rate fighter, as it was unable to deal with the dangerous Fokker monoplane. An experimental mounting of twin Lewis guns was tried out in 11 Squadron, which did not give up its Gun Buses until July 1916.

There were some experimental models of the type: an armoured version with the 110 h.p. Clerget rotary engine, and two F.B.5s built for the Navy, with the unsuccessful Smith Static radial engine.

The F.B.9 was an improved Gun Bus which came out in December 1915. The Gnôme Monosoupape was the standard engine, but the 110 h.p. Le Rhône rotary was also used.

Wings and tail-plane had rounded ends; the nacelle first had a semicircular profile, but later machines had a pointed nose. The Lewis gun was given a new mounting which enabled it to be rotated. The old twin-skid under-carriage was replaced by plain vees, and streamlined 'Raf-wires' were used instead of bracing cables.

There is some doubt whether the F.B.9 was used operationally; it saw considerable service at training units.

1. Early Vickers Fighting Biplane with Vickers gun and transparent side panels. 2. The F.B.4. Note the angular rudder and mounting for a Lewis gun. 3. Production F.B.5 with enlarged rudder. 4. and 5. Vickers F.B.9 with early form of nacelle.

VICKERS F.B.5

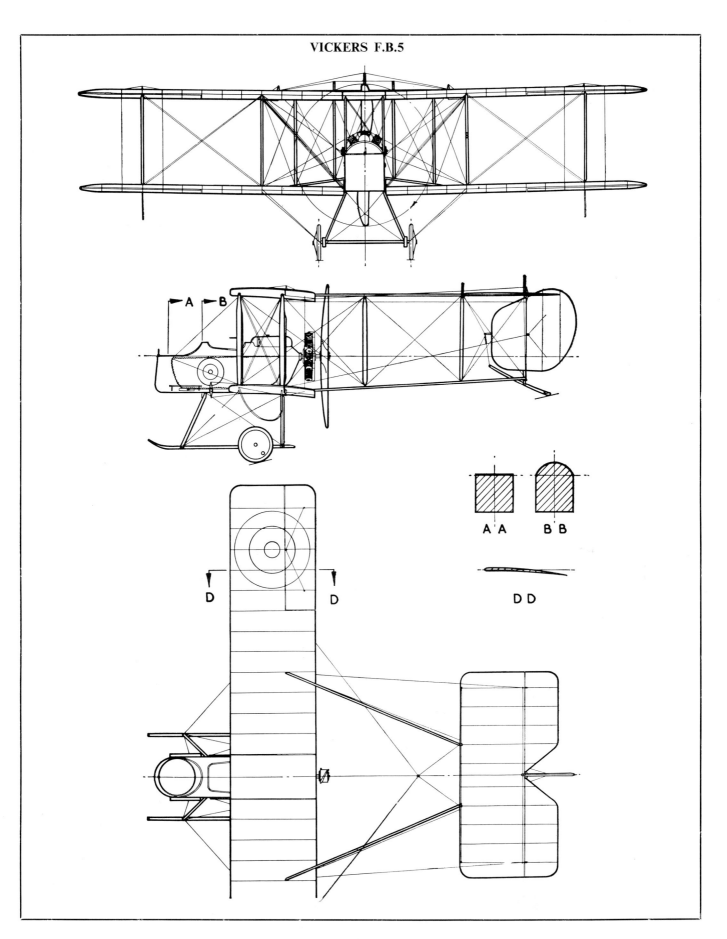

A A   B B

D D

VICKERS F.B.12, 12a, 12b AND 12c

In June 1916, when most single-seater fighter designers were engaged on the development of tractor biplanes armed with one or two synchronised guns, the Vickers company brought out a pusher scout, the F.B.12.

Basically it resembled the D.H.2 and F.E.8 single-seater pushers of the previous year; it had an 80 h.p. Le Rhône rotary engine which drove a two-bladed propeller. The wood and fabric wings were relatively short in span and had rounded tips. In front elevation the outer bays of interplane struts were inclined outwards, while in side elevation each pair of struts was closer together at the bottom than at the top. Mounted between the wings, the nacelle, framed in steel tubing, was faired to a circular cross-section, and a small head-rest was fitted behind the open cockpit.

Like those of the F.E.8 the steel-tube tail-booms converged in side view and connected to the rear spar of the tail-plane. Fin and rudder were set symmetrically about the tail, and the undercarriage vee struts were fixed to the lower centre section. A Lewis gun was mounted inside the front of the nacelle with only part of the barrel protruding. A 100 h.p. Gnôme Monosoupape rotary was also installed in this machine.

Modifications were made to the design: new wings of larger span and area, with raked tips, were fitted, and the front undercarriage struts were lengthened and connected to the bottom of the nacelle. The new version, which was probably designated the F.B.12a, had the Mono-Gnôme engine. In December 1916 it was sent to France for operational trials; there it was considered to be as good as the D.H.2 and F.E.8, but as the latter types were by then quite outclassed by contemporary German fighters, this was scarcely a recommendation.

The next variant, the F.B.12b, is believed to have been powered with the unsuccessful 150 h.p. Hart radial engine. The one example, built by the Wells Aviation Co. Ltd., crashed during tests. A flat-sided wooden nacelle and a larger fin and rudder were fitted to the F.B.12c. Fifty machines of this type (A7351–A7400) were ordered in November 1916, and it was intended to utilise the Hart engine. Only eighteen examples, however, are said to have been completed, at the Weybridge works of Messrs. Vickers. A number of alternative power units were installed: A7351 had a 110 h.p. Le Rhône rotary, while A7352 had a 100 h.p. Anzani radial.

These machines were tested in May and July 1917, but by that time the pusher single-seater type had become outmoded. One F.B.12c was supplied to a Home Defence unit during 1917.

Yet another version, the F.B.12d, is believed to have been powered by the 110 h.p. Le Rhône or 100 h.p. Gnôme Monosoupape. The Vickers concern continued their pusher design work; the F.B.26 and 26a fighters of 1917–1918 (Vampire I and II) were developments of the F.B.12. One Vickers F.B.26 was flown experimentally by Nos. 39 and 141 Home Defence Squadrons R.F.C. The F.B.26a powered by the 230 h.p. B.R.2 rotary was designed as an armoured trench-fighting aeroplane. After the Sopwith Salamander was adopted, the F.B.26a type was abandoned.

1. and 2. The first version of the F.B.12 with undercarriage struts attached to the lower wing. 3. F.B.12 with modified wings and undercarriage. 4. F.B.12c with flat-sided nacelle. 5. F.B.12c with 100 h.p. Anzani radial. This aircraft was probably A.7352.

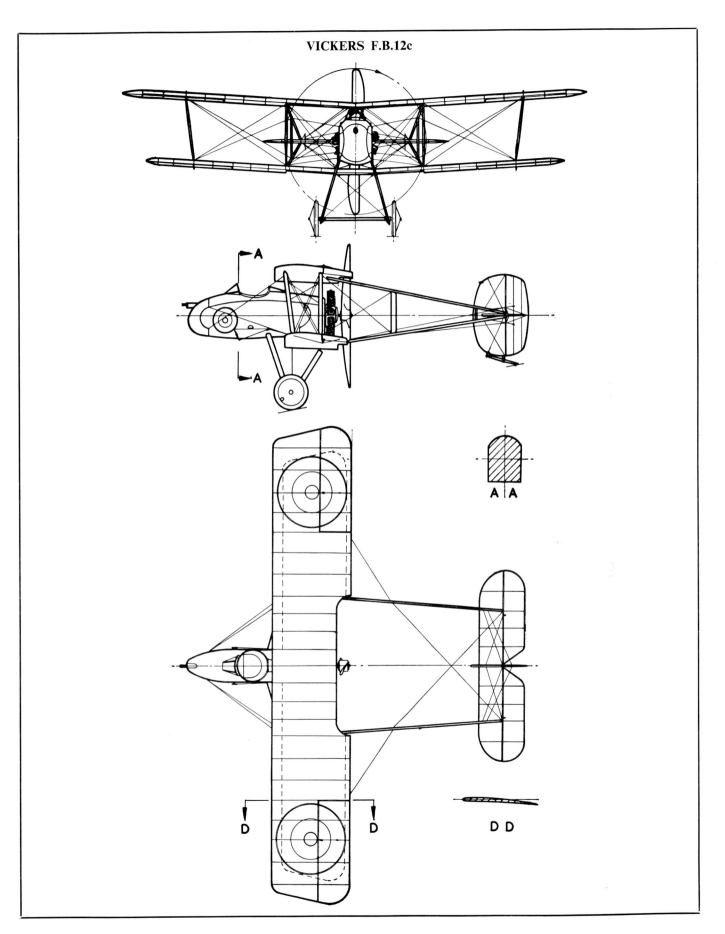

VICKERS F.B.12c

VICKERS F.B.19

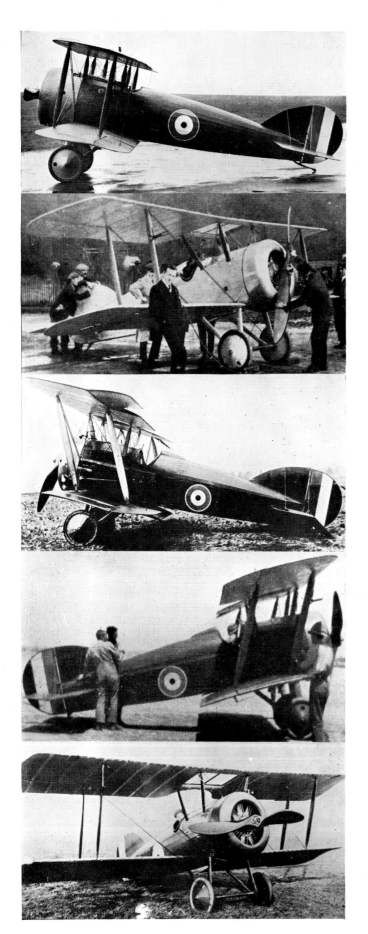

The forerunners of the Vickers F.B.19 were two single-seater biplane types produced by Vickers Ltd. in 1915: the E.S.1 and E.S.2.

The E.S.1 had a 100 h.p. Gnôme Monosoupape rotary engine installed in an open-fronted long-chord cowling. The wings and tail-plane, of the usual fabric-covered wooden construction, were square-cut. Ailerons were fitted to both wings. The fuselage was a wire-braced wooden box girder faired to a circular cross-section.

Although the 'Bullet', as it was called, was extremely fast for 1915 (114 m.p.h. at 5,000 feet), the position of the mainplanes and the tubbiness of the fuselage considerably obscured the pilot's view. For this reason the type was not considered suitable for production.

Two E.S.2s were built. At first the 110 h.p. Clerget was fitted; the 110 h.p. Le Rhône was also used experimentally. Improvements on the E.S.1 design included rounded wing-tips, a clear-view cut-out in the centre section and a shorter-chord cowling. The mechanical synchronising gear developed by George H. Challenger for the Vickers company was now available, and by this means a Vickers gun fixed in a recess on the port upper longeron fired forwards through the revolving airscrew. These modifications reduced the maximum speed of the E.S.2 to 98 m.p.h., but its chief defect appears to have been the poor view from the cockpit. It was not accepted by the R.F.C.

In August 1916 the Mark I F.B.19 appeared; superficially its shape was very similar to that of the E.S. types. The power unit was the 100 h.p. Gnôme Monosoupape engine. The wings were unstaggered and had slightly raked tips; there was a cut-out in the centre section. A modified version existed, with the 110 h.p. Le Rhône rotary, a shallower cowling and a faired head-rest behind the cockpit. This may be the model which went into production.

The Mark II F.B.19 had staggered wings, which further improved the view of the pilot. Both marks were fitted with a Vickers gun which fired through the airscrew arc; its mounting was interesting, the gun being fixed in a trough on the port side of the fuselage and the bullets passed through a hole in the cowling.

The F.B.19 inherited the name 'Bullet' from the earlier E.S. machines.

Small numbers of both marks were constructed; six went to France for service trials late in 1916, and a batch was dispatched to Russia.

It is believed that the type was flown for a time by No. 11 Squadron, R.F.C.

The F.B.19 failed to impress the authorities and it was decided not to use it on the Western Front. In June 1917 No. 111 Squadron R.F.C. in Palestine received five machines, including Nos. A5223 and A5224, and a few were used by Nos. 17 and 47 Squadrons in Macedonia. In neither theatre of war did the type prove to be satisfactory.

Although it was of some use as an interceptor, the view from the cockpit was poor, and, in a dog-fight, the pilot tended to lose sight of the enemy.

The rest of the F.B.19s were supplied to·Home Defence squadrons (six machines) and various training units (twelve machines). 36 of the type were issued to the Royal Flying Corps.

1. One of the two E.S.2s, 7759 and 7760. The recessed Vickers gun can be seen. 2. The Le Rhône-powered Mk. I F.B.19. 3. Production Mk. II. 4. Mk. II with No. 14 Squadron, R.F.C. in the Middle East. 5. Production Mk. II. Note the 'glazed' panels in the top wing.

VICKERS F.B.19

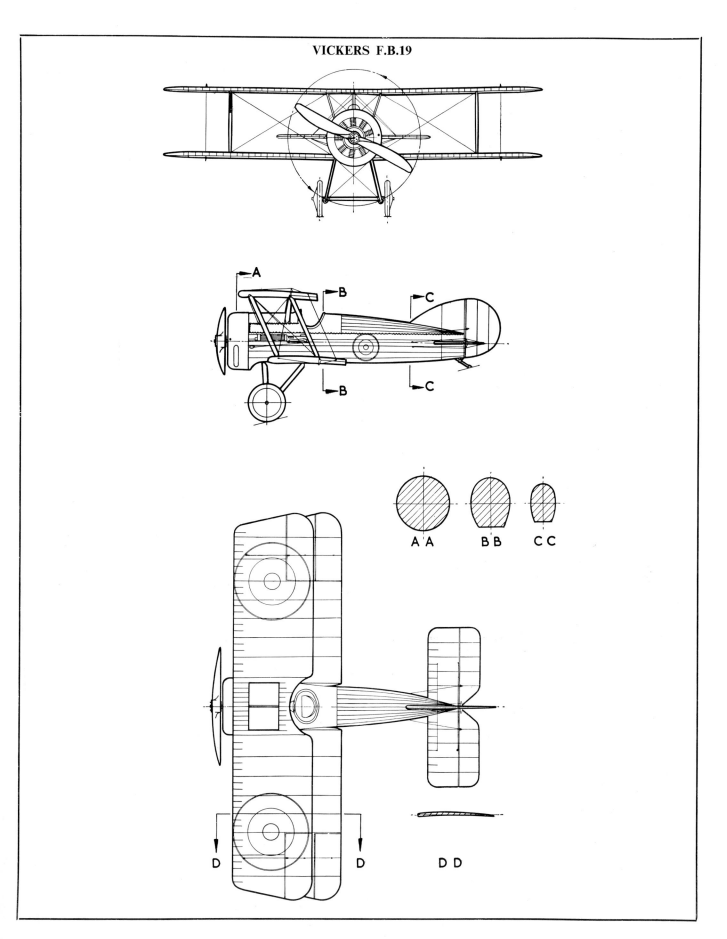

A A   B B   C C

D   D   D D

HANRIOT HD-1

The original Hanriot concern built a number of monoplanes in the pioneer days of flying. After the outbreak of war M. Hanriot formed a new company which manufactured some types under licence.

In 1916 appeared the Hanriot HD-1, a single-seater fighter biplane designed by M. Dupont, a type which proved most successful with Italian and Belgian units, but which was strangely neglected by the French authorities. The standard engine was the 110 Le Rhône rotary, housed in a circular open-fronted cowling provided with cooling holes in varying positions and of varying shapes. Some late production machines had the experimental and unsuccessful 150 h.p. Le Rhône. The staggered wings had wire-braced wooden spars, steel-tube compression members, and were fabric-covered. There was no centre section; the top wing had 4/4½ degrees of dihedral and carried the ailerons; the lower had no dihedral and was of shorter span. Splayed-out spruce interplane struts were fitted; the cabane bracing, of steel tubing, recalled that of the Sopwith 1½-Strutter, a type that had been built under licence by the Hanriot company.

The fuselage was the usual fabric-covered wire-braced wooden box girder with a top decking and head-rest built up of three-ply formers and stringers. Metal panels, which reached back as far as the cockpit, faired the round cowling into the flat-sided fuselage. The empennage was fabric-covered; fin and rudder were framed in steel tubing, while the tail-plane was of mixed metal and wooden construction, braced by four struts from below. A modified rudder of rounded outline was fitted to some HD-1s. The under-carriage was of the plain vee type. A single synchronised Vickers gun was mounted to port of the fuselage. This was the Hanriot's chief drawback; it was found that twin guns much reduced the ceiling, and consequently the standard model suffered from lack of fire-power.

In addition to being produced in France for the Italian and Belgian Governments, the HD-1 was built by Nieuport-Macchi of Varese, Italy. It became very popular with its pilots, for it was highly manœuvrable and far stronger than it looked.

Major le Chevalier Willy Coppens de Houthulst (thirty-seven victories), the Belgian ace of aces, was the most successful HD-1 pilot. One of his aeroplanes, Hanriot No. 23, was equipped with a Lanser fireproof petrol tank, a gift from M. René Hanriot. In Italy the type became the standard fighter; by November 1918 sixteen of the eighteen operational fighter squadrons flew HD-1s. Tenente Scaroni, the highest-scoring Italian pilot to survive the war, flew a Hanriot fitted with twin Vickers guns. It is possible that this aeroplane carried less fuel to compensate for the increased weight.

A small number of Hanriots were used by France; one at least had a hydrovane fitted to its undercarriage and flotation bags to facilitate forced landings in the sea. The French and U.S. Navies operated a few naval stations on the French coast. After the war the type equipped units of the Swiss Air Force, and ten were constructed at the U.S. Naval Aircraft Factory, Philadelphia, for use as trainers.

The latter machines were equipped with twin guns.

1. Italian Hanriot HD-1. 2. Rear view of HD-1. 3. A late machine with rounded fin and rudder. 4. French Naval Hanriot HD-1 at Dunkirk, with twin guns, hydrovane and flotation bags under lower wings. 5. HD-2 seaplane, with modified tail unit.

HANRIOT HD-1

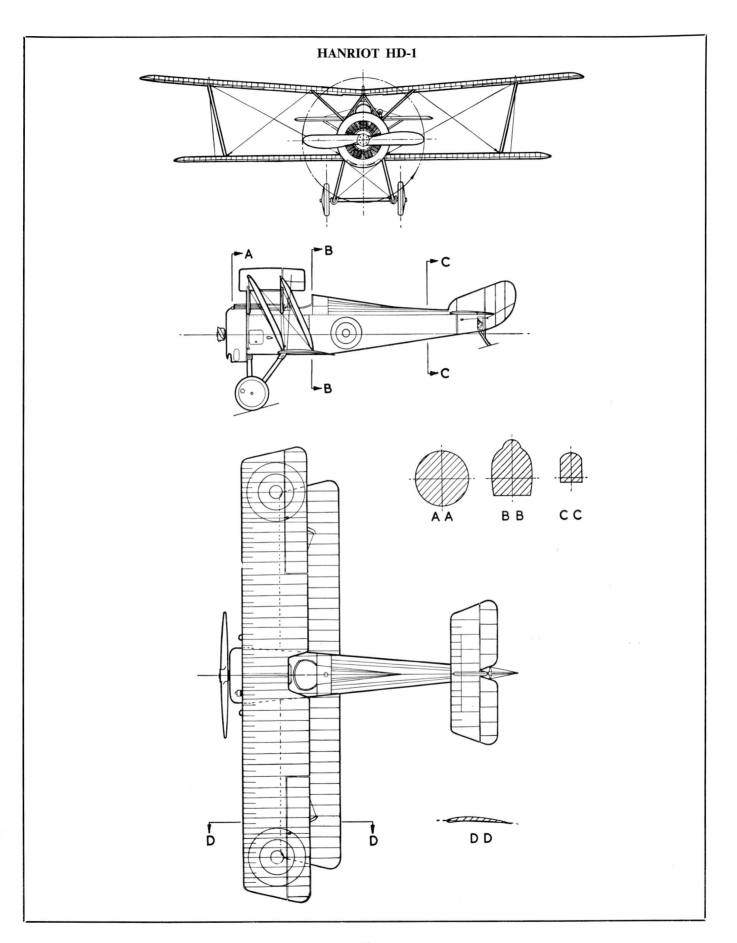

MORANE-SAULNIER AI

By the autumn of 1915 the Morane-Saulnier Type N single-seater monoplane had been rendered obsolescent by the appearance of the Nieuport 11 'Bébé'. Subsequent developments of the N were all inferior to the Nieuport, so that the bulk of the Morane-Saulnier aircraft built during 1916 were reconnaissance types. These included the twin-engined T and two models which served with both French and British units, the single-bay BB biplane and the P parasol monoplane.

Two new single-seaters were brought out in 1917; the AF biplane and its parasol monoplane equivalent, the AI.

The AF was powered by the 120 h.p. Le Rhône 9J rotary engine, and had staggered wings without dihedral and N-shaped interplane struts. The fuselage was round in section, tapering to a point at the tail, and the triangular fin and rudder were typically Morane. Little is known about the AF, which was evidently not a success. The AI, on the other hand, went into production, the first examples being delivered late in 1917. It had either the 120 h.p. Le Rhône or the 160 h.p. Gnôme Monosoupape 9N rotary engine, mounted in a circular open-fronted cowling, the lower half of which was fretted with seven ventilation holes. The parasol wing was swept back and carried horn-balanced ailerons; the wing-tips were raked and there was a large semicircular cut-out in the trailing-edge of the centre section. Spars and ribs were of wood, wire-braced and covered with fabric. An astonishing complexity of struts connected the wing to the fuselage, extra bracing being necessary to withstand the stress of combat manœuvres. Owing to the swept-back form of the wing, the main struts sloped slightly backwards in side elevation. The fuselage, of circular section tapering to a point at the rear, was built up of wooden formers and stringers, covered with fabric except for the panelled portion between cowling and cockpit. Braced from below by struts, the tail-plane was small in area, but carried fairly large elevators; the fin and balanced rudder were triangular in shape. As on most Morane-Saulniers the undercarriage was additionally braced by a vee strut to the centre point of the spreader bar. Either one or two synchronised Vickers guns were fixed to fire forwards through the airscrew arc.

One unit, *Escadrille 156*, was equipped with AIs in January 1918. Some structural trouble was experienced initially, but many pilots liked the type's handling qualities. Other units are believed to have had one or two AIs on their strength for evaluation. In March 1918 the type was withdrawn from the front, and thereafter served as an advanced trainer. Twelve hundred AIs were built, fifty-one of them being purchased by the American Expeditionary Force for use as pursuit trainers.

The version with one gun was designated the M.S.27 C-1, that with two guns, the M.S.29 C-1, and the training model the M.S.30 E-1.

After the war many continued in service; a number of these being re-equipped with 130 h.p. Clerget rotaries. One machine, piloted by Fronval and Joyce, was looped 1,111 consecutive times! A great number of parasol monoplanes were produced by Morane-Saulnier between the wars, the best known perhaps being the M.S.130 and M.S.230.

1. and 2. A standard Morane-Saulnier AI trainer (M.S.30 E-1). 3. AI with twin Vickers guns. 4. Two AIs of a French training unit. 5. One of the many machines which was added to the French Civil Register after the war— F-ABAD.

MORANE-SAULNIER A-I

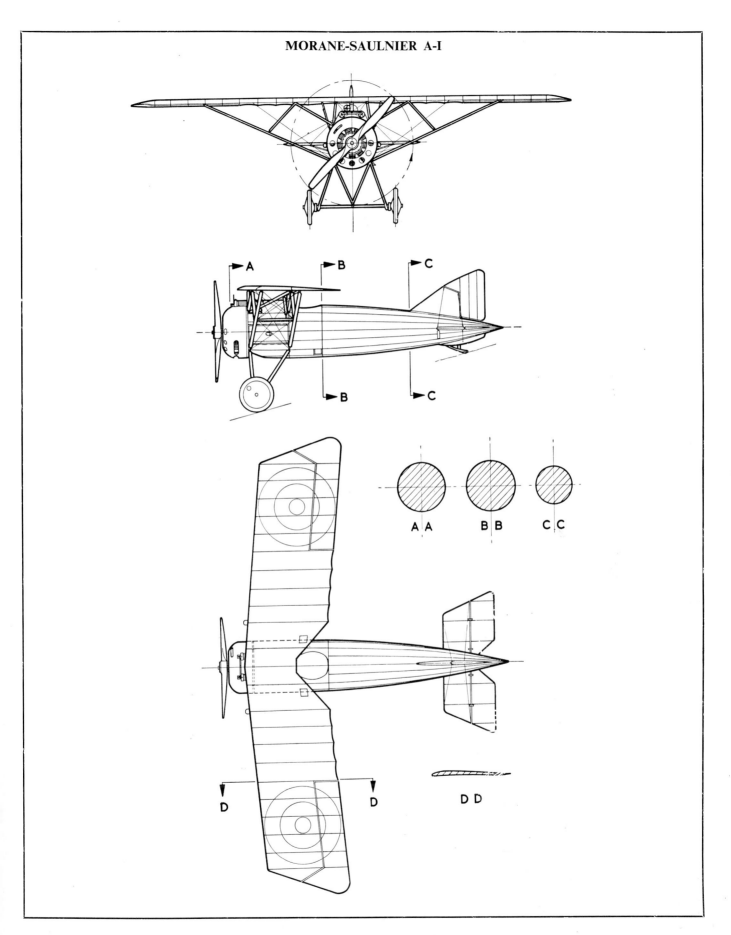

AA BB CC

DD

MORANE-SAULNIER L

The brothers Robert and Léon Morane with their associate Saulnier began to build aeroplanes in 1911, and their monoplane designs quickly became famous. The earliest of their 'Parasol' monoplanes, the type L, which appeared in 1913, can claim to be the first successful fighter aeroplane.

Its power unit was the 80 h.p. Gnôme rotary engine, or, alternatively, the more reliable 80 h.p. Le Rhône, partially enclosed in an aluminium 'horseshoe' cowling, embossed with the Morane-Saulnier trade mark. The broad-chord wings had raked tips and were of orthodox wood-and-fabric construction; there was a large cut-out in the trailing-edge, above the observer's cockpit. Lateral control was by means of wing warping; the upper control wires ran up over a pulley in the apex of the tall wing pylon, the lower wires connected to cranks pivoting at the apex of the inverted pylon situated behind the undercarriage. The crank pivot was connected to the control stick in the cockpit. The fuselage was a wooden wire-braced box girder which tapered to a horizontal knife-edge; the front panels were of plywood, the remainder was fabric-covered. There were no fixed tail-surfaces; both elevator and rudder were remarkably small in area. Early Parasols had wide undercarriage vees; the front struts were later moved back in line with the front of the pilot's cockpit. Other modifications included cut-away cowlings and additional pylon and cabane struts.

The type was ordered by the French Army in fairly large numbers. Very early in the war the commanding officers of the *Escadrilles MS. 23* (de Vergnette), *MS. 12* (de Rose) and *MS. 3* (Brocard) encouraged aggressiveness in their air crews; the Parasol was speedier than the opposing Albatros and Aviatik two-seaters, which were pursued and engaged with carbine fire on every possible occasion. German machines were brought down on January 10th, 1915, by Gilbert and his observer Puechedron, on April 1st by Navarre and Robert, on April 2nd by Pelletier-Doisy and Chambe, on April 23rd by de Bernis and Jacottet, and on May 26th by Méseguich and Jacottet—considerable achievements which attest to both the skill of the pilots and the marksmanship and coolness of the observers.

On July 19th, 1915, a German two-seater was shot down in flames by Caporal Guynemer and Mécanicién Guerder of *MS. 3*. This was Guynemer's first success, although Guerder operated the Parasol's Lewis gun, which was mounted on the top wing to fire above the revolving airscrew.

L-type Parasols were purchased direct from the firm by the British Expeditionary Force in France. They partially equipped No. 3 Squadron, R.F.C., and No. 1 Wing, R.N.A.S. The Victoria Cross was won by a Parasol pilot, Flight Sub-Lieutenant Warneford, who intercepted the Germany army Zeppelin L.Z.37 on June 7th, 1915, and destroyed it with bombs. A number of Ls were used by the R.N.A.S. in the Aegean, and the type was also flown by Russian units.

Improved two-seater Parasols were designed; the LA, equipped with a spinner, ailerons and a fin, and the more powerful P types. These machines, however, were used for reconnaissance work.

1. French Morane L. 2. 3253, in which Warneford destroyed a Zeppelin; one of the two impressed Sopwith Gordon Bennett Racers (1214-15) is behind. 3. R.N.A.S. 'L' at Mudros, protected from blowing sand. 4. Pegoud's armed 'L' type. 5. Late version, with fin.

MORANE-SAULNIER L

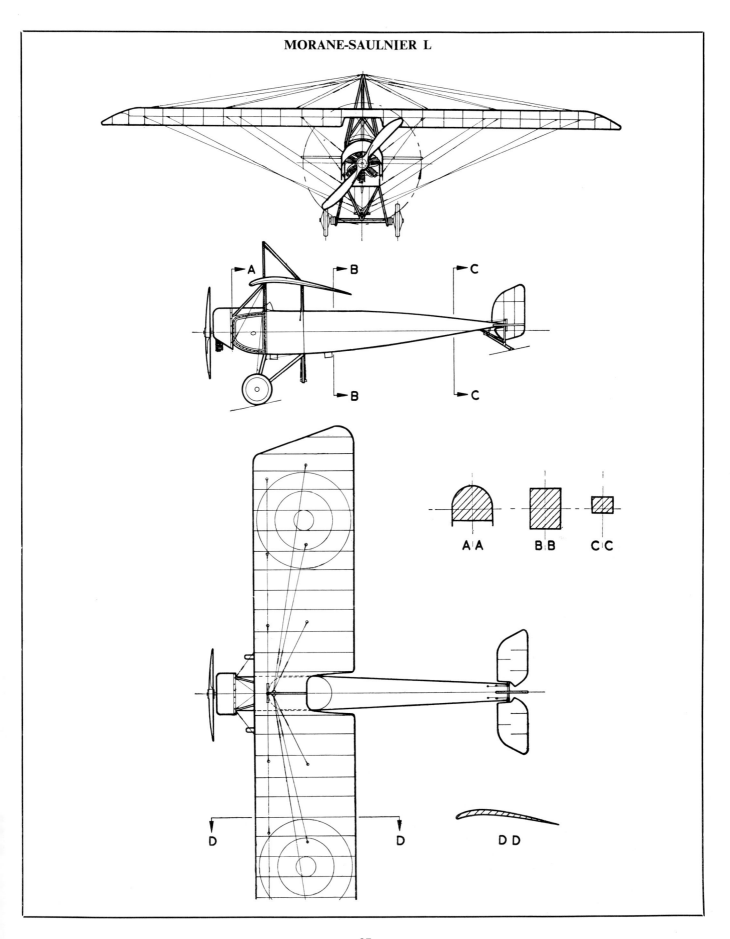

A   B   C

B   C

A A   B B   C C

D   D   D D

MORANE-SAULNIER N

By 1913 monoplane design had reached a very high
level in France, and the Deperdussin and Morane single-
seaters of that year were remarkably well streamlined.

The Type N or Monocoque-Morane was a mid-wing
monoplane powered by the 80 h.p. Gnôme or 110 h.p. Le
Rhône engine. The airscrew had a large spinner, nicknamed *'la casserole'*, which left only a small annular opening for cooling the engine, so that it was often discarded in
hot weather. The typical Morane wings were of wood-and-
fabric construction with flexible tips to allow for warping.
The fuselage was not a true monocoque; its circular section
was formed by fitting light stringers over a wooden frame.
A balanced elevator was fitted; the triangular fin and plain
rudder were of low aspect-ratio. Like most of the Morane
types, the undercarriage struts were of 'M' shape when
viewed in front elevation.

Early in 1914 Raymond Saulnier devised a true synchronising gear, using a Hotchkiss gun borrowed from the
French Army. Difficulties were caused by the faultiness of
the standard ammunition supplied, and Saulnier replaced
his gear with a crude arrangement of steel deflectors fixed
to the airscrew blades; those bullets which did not pass
between the blades were deflected by the steel plates. On
the outbreak of war, the idea was temporarily abandoned.

Among the well-known pre-war pilots serving with
Escadrille M.S. 23 early in the war was Roland Garros.
The unit commander, Capitaine de Vergnette, on his own
initiative sent Garros to Villacoublay to co-operate with
Saulnier. In March 1915 Garros returned with a Morane
N armed with a fixed Hotchkiss gun capable of firing
through the airscrew arc. Deflector plates were fitted to the
airscrew blades. A German two-seater was shot down in
flames on April 1st, 1915, and other victories followed on
the 13th and 18th of the same month. The next day he
forced-landed on the wrong side of the lines, and the device
fell into German hands. As a direct result of this capture,
the Fokker synchronising gear was developed.

Other French pilots quickly obtained Morane single-
seaters; the N was flown by Navarre, the first French ace,
and by Pégoud, the pre-war exhibition pilot, who shot
down six enemy aeroplanes before being killed on August
31st, 1915. Later machines were armed with a synchronised
Vickers gun.

The British purchased a few Ns, which were used by
Nos. 3 and 60 Squadrons, R.F.C., during the summer
of 1916. The type became known as the 'Bullet' in the
R.F.C.; it was armed with a Lewis gun. Ns were also
supplied to the Russian 19th Squadron.

A captured Fokker monoplane (probably an E-III)
and a 'Bullet' were flight-tested together in April 1916, and
the Morane was found to have the better performance. It
was not an aeroplane for a beginner, however, having a
very high landing speed and extreme fore-and-aft sensitivity.

Some Monocoque-Moranes had strengthened undercarriages, modified cowlings and smaller spinners. The V
and AC were 1916 developments; some thirty of the latter
type were constructed, but it is doubtful if it formed the
equipment of any operational unit. The wings were strut-
braced from below.

*1. Morane N with Hotchkiss gun. 2. N with Vickers gun;
the synchronising linkage could be adjusted by a nut on
the projection above the muzzle. 3. British Morane
'Bullet'. 4. Machine with modified spinner, cowling and
undercarriage. 5. Morane AC.*

MORANE-SAULNIER N

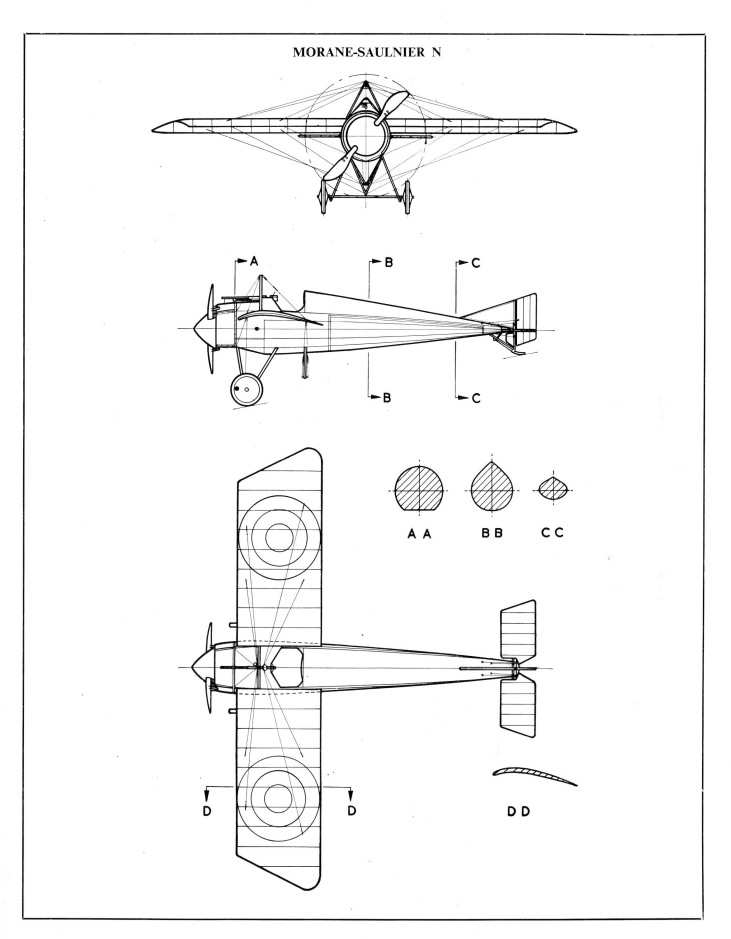

A A   B B   C C

D D

NIEUPORT 10 AND 12

Founded by Edouard de Niéport, the Société Anonyme des Etablissements Nieuport produced a successful series of monoplanes before the outbreak of the First World War. In January 1914 the firm acquired the services of Gustave Delage, a former naval engineer, who was chief designer during the war period.

Delage's first design to go into production was the Type 10 or '18 (square) metre' Nieuport, a two-seater biplane powered by the 80 h.p. Gnôme or Le Rhône rotary, installed in a horeshoe-shaped cowling. The wing arrangement was of the unusual sesquiplane form soon to be universally recognised as characteristically Nieuport; both wings were of orthodox wood-and-fabric construction, but whereas the flat swept-back upper plane had the usual two main spars, the lower had only one, which was a mere streamlined support for the interplane bracing struts. Unequal-chord ailerons, actuated by vertical rods, were fitted to the top wing only; the lower wing had slight dihedral. The wooden vee-shaped interplane struts were bound with tape and braced with wire; in side elevation the front supports to the centre section were of inverted vee shape.

Small metal fairings streamlined the cowling to the fuselage, which was constructed as a wooden box girder with a rounded top decking and a slight amount of vertical taper. Framed in tubular steel and fabric-covered, the tailplane and elevators had raked tips; the balanced rudder was of typical Nieuport shape. Vee-shaped undercarriage struts and a leaf-spring-type tail-skid were fitted.

Two versions were constructed, the 10 AV, with the observer in front of the pilot, and the 10 AR, with the observer behind. A rectangular aperture was provided in the centre section for a machine-gun, but at first only a carbine or pistol was carried. Nieuport 10s were supplied to the *Escadrilles* and the R.N.A.S. in 1915; as they were rather underpowered, they were frequently flown as single-seaters. On July 3rd, 1915, Capitaine Brocard, later to command the Stork Group, shot down a German aeroplane with a pistol when flying solo in his '18 metre' Nieuport. Various gun mountings were often fitted, including an arrangement in which the observer stood with his head through a hole in the top wing to fire his gun.

Nieuport 10s were also used by the R.N.A.S. in the Aegean; some were converted to single-seaters, armed with a Lewis gun pointing through the top plane. The type was manufactured by Nieuport-Macchi for use on the Italian front.

The Nieuport 12 was a larger and more powerful development of the 10. With either the 110 h.p. or 130 h.p. Clerget engine, the type equipped both French and British units. A transparent 'skylight' was provided in the centre section, and some machines had small cut-outs in the leading-edge of the lower wing adjacent to the fuselage. A Lewis gun on a Nieuport-type mounting was provided for the observer; when a synchronising gear became available, a fixed Vickers gun was fitted for the pilot.

Nieuport 12s were built under licence by the Beardmore Company of Dalmuir, Scotland; the later models had circular cowlings and small fixed fins, and presented a well-streamlined appearance.

1. Nieuport 10 AV with hole in top wing through which the observer operated a Hotchkiss gun. 2. 10 AR. 3. Nieuport 12 with Lt. Brisley, 2 Wing, R.N.A.S., Mudros. 4. Nieuport 12 of No. 46 Squadron R.F.C. 5. Late model 12 built by Beardmore.

NIEUPORT 12

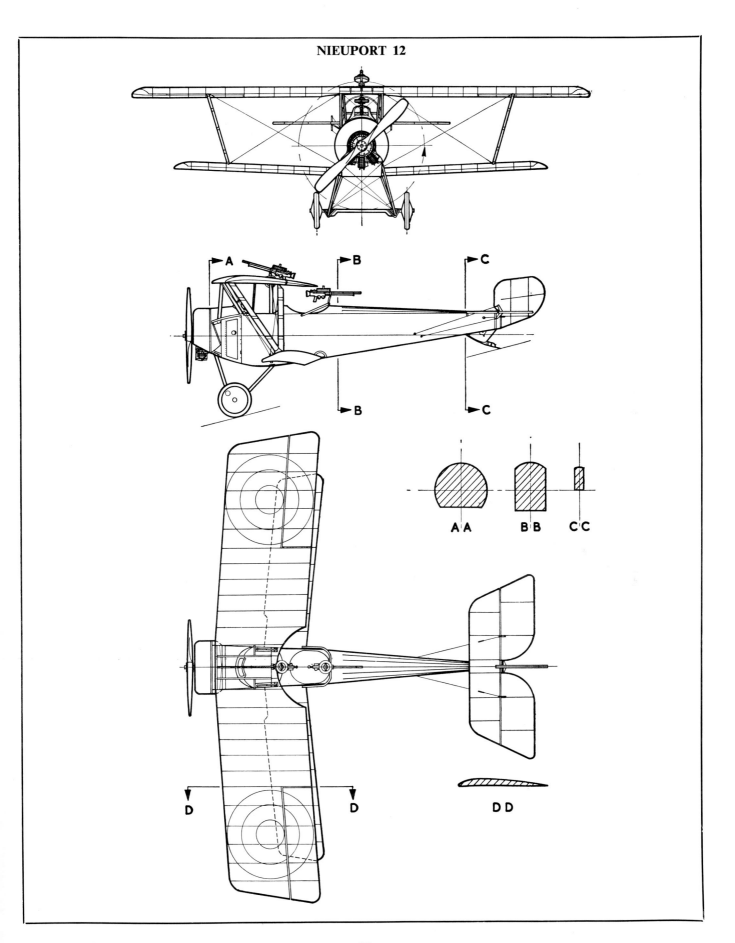

A A   B B   C C

D D

NIEUPORT 11 AND 16

Delage's next design was a small single-seater biplane, the Type 11, which it was intended to enter for the Gordon Bennett Cup contest.

The prototype took four months to construct; the power unit was the 80 h.p. Gnôme rotary engine, installed in a horseshoe-shaped cowling. The wing arrangement was unusual; both planes were of orthodox wood-and-fabric construction, but (like the Nieuport 10 and 12) the flat swept-back upper plane had two main spars, and the lower had only one, which was a mere streamlined support for the interplane bracing struts. Unequal-chord ailerons, actuated by vertical rods, were fitted to the top wing only; the lower wing had slight dihedral. The wooden vee-shaped interplane struts were bound with tape and braced with wire; the front centre-section struts were parallel but the rear struts formed an inverted vee.

Small metal fairings streamlined the cowling to the fuselage, which was constructed as a wooden box girder with a rounded top decking and a slight amount of vertical taper. Framed in steel tube and fabric-covered, the tail-plane and elevators had raked tips; the balanced rudder was of the characteristic Nieuport shape. Vee-shaped under-carriage struts and a leaf-spring-type tail-skid were fitted.

First the British then the French governments placed orders for the type. It was armed with a stripped Lewis gun, mounted in various ways above the centre section to fire above the airscrew arc.

The little biplane quickly became popular, for it had a fine rate of climb and was very manœuvrable. It was usually referred to as the 'Bébé', the '13 (square) metre Nieuport' or the '1½ plane'. French units received the type during the late summer of 1915, and together with the D.H.2 it mastered the Fokker Monoplane and helped to win temporary air superiority for the Allies.

The R.N.A.S. used the Nieuport 11 as early as July 1915 at the Dardanelles. This type also saw service with the R.N.A.S. in France. Large numbers were built in Italy by Nieuport-Macchi, and until mid-1917, the 'Bébé' was the standard Italian fighter. The type was also used by the Russian Air Service.

Some 11s had wide-track undercarriages, which greatly improved their handling qualities on the ground.

Admirable design though it was, the Type 11 was structurally weak; several pilots were killed when the wings of their machines broke in the air. The fault lay in the single spar of the lower wing, which tended to twist and break under stress; a defect common to all aeroplanes of the 'vee-strut' type.

With the same overall dimensions the Nieuport 16 was powered with the 110 h.p. Le Rhône engine and had an improved performance. This version was used by the British as well as by the French; two examples of the Type 16 which served with the R.F.C. in April 1917 were A.131 and A.223 of Nos. 29 and 60 Squadrons respectively. It is probable that the nose-heavy Nieuports flown by the 1st Belgian Squadron in the summer of 1917 were 16s. They had a tendency to dive headlong with engine off.

Nieuport 16s (and 17s) were often equipped with Le Prieur rockets, which could be fired electrically.

1. Early Nieuport 11. 2. French 'Bébé' in German hands. 3. No. 3993, a machine purchased by the Royal Naval Air Service, with Lewis gun. 4. Italian Type 11 built by the Nieuport-Macchi company. 5. Nieuport 16 fitted with Le Prieur rockets.

NIEUPORT 11

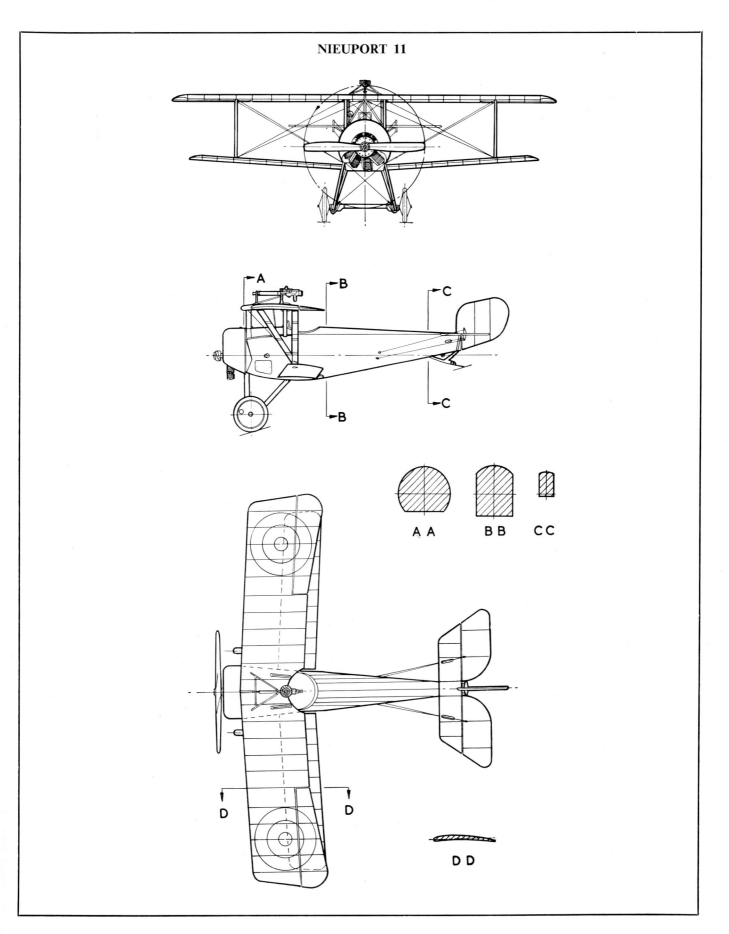

A A   B B   C C

D D

NIEUPORT 17, 21 AND 23

Most famous of the Nieuport designs, the Type 17 or '15 (square) metre' Nieuport, made its appearance early in 1916. A larger, stronger and more powerful development of the successful '*Bébé*', the 17 was truly one of the outstanding aeroplanes of its time. Its standard engine was the 110 h.p. Le Rhône rotary, but the 130 h.p. Clerget was also fitted; machines with the latter power unit were designated 17bis.

The cowling, occasionally provided with strengthening ribs, had two ventilation holes in its lower starboard side; it was streamlined into the fuselage by curved side fairings, fitted with large oval access panels. The wing structure was basically similar to that of the '*Bébé*', with the same vee-strut interplane bracing. Some machines had transparent celluloid 'skylights' in their centre sections. Of typical Nieuport construction, the fuselage was a wire-braced wooden box girder with both horizontal and vertical taper, internally strengthened with plywood sheeting in front of the tail, and with a covering of fabric. Behind the cockpit was a faired head-rest. The empennage was framed in steel tubing and covered with fabric; the vee-type undercarriage was sprung with rubber cord and the tail-skid was of the leaf-spring variety.

At first the armament consisted of a single Lewis gun mounted in various ways above the centre section; later the Lewis gun was either replaced or augmented by a mechanically synchronised Vickers gun fixed centrally in front of the pilot or offset to starboard. British Nieuport 17s carried a Lewis gun on an improved sliding rail mounting invented by Sergeant Foster of No. 11 Squadron, R.F.C. For balloon attacks Le Prieur rockets were fitted to the interplane struts.

The Nieuport 17 reached the front in March 1916 and gradually replaced the '*Bébé*' in French fighter units. Many famous French pilots flew the type. The early Fokker and Halberstadt D-types were inferior to the agile, fast-climbing little machine, and in desperation the Germans ordered the Nieuport to be copied. Not until the Albatros D-I came out in September were they able to find a match for the '15 metre'.

Only six of the type were on the strength of the British Flying Corps on July 1st, 1916; more were soon obtained, however, for it became obvious that there would be no new British fighters for many months. By the early spring of 1917 four R.F.C. squadrons, Nos. 1, 29, 40 and 60 were partially equipped with the 17.

French-built machines were also supplied to Belgium and Russia. The type was constructed in Italy by Nieuport-Macchi and in Russia by the Dux Company, the Russo-Baltic Works and Shchetinin & Company.

Seventy-five Nieuport 17s, purchased by the A.E.F. in September 1917, were used as trainers; one 17bis went to the U.S.A. for evaluation.

The Nieuport 21 had the same overall dimensions. It was powered by either the 80 h.p. or 110 h.p. Le Rhône, and was used as a trainer by the French, Russians and Americans. The Type 23 (80 or 120 h.p. Le Rhône) which served with French, British and American units, closely resembled the 17, but was slightly heavier.

1. Standard Nieuport 17. 2. Bearing the 'Hunting Horn' insignia of Escadrille N.68, this 17 had an airscrew spinner and three guns. 3. Russian Nieuport 17 in the service of the Bolsheviks. 4. Nieuport 21 with Russian markings. 5. Nieuport 23.

NIEUPORT 17

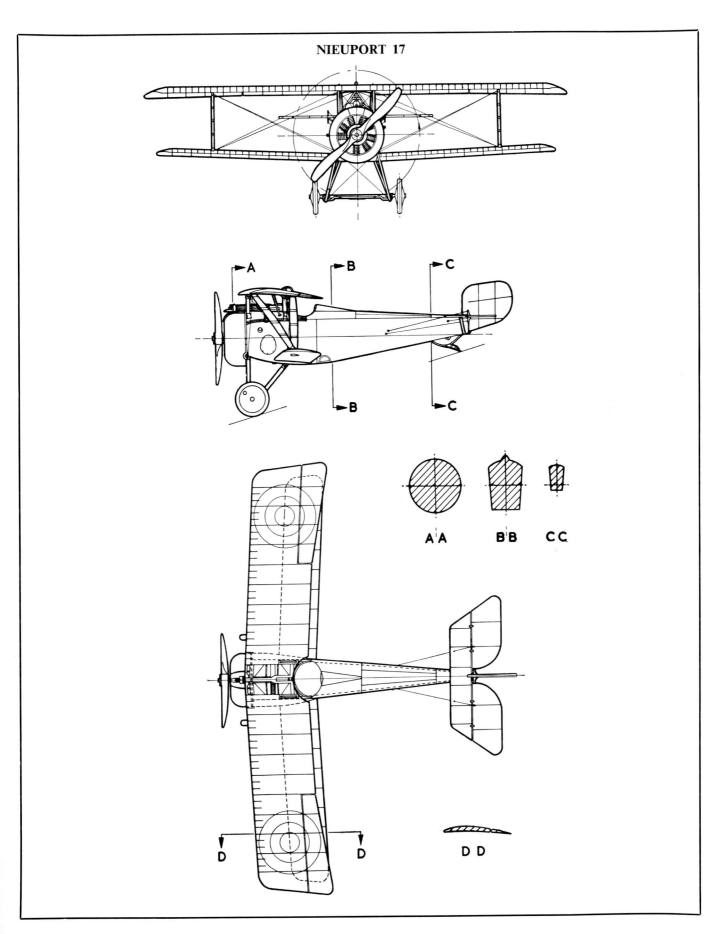

A A   B B   C C

D D

NIEUPORT 24 AND 27

The immediate successors to the excellent Nieuport 17 were also of the sesquiplane vee-strutted type, but they incorporated a number of refinements.

The Nieuport 24 was better streamlined and resembled the experimental Type 18; its power unit was the 130 h.p. Le Rhône. Rounded sides were given to the fuselage by means of horizontal stringers, the tail-plane had a curved leading-edge and a small fin and rounded horn-balanced rudder were fitted. At least one example had inverted-vee front centre-section struts. The tail-skid was internally sprung.

A variant, designated the 24bis, had the same engine and fuselage, but reverted to the earlier Nieuport empennage, with angular tail-plane and finless balanced rudder. Some 24bis retained the angular upper wing-tips of the earlier types; others had rounded tips to their upper wing trailing-edges, and occasionally rounded tips to their tail-planes as well. There was a lack of uniformity in the Nieuports of the mid-1917 period. Machines flown by French units were usually armed with single synchronised Vickers guns, while those used by the British conservatively retained the wing-mounted unsynchronised Lewis.

By the summer of 1917 the more powerful Spad had replaced the Nieuport in many *Escadrilles de chasse*; a number of units, however, were still equipped with the rotary-engined single-seater, which was indeed preferred by some pilots, including the famous Nungesser. 24bis supplied to the British remained in service both on the Western Front and in the Middle East until well into 1918, owing to a shortage of S.E.5as. A batch of 24bis, numbered N5860–5909, were built in England for the R.N.A.S. by the British Nieuport and General Aircraft Co. Ltd. In November 1917 the United States purchased 121 24s and 140 24bis from France and used them as advanced trainers.

Last of the Nieuport vee-strutters, the Type 27 was powered by the 120 h.p. Le Rhône rotary. It had rounded wing-tips, a fuselage with curved sides and a rounded tail-plane and curved fin and rudder like that of the Nieuport 24. An internally sprung tail-skid was provided. The standard armament, a Vickers gun on French machines, a Lewis on British, remained the same, in order to retain a reasonable performance.

The type served in limited numbers with the French Flying Service, and French-built machines were used by the British from the summer of 1917 until the spring of 1918. 27s were supplied to Italy and in addition were constructed there by the Nieuport-Macchi company at Varese. Two hundred and eighty-seven machines were purchased by the United States for use at their training schools in France.

In spite of its improved aerodynamic shape, the performance of the 27 was little better than that of the earlier Nieuport models, and its armament was scarcely good enough for the intensive air fighting of 1917–1918. It could not compete with the speed, strength and fire-power of the later Spads. The vee-strutted design was in fact incapable of further development, and the designer Delage and his associates had already begun to work on biplanes of more orthodox configuration.

1. An American 24bis in France. 2. Nungesser, the famous French pilot, with his 24bis at St. Pol, 1917. 3. 24bis of a French Escadrille. *4. Nieuport 27 in the U.S.A. 5. 27s (which were the last of the 'vee-strut' type) at an American training unit.*

NIEUPORT 27

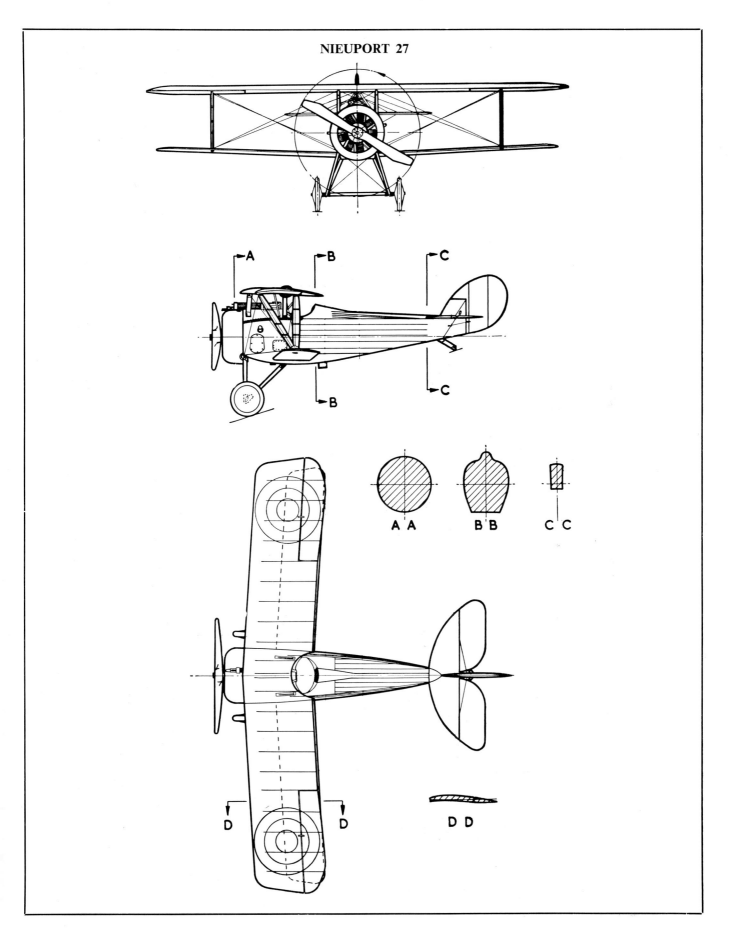

A A   B B   C C

D D

NIEUPORT 28 C-1

Described as the 'most elegant aeroplane of the First World War', the Nieuport 28 C-1 was radically different from the familiar line of Nieuport sesquiplanes.

The first prototype, which had dihedral on both wings, underwent trials on June 14th, 1917. During the second week of November 1917 it took part in a series of comparative tests with two other prototypes; one of these had flat wings, while the other had dihedral only on the top plane, which was set close to the fuselage.

As a result of these trials a fourth version was evolved, which went into production; its top plane had a slight dihedral angle and was fixed at a more orthodox height above the fuselage; its lower plane was flat. The power unit was the 160 h.p. Gnôme-Rhône Monosoupape 9N rotary, neatly installed in a circular cowling fretted with cooling apertures in varying positions. The wings were staggered, with elliptical tips; rather unusually, the lower wing carried the ailerons. Two pine spars on which were fitted wire-braced wooden ribs made up the basic wing shape; the thin-sectioned leading-edges were covered with plywood veneer, to which was tacked the fabric wing covering. The interplane and centre-section struts, of wood, were set closely together in side elevation.

The slim and comparatively long fuselage was given a circular cross-section by means of wooden formers and longitudinal stringers; it was fabric-covered, except for the plywood portion between the cowling and the rear of the cockpit. Two inspection panels of sheet duralumin were provided on each side. The pilot sat fairly high in the cramped cockpit, inadequately protected by a small windshield; behind his shoulders was a streamlined fairing. The strut-braced tail-plane, the elevators and balanced rudder were of wood-and-fabric construction. Steel-tube undercarriage struts, streamlined with wooden fairings, were fitted; the tail-skid was internally sprung. Two synchronised Vickers guns were provided; owing to the narrowness of the centre section one gun was mounted on top of the fuselage to port; the other was set on a shelf below the port struts of the centre section.

Limited numbers of the type were used by the French Flying Service. The 28 is more famous, however, as being the machine which equipped the first American fighter squadrons. Two hundred and ninety-seven were purchased by the American Expeditionary Force, the first delivery being in March 1918.

On April 14th, 1918, Lieutenants D. Campbell and A. Winslow of the 94th 'Hat-in-the-Ring' Squadron shot down a German single-seater apiece, the first to fall to an all-American unit. Captain E. Rickenbacker, greatest of the United States aces, scored several of his twenty-six victories in a Nieuport 28.

Nevertheless the little biplane was not popular with American pilots. Though very manœuvrable and with a good rate of climb, when dived too steeply it had a tendency to shed the fabric from the leading-edges of its wings. Steps were taken to strengthen the wing-fabric of the Type 28, and a satisfactory solution to the problem had been evolved by July 1918. This was too late unfortunately, for by then the Nieuports in the American fighter squadrons had been replaced by sturdier Spad 13s.

1. and 2. Two views of the flat-winged prototype. 3. Prototype with the top wing set close to the fuselage. 4. Standard model Nieuport 28 on test in the U.S.A. 5. Production model, as used by American squadrons.

NIEUPORT 28

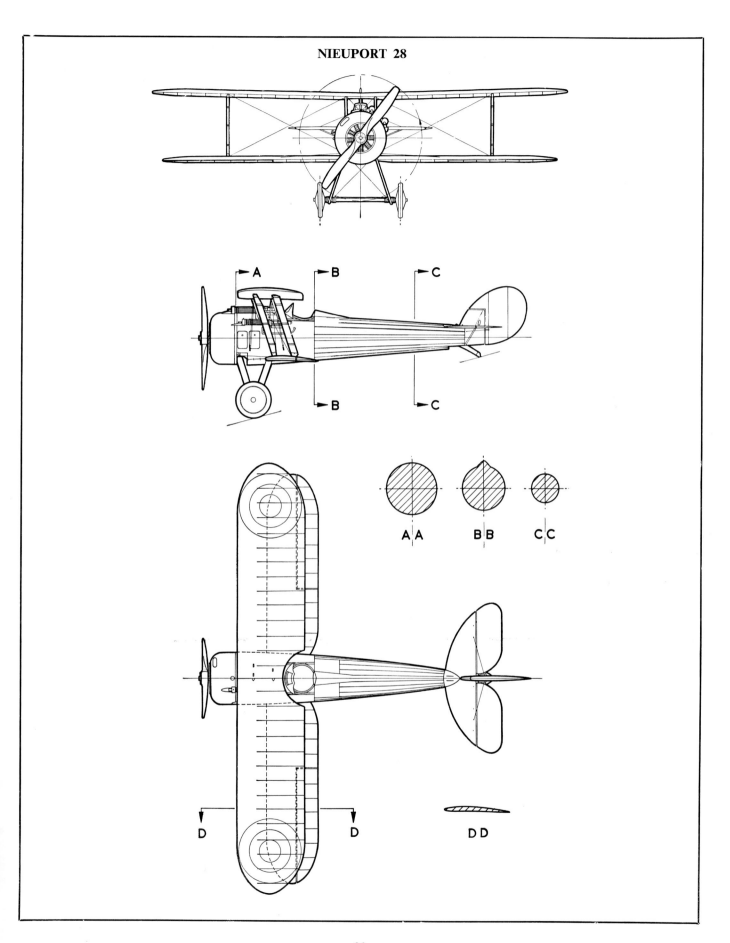

A A   B B   C C

D D

NIEUPORT-DELAGE 29

The Nieuport-Delage 29 C-1, designed in 1918 by M. Delage, was in every way an outstanding fighting aeroplane. With its heavy stationary engine and double bays of interplane struts it presented a complete contrast to the earlier Nieuport Scouts. The power unit was the 300 h.p. Hispano-Suiza engine, entirely enclosed in a metal cowling, the exhaust gases discharging through four stubs on each side of the nose. Between the undercarriage vees were two Lamblin radiators; the lower surface of the oil tank, which was fitted below the engine crankcase, formed part of the outer surface of the cowling, and was corrugated to provide cooling. The wings, of the normal wire-braced wooden and fabric construction of the time, had 10 degrees of stagger; there was no centre section, the wooden cabane bracing being of the trestle type more often seen on German machines. The top wing had slight dihedral and carried two gravity fuel tanks. Only the flat bottom wing was fitted with ailerons, which were of the long-span variety. The interplane struts were of wood, bound with tape and braced with wires.

Great care was taken to obtain a well-streamlined fuselage; it was a true monocoque, built up of spiral layers of tulip-wood veneer fixed alternately right- and left-handed over plywood bulkheads in front of the cockpit, and over light stringers behind. A high faired head-rest was fitted behind the pilot's seat. Built-in fairings were provided to take the lower wing-roots, and the low aspect-ratio tail-plane and upper and lower fins, covered with a tulip-wood skin, were also integral parts of the fuselage. Elevators and rudder were horn-balanced.

The undercarriage vees were built up of multi-ply wood and the wheels had a hinged axle. In the fuselage behind the engine was the main fuel tank; a wind-driven generator supplied electricity for lighting purposes and to heat the pilot's flying suit. Twin Vickers guns mounted in front of the pilot were synchronised to fire through the airscrew arc.

The 29 C-1 was fast and manœuvrable, and performed well in its official trials. It was not, however, destined to come into use before the Armistice was signed.

In the immediate post-war years the 29 C-1 was the standard French single-seater fighter, and examples were supplied to Belgium and Japan. As late as 1922 the machine was described by an authority as the 'finest fighting machine now in commission'.

At one time the Nieuport-Delage held the world's height record. In 1920 a modified machine was entered for the Gordon Bennett Cup. It had a reduced wing-span, single-bay interplane bracing, and, rather oddly, the lower wing was some twenty-one inches longer than the upper. After a tremendous struggle, Nieuport-Delage No. 10, piloted by M. Sadi-Lecointe, won the race and at the same time broke the world's speed record. The same machine also won the 1922 Deutsch Cup competition.

A version of the 29 C-1 was built in 1918 for the Ministry of Marine. The 29G, as it was designated, had the 180 h.p. Le Rhône rotary engine installed in a round open-fronted cowling. Full-span, horn-balanced ailerons were fitted to the bottom wing only.

1, 2 and 3. Standard Nieuport 29, with twin Lamblin radiators. 4. Nieuport 29 with frontal radiator, single Lamblin radiator and horn-balanced ailerons to its lower wing. 5. The Nieuport 29G supplied to the French Ministry of Marine.

NIEUPORT-DELAGE 29

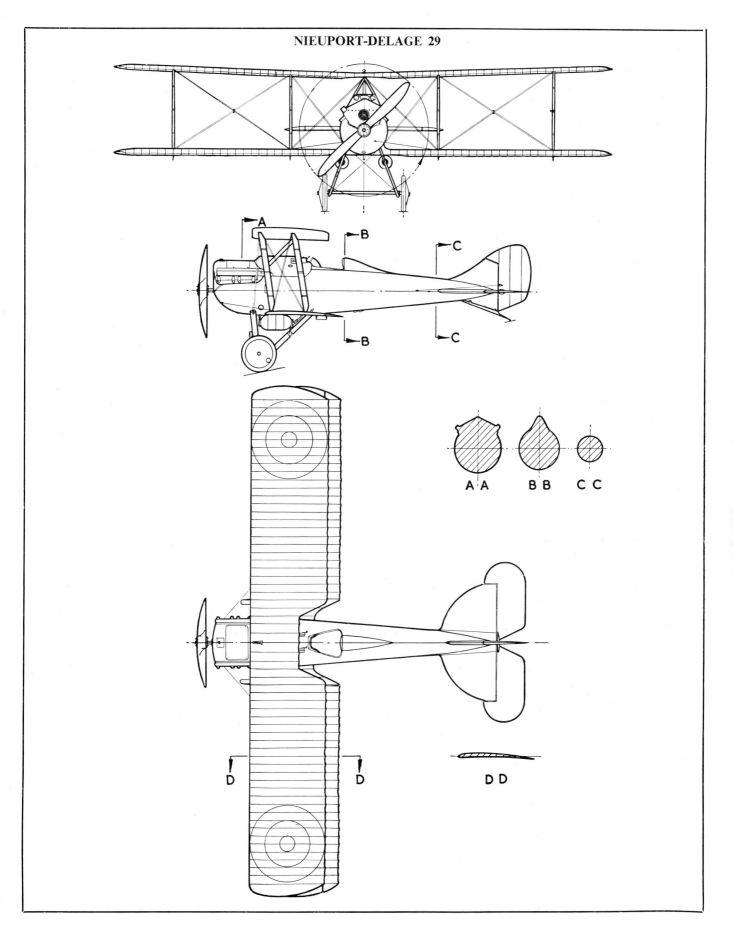

A A   B B   C C

D   D

D D

SPAD A.2 AND A.4

Fastest of all pre-war aeroplanes were the Deperdussin monoplanes, designed by M. Béchereau of the Société pour les Appareils Deperdussin. In 1914 the proprietor of the firm, Armand Deperdussin, was implicated in a financial scandal, and the concern was taken over by Louis Blériot, who renamed it the Société pour Aviation et ses Dérivés, thus preserving the original initials.

Béchereau's first wartime model, the Spad A.2, was designed as a reasonably fast tractor aeroplane with forward armament. An interrupter gear which permitted a machine-gun to fire through the revolving airscrew of a tractor aeroplane had been demonstrated as early as 1912, but the designers were strangely reluctant to utilise this system. Every possible alternative was investigated, the most extraordinary perhaps being the 'pulpit'-type design, a tractor aeroplane with a nacelle for the observer in front of the airscrew.

The A.2, a 'pulpit' tractor biplane, first flew on May 21st, 1915. Its power unit was the 80 h.p. Le Rhône rotary, mounted immediately below the front pair of centre-section struts, and almost entirely enclosed in a flat-fronted metal cowling provided with ventilation apertures. The flat unstaggered wings, of wire-braced wood-and-fabric construction, had blunt tips; above the pilot's head was a large rectangular cut-out, and there were cut-outs in the leading-edges of the wings to provide clearance for the airscrew blades. Ailerons of the plain equal-chord type were fitted to the top plane only. Interplane bracing was that of a single-bay biplane, but light additional struts braced the intersections of the wires to the main spars. The fuselage was a wooden wire-braced box girder with a rounded top decking; from a point approximately two feet behind the pilot's seat back to the stern-post the underside was rounded also. The tail-plane, braced from below by a strut on each side, had a straight leading-edge and raked tips, and carried plain equal-chord elevators. The unfortunate observer was accommodated in a small pointed plywood nacelle, which afforded him little protection from the slipstream. An extension to the airscrew shaft revolved in a ball-race attached to the rear of the nacelle, which was braced to the top plane by steel tubing and to the undercarriage by wooden vee struts. The usual armament was a Lewis gun mounted on a crude arrangement of steel tubes connected to a vertical pylon, which permitted some movement. A semicircular mesh screen fixed to the rear of the nacelle guarded the observer from the airscrew. Forty-two Spad A.2s were supplied to France, and fifty-seven to Russia. Naturally the type was unpopular with observers, who would certainly be crushed by the engine in even the mildest crash. Very soon the A.2 was abandoned by the French Flying Service, but owing to a general shortage of equipment the Russians continued to use theirs for a considerable time. Some Russian A.2s were fitted with skis.

The Spad A.4, which first flew on February 22nd, 1916, had the same dimensions, but the more powerful 110 h.p. Le Rhône rotary was installed. Only one example was purchased by France; ten went to Russia, where presumably they were used on operations.

1. An early model Spad A.2. Note three exhaust outlets above lower wing leading edge. 2. A later version with more streamlined exhaust system and without lower wing cut-out. 3, 4. and 5. A.2s in Russian markings. Number 4 shows means of access to engine.

SPAD A.2

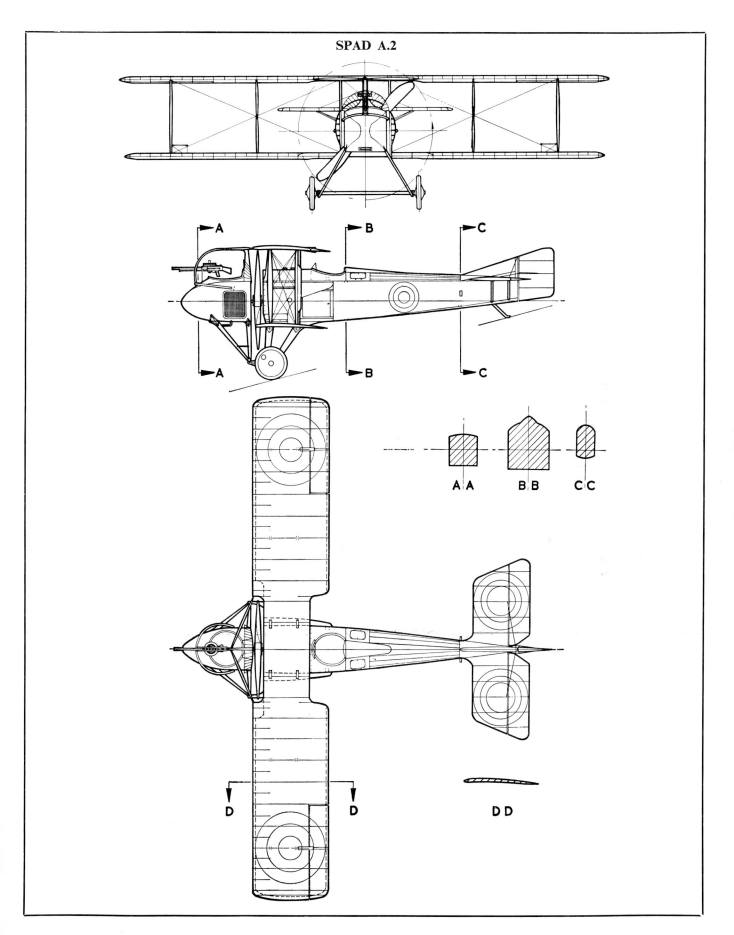

A A   B B   C C

D D

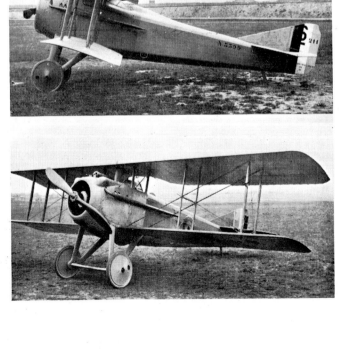

SPAD S.7

In late 1915 M. Béchereau of the Société pour Aviation et ses Dérivés designed a trim little single-seater biplane which proved to be one of the outstanding aeroplanes of the First World War. Piloted by Bequèt, it made its first flight in May 1916; in appearance it resembled a Spad 'A', without the frontal nacelle.

The prototype had the 140 h.p. Hispano-Suiza engine; the 150 h.p., 180 h.p. and 200 h.p. Hispano engines were installed as they became available. One S.7 was experimentally fitted with the 150 h.p. Renault. The characteristic metal cowling had a round frontal radiator, which was provided with shutters on the later models; twin exhaust pipes passed horizontally along each side of the fuselage. The engine had large inspection panels on either side, which were occasionally fitted with louvres; these panels were removed in hot weather. The straight wings, of wire-braced wood-and-fabric construction, had no dihedral, and were of unequal chord; ailerons were carried on the top planc only. Wire trailing-edges gave a 'scalloped' effect; above the pilot's head was a semicircular cut-out. The interplane bracing was that of a single-bay biplane, but the cable intersections were connected to the spars by light auxiliary struts. Four vertical centre-section struts were fitted; in the centre section was a header tank for the radiator and a gravity fuel tank. The wire-braced wood-and-fabric fuselage had flat sides with streamlined top and bottom decking; behind the cockpit was a faired head-rest. The tail-plane, of wood-and-fabric construction, had raked tips and was braced from below by a strut on either side. Elevators had 'scalloped' trailing-edges, as did the rudder, which, in the 180 and 200 h.p. models, was of increased area. The sturdy wooden undercarriage vees were joined by double steel-tube spreader bars, covered by a fairing. The standard armament was a single synchronised Vickers gun mounted in front of the pilot, slightly to starboard; at least one British Spad carried an extra Lewis gun above the centre section.

Production machines reached the front in the autumn of 1916, and the type quickly became popular. The S.7 will always be associated with the Stork Group (*Les Cicognes*) and the names of Fonck and Guynemer.

As early as October 1916 a single Spad was attached to No. 60 Squadron R.F.C., for evaluation. In addition to S.7s purchased by the R.F.C. in France, 100 (A8794–A8893) were built in England by the British Blériot and Spad Company of Addlestone. Further machines, numbered from N6210, were ordered by the British Navy from Mann, Egerton & Co., Norwich, but as has been related in the Sopwith triplane section, these were handed over to the R.F.C., which renumbered them A9100–A9161, B1351–B1388 and B9911–B9930. Nos. 19 and 23 Squadrons, R.F.C., flew the type on the Western Front, and a few machines were sent to Mesopotamia. S.7s were used by the *5me* and *10me Escadrilles*, Belgian Aviation Militaire, by the Italian *91a Squadriglia*, the 'Squadron of Aces', and in Russia. In December 1917 189 machines were bought by America. Compared to the Nieuport Scouts, the S.7 lacked manœuvrability, but it more than made up for this by its great strength and high speed.

1. Prototype Spad S.7. 2. French-built S.7 sent to England as a pattern, with R.F.C. serial A.8965. 3. R.F.C. A.9100, ex-R.N.A.S. N.6210, with extra Lewis gun. 4. French-built S.7 with R.N.A.S. serial N.3399. 5. A British-built machine.

SPAD S.7

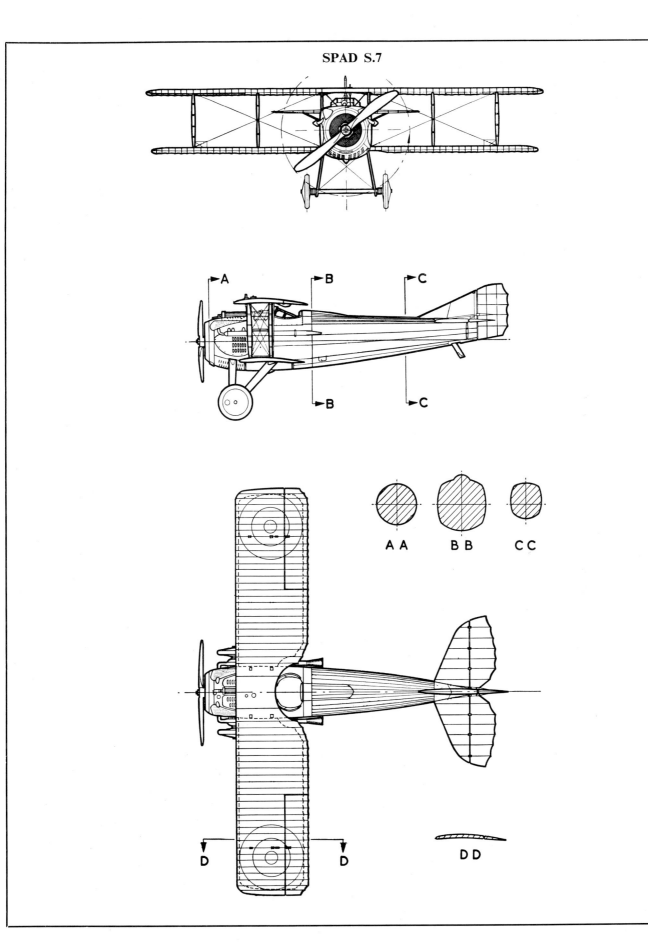

A A   B B   C C

D D

SPAD S.12, S.13, S.14 AND S.17

The Spad S.13, designed by M. Béchereau towards the end of 1916, was a larger and more powerful development of the very successful S.7. Hispano-Suiza engines of ever-increasing horse-power were installed, ranging from the 200 h.p. to the 235 h.p. models. Apart from its increased size and bulkier engine cowling, the S.13 differed from the S.7 in having unequal-chord ailerons, rounded tips to the tail-plane and elevators and twin Vickers guns. The rudder was of the larger type used on some of the later S.7s; on late production S.13s the lower wing-tips had curved leading-edges, and inverted vee-shaped front centre-section struts were fitted.

During the summer and autumn of 1917 the S.13 gradually replaced the S.7 in the *Escadrilles de chasse*, and by early 1918 had become the standard French single-seater fighter. A total of 8,472 machines was built, by Spad (1,141), Blériot (2,300), Bernard (1,750), Kellner (1,280), Nieuport (700), Borel (300), Levasseur (340), SCAP (300) and ACM (361), and the U.S.A. purchased 893 of these Spads in March 1918. The type's speed and robustness made it popular with American pilots, and by November 1918 it equipped sixteen A.E.F. pursuit squadrons. Three contracts placed in the United States for the construction of 6,000 S.13s were cancelled when the war finished. Eleven Italian fighter squadrons flew the type, although several of these were re-equipped with the more popular Hanriot during 1918. Only one Belgian unit, the *10me Escadrille*, had S.13s. In France the Spad S.13 continued to be used until 1923.

Based on the S.13 design, the Spad S.12 Ca-1 appeared in early 1917. A shell-firing gun was fixed in the vee of its 220 h.p. Hispano-Suiza engine and fired through the hollow shaft of the airscrew. The breech of the gun protruded into the cockpit. A single Vickers gun was mounted on top of the cowling; the procedure was to fire a sighting burst from the Vickers before discharging the '*moteur-canon*'. Although Guynemer and Fonck achieved some success with this new weapon, its tremendous recoil and slow rate of fire led to the abandonment of the S.12 after 300 had been constructed.

The Spad S.14 was a seaplane version of the S.12, developed by Béchereau and Herbemont, with floats supplied by the flying-boat designer Tellier. The prototype, built by the Levasseur concern, first flew on November 15th, 1917. Forty of the type were constructed for the Ministry of Marine.

The S.14's fuselage was identical to that of the S.12, and it had the same armament—a *moteur-canon* and a Vickers machine-gun. Its maximum speed of 128 m.p.h. was particularly good for a seaplane.

Operational trials of an improved S.13, the S.17, fitted with the 300 h.p. Hispano-Suiza engine, were carried out by Capitaine de Slade in June 1918. A larger and heavier aeroplane, with reinforced interplane and empennage bracing, it had an excellent performance. Twin synchronised Vickers guns were fixed to fire through the airscrew arc. Twenty S.17s were constructed; most of these were issued to the Stork Group, the crack unit of the French flying service.

1. and 2. Late model S.13s with strengthened centre-section bracing. 3. The 'moteur-canon' S.12. 4. The S.14 seaplane, which also carried a cannon; a few are believed to have operated from Corfu. 5. The 300 h.p. Spad S.17, which was introduced in 1918.

SPAD S.13

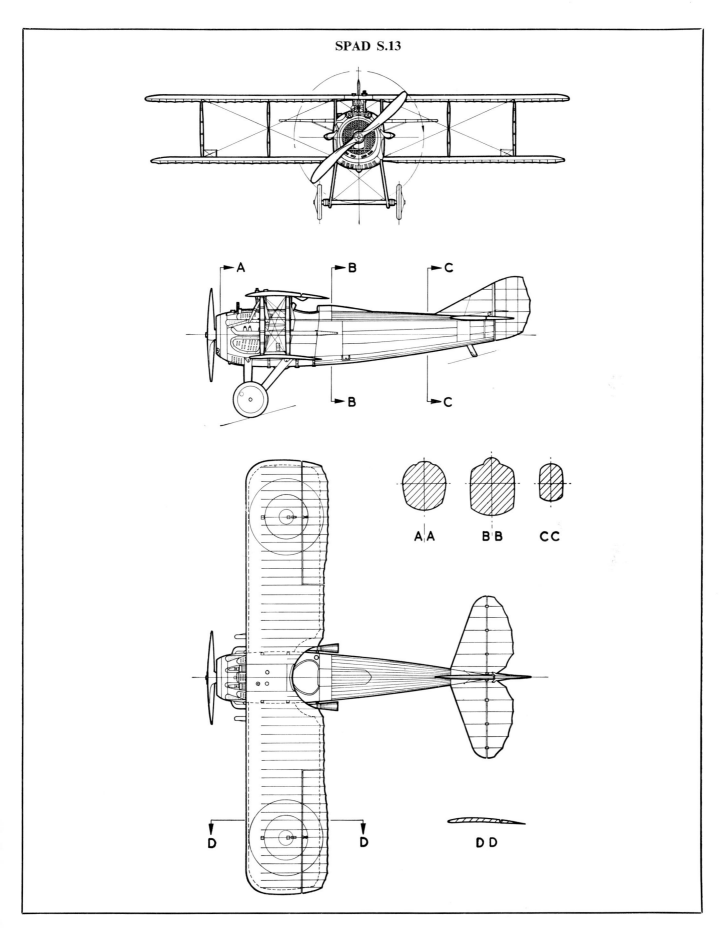

A A   B B   C C

D   D   D D

ALBATROS D-I AND D-II

In July 1916 the Allies had complete command of the air; the German High Command therefore began to organise units completely equipped with single-seater fighters, called *Jagdstaffeln* or '*Jastas*'. The difficulty was to find an outstanding new type for these units; one that would be able to deal with the Allied Nieuport 11 and D.H.2. As the available Fokker and Halberstadt biplanes were not good enough, the rather desperate decision was made to build copies of the French Nieuport.

Meanwhile the Albatros engineers Thelen, Schubert and Gnädig had developed a little biplane of advanced design which was to provide the answer to the problem.

The Albatros D-I was brought out in August 1916. Its power unit was either the 160 h.p. Mercedes or the 150 h.p. Benz, cooled by two box-like radiators fixed on each side of the fuselage. A 'chimney'-type exhaust pipe was fitted to the prototype, but production models had horizontal manifolds discharging to starboard. The square-cut wings had orthodox fabric-covered wooden spars and ribs; ailerons were carried on the top wing only. The lower wing was in two parts, connected to projections on either side of the fuselage. Interplane struts were of wire-braced steel tubing; the cabane struts of the trestle type. A frame of longerons and formers covered with plywood, the fuselage was a semi-monocoque structure. A large spinner provided a smooth 'entry'. Upper and lower empennage fins were of wood covered with three-ply, the tail-skid being attached to the lower fin. The fish-like tail-plane was wooden-framed and fabric-covered; the balanced elevators and rudder were of fabric-covered steel tubing. Sockets in the fuselage bottom took the tops of the plain vee under-carriage struts. Twin Spandau guns were synchronised to fire through the airscrew arc.

The authorities had only one criticism of the D-I: that the top wing obscured the view of the pilot in a forward and upward direction. The Albatros Werke therefore brought the top wing closer to the fuselage and replaced the trestle-type cabane with splayed-out steel tube 'N' struts. The modified machine was designated the D-II. The later D-IIs had radiators inset in their top planes in place of side radiators.

On September 17th, 1916, Hauptmann Boelcke led the picked pilots of *Jasta 2* into action with great success. The Albatros proved to be overwhelmingly superior to contemporary Allied machines in both rate of climb and fire-power. Within a few weeks the scales had again tipped in Germany's favour.

A number of Albatros D-IIs were built under licence by the Luft Verkehrs Gesellschaft (L.V.G.) at Köslin, with the designation L.V.G. D-I. Twenty D-IIs (53.01 to 53.20) were constructed for Austro-Hungary by the Oeffag concern at Wiener-Neustadt. Their 185 h.p. Austro-Daimler engines were completely enclosed; six exhaust stubs replaced the long pipe of the German model, and their radiators were in the top wing.

After the war, to circumvent the Armistice Commission's veto on warplane construction, Albatros products were re-designated in an 'L' series. The D-I became the L.15, the D-II the L.17.

1. The D-I prototype. 2. D-I 391/16 (Leut. Büttner, Jasta Boelcke) captured by the British 1.12.16. 3. and 4. Early D-IIs. 5. 53.01, an Oeffag-built Austro-Hungarian D-II. Note wing-radiator and cylinder-heads enclosed in an aluminium cowling.

ALBATROS D-II

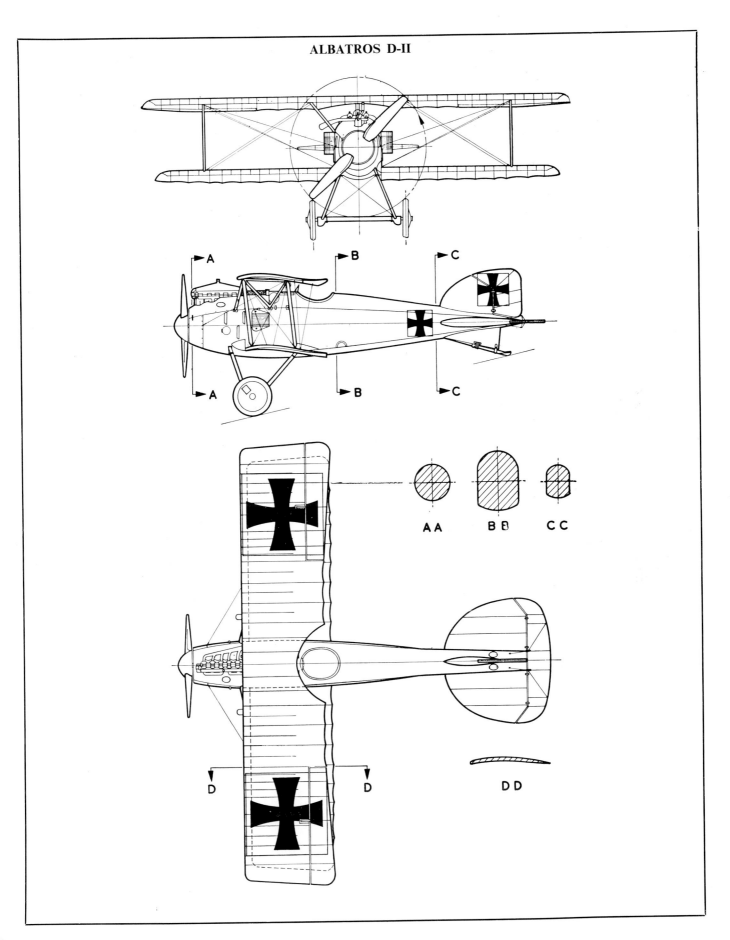

A A   B B   C C

D   D   D D

ALBATROS D-III

The Albatros D-I and D-II had proved to be superior to any of the available Allied types. German fighter pilots, therefore, congratulated themselves when in January 1917 a third and even better Albatros Scout arrived at the front; the D-III.

The D-III's engine was a high-compression model of the 160 h.p. Mercedes; the radiator was situated in the top wing; centrally on the early models, offset to starboard on the later machines. The exhaust pipe was carried along the starboard side of the nose.

In order to improve the pilot's downward view, the 'vee strut' sesquiplane layout of the French Nieuport was adopted. The top wing had the two wooden spars of its predecessor, but the lower wing, of much narrower chord, had only one. Both wings had raked tips; ailerons were fitted to the top wing only and were of unequal chord. The vee-shaped interplane struts and N-shaped cabane struts were of streamlined steel tubing.

The fuselage was very similar to those of the D-I and D-II: a semi-monocoque with wooden longerons and formers over which was fixed the plywood covering. The upper and lower tail-fins were wooden-framed and covered with three-ply. The tail-plane was also framed in wood, but had a fabric covering. Elevator and rudder, framed in steel tubing and covered in fabric, were balanced. A few late model D-IIIs had the Albatros D-V rudder, with rounded trailing-edge. The undercarriage was identical to that of the D-II. Twin synchronised Spandau guns were fixed to fire through the airscrew arc.

Some of the first D-IIIs were supplied to *Jasta 11*, commanded by Baron Manfred von Richthofen. On January 24th, 1917, when von Richthofen was attacking an F.E.2b, a dangerous crack appeared in the lower wing of his machine. He was able to land safely, but his trust in Albatros designs was temporarily shaken, and he flew a Halberstadt D-II for a time. On the same day two pilots of the *Jasta Boelcke* were killed through similar wing failures. The source of the trouble lay in the single spar of the lower wing; it was positioned too far back from the leading-edge and tended to twist under stress. The D-III had inherited the structural weakness of the Nieuport Scout!

In spite of this drawback, the D-III had a better rate of climb than its predecessors, and its pilots ran up considerable personal scores; January to May 1917 were successful months for the *Jagdstaffeln*.

D-IIIs built by the Ostdeutsche Albatros Werke at Schneidemühl were designated Alb. D-III (O.A.W.). Three series of D-IIIs (53.2, 153 and 253) were manufactured by the Oeffag firm for Austrian use. They had Austro-Daimler engines of 185, 200 and 225 h.p., respectively, with six exhaust stubs in place of the pipe of the German D-III. Normally fully cowled, the cylinder heads were exposed in hot weather. The 253 series did not have spinners, because of the increased length of the engine.

D-IIIs were used by German units in Macedonia and Palestine. The type was re-designated the Albatros L.20 in post-war years, a device which enabled the firm to thwart the Armistice Commission's ban on warplane construction.

1. Prototype. 2. D2096/16 'Vera' in the U.S.A. 3. D.3066/16, which was successfully air-launched from the Zeppelin L.35. 4. 53.21 one of the Oeffag-built D-IIIs for Austro-Hungary. 5. The Austrian pilot Oberleutnant Selinger with his 253 series D-III.

ALBATROS D-III

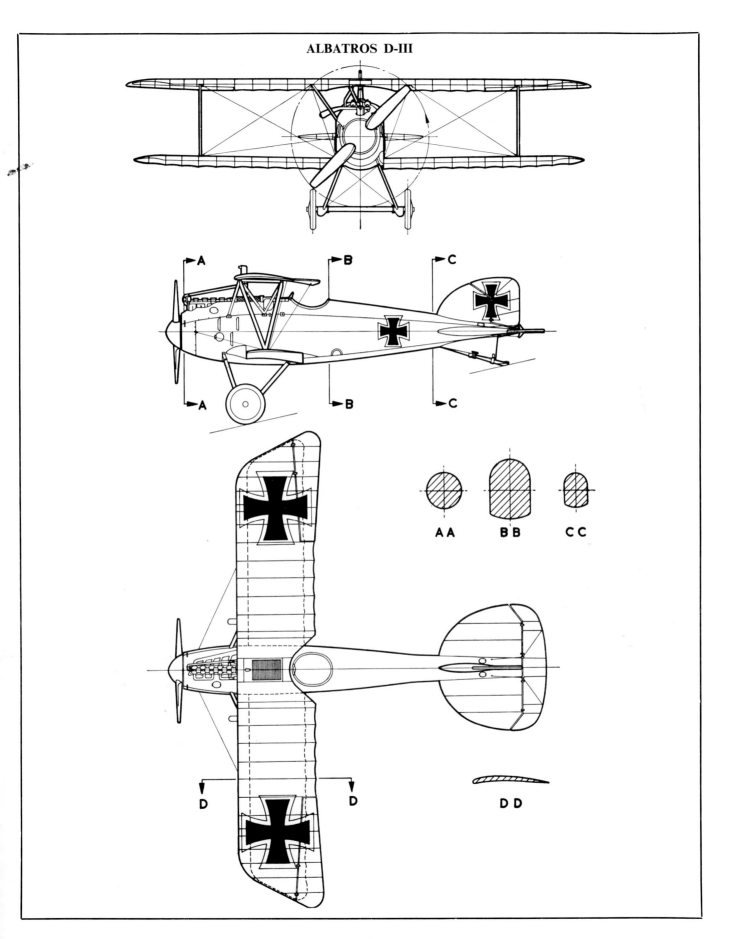

AA   BB   CC

D   D   DD

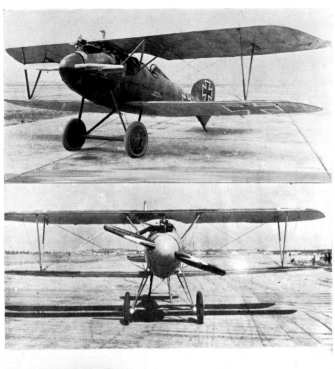

ALBATROS D-V AND D-Va

The tremendous success of the Albatros Scouts in the early months of 1917 encouraged a feeling of complacency in the *IdFlieg* (Inspectorate of Flying Troops). It was felt that the Albatros Werke would continue to produce war-winning fighters. By May 1917 such Allied types as the Spad, Sopwith Pup and Triplane and S.E.5, each able to out-fly the Albatros D-III, were appearing in numbers. With some dismay it was then realised that the new Albatros D-V was little better than its predecessor.

The engine fitted to the D-V was the 180 h.p. Mercedes (the 160 h.p. Mercedes with an increased compression ratio). The 220 h.p. Mercedes and the 200 h.p. Benz were installed experimentally. The radiator was set in the top wing to starboard of the centre-line; machines operating in Palestine had two radiators. Wings, interplane struts and tail were identical to those of the D-III, but the D-V's aileron cables passed through the top wing and had small shrouds, while the D-III's ran through the lower wing and thence up to crank levers on the top wing. The prototype's rudder had a straight trailing-edge, but later machines had trailing-edges of rounded outline. The lower fin was taken back to the horizontal knife-edge of the fuselage—the D-III's lower fin terminated below the rudder-hinge line. In contrast to the flat-sided D-II fuselage, that of the D-V was oval in cross-section and deeper, so that there was a smaller gap between it and the top plane. A faired head-rest was fitted behind the cockpit, but it was frequently taken off. The undercarriage was of the steel-tube type with a fairing over the axle, which provided extra lift. Twin synchronised guns were mounted.

The D-Va differed from the D-V in having aileron cables as on the D-III. Its head-rest was generally removed to improve the pilot's view rearwards.

The *Jagdstaffeln* received the D-V in May 1917; the D-Va was supplied in the following month. From the beginning fatal crashes, caused by wing failure, occurred, and extra bracing wires were added to remedy wing flutter. In order to prevent the twisting of the single spar of the lower wing under stress, small struts were taken from the leading-edge to the lower part of the interplane struts. Finally, the factory fitted a metal box-like sleeve to the centre section of the lower wing; the sleeve enclosed the main spar and strengthened it. The aircraft parks were ordered to modify those machines already issued, but subsequently an Albatros official visiting the front discovered that this work had not been done, and that wing failures were still occurring! Even after these alterations, pilots were advised not to dive too steeply, which hardly raised their morale.

Nevertheless the type was used in large numbers, for the only alternatives were the suspect Fokker Triplane and the second-rate Pfalz D-III and many machines were still in operational use up to the time of the Armistice.

The D-V/Va flew in Italy with German units, and operated in Palestine. Machines built by the Ostdeutsche Albatros Werke were designated Alb. D-V or D-Va (O.A.W.).

When the Albatros types were re-designated after the war (in order to circumvent the terms of the Armistice), the DV/Va was given the title L.24.

1. The D-V prototype, probably D.1021/17, which had a straight trailing edge to its rudder. 2. Alb. D-V (O.A.W.) 2004/17, first of the type built by the Ostdeutsche Albatros Werke. 3. Alb. D-V 1178/17. 4. D-Va in French hands. 5. D-Va captured by No. 3 Squadron, A.F.C.

ALBATROS D-Va

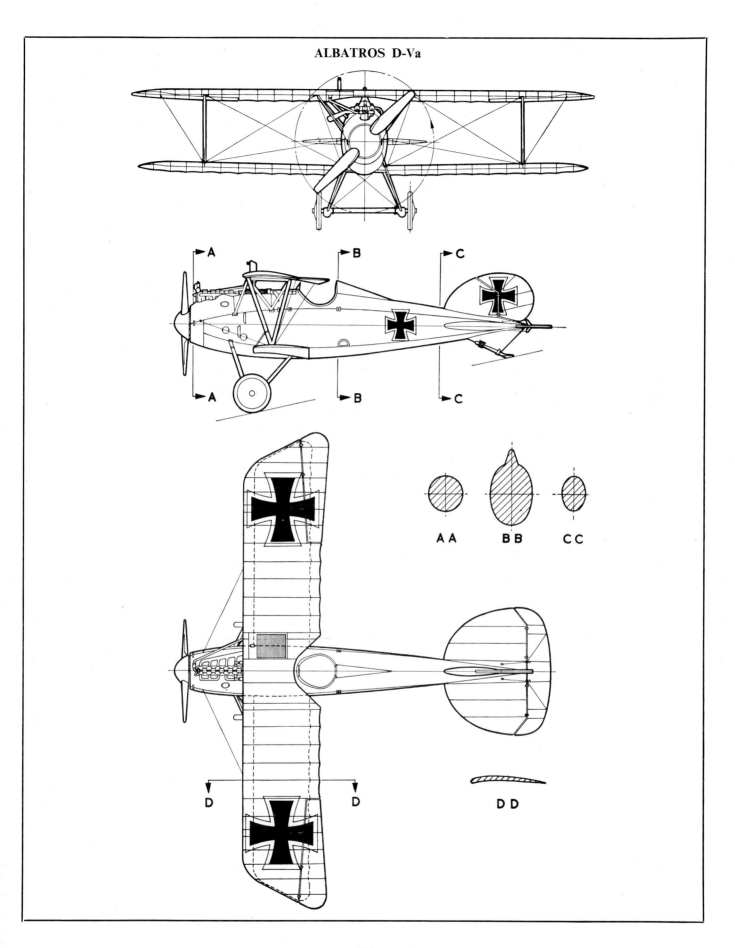

A A   B B   C C

D D

ALBATROS D-XI

By the autumn of 1917 the reputation of the Albatross company had been adversely affected by the numerous accidents caused by the failure of the lower wings of the D-V and D-Va fighters. Strenuous efforts were therefore made by Robert Thelen and his associates to design an outstanding new single-seater which would regain for the firm its earlier pre-eminent position.

The Albatros D-VI was provided with heavily braced wings to ensure complete structural safety; it was powered by an Argus engine of 180 h.p. and had the same fuselage as the D-Va. The machine took part in the first Adlershof fighter competition in January 1918, but performed poorly in comparison with the Fokker D-VII and Roland D-VI. The outcome of the contest was unfortunate for the Albatros Werke; to the chagrin of their designers the firm was ordered to build Fokkers under licence.

Further Albatros fighters were, however, produced; the Dr.-I (160 h.p. Mercedes) and the D-VII, D-IX and Dr.-II, all equipped with 195 h.p. Benz engines, but none of these types proceeded beyond the experimental stage.

With the D-XI, which appeared in the first months of 1918, the company departed from the traditional stationary-engined Albatros formula. It used the 160 h.p. Siemens-Halske Sh IIIa geared rotary, *in which the cylinders revolved in the opposite direction to that of the airscrew.* This engine was enclosed in a deep horseshoe-shaped cowling provided with two ventilation holes; a large spinner left only a small frontal gap for cooling purposes. The first prototype, D2208/18, had a large four-bladed airscrew to utilise the advantages of the slow-revving engine (which, of course, revolved at half the usual engine speed).

Of wood and fabric construction, the wings were staggered but without dihedral. The upper wing, of much greater span and chord than the lower, carried horn-balanced ailerons. Both wings had raked tips; there was a peculiarly shaped cut-out in the trailing-edge of the centre section of the top wing, and two small cut-outs in the lower wing-roots. The interplane bracing was unusual in that the lower ends of the large I-struts were braced to the upper longerons by two faired struts on each side. The cabane was of the trestle type.

Framed in wood with a covering of plywood, the stumpy fuselage had flat sides and a rounded top decking. The tail-plane was of typical Albatros shape, with a single balanced elevator; the plywood fin and balanced fabric-covered rudder were mounted well forward.

To provide clearance for the large airscrew blades, the steel-tube undercarriage vees were unusually long; a small lower fin of plywood helped to support the tail-skid. The machine was armed in the standard fashion with twin synchronised Spandau guns.

D2209/18, the second prototype D-XI, was fitted with a two-bladed airscrew of large proportions, and had plain equal-chord ailerons. It was entered for the second and third fighter contests of April and June 1918. The excellent Sh IIIa rotary gave it a good rate of climb, but otherwise it was inferior to its competitors, and failed to obtain a production order.

1 and 2. The first Albatros D-XI 2208/18 with four-bladed airscrew and horn-balanced ailerons. 3, 4 and 5. The second machine, 2209/18 with two-bladed airscrew and plain ailerons, which took part in both the second and third fighter competitions.

ALBATROS D-XI

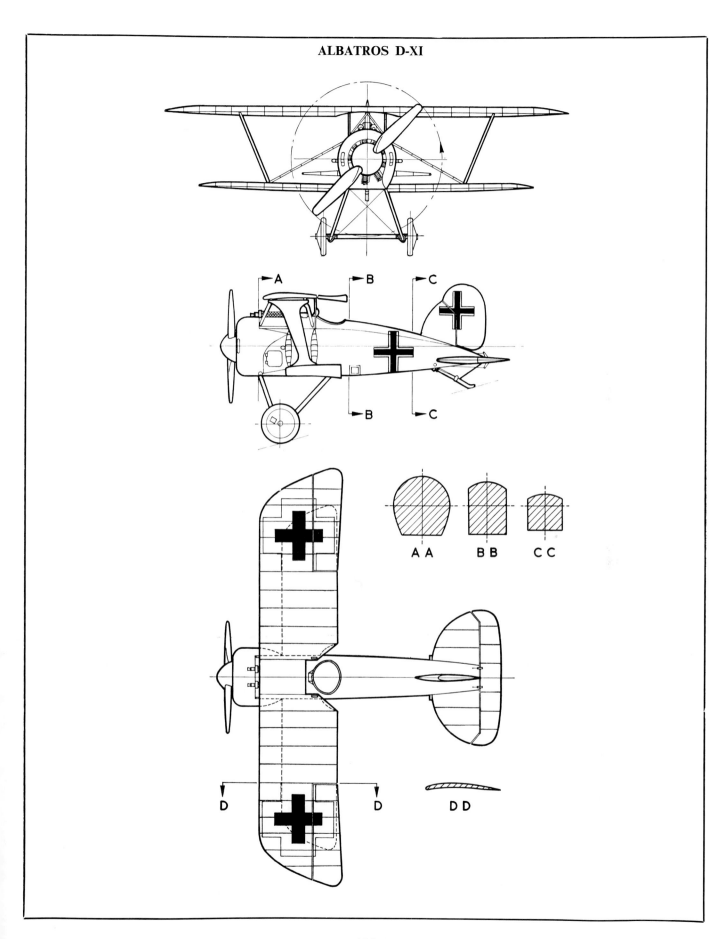

A A   B B   C C

D D

ALBATROS W.4 SEAPLANE

A single-seater fighter seaplane, the W.4, was designed by the Albatros Gesellschaft in the summer of 1916. It had a family resemblance to the D-I and D-II landplanes, but its overall dimensions were somewhat larger. The first production machine, No. 747, was ordered in June 1916 and was delivered in September. It was equipped with the excellent 160 h.p. Mercedes engine neatly cowled with only a portion of the cylinder heads protruding; the exhaust pipe passed rearwards and downwards along the starboard side of the nose. A rounded spinner was fitted to the airscrew hub and box-like radiators were fixed on each side of the fuselage. The wood-and-fabric wings, of equal span and chord, were quite flat, and had square-cut tips with some wash-out of incidence. Unequal-chord ailerons were carried on the upper plane only. The interplane and cabane struts were of wire-braced steel tubing; the latter were splayed out in front elevation. The gap between the wings was larger than that between those of the D-I or D-II. Framed in wood with a covering of plywood, the semi-monocoque fuselage tapered to a horizontal knife-edge at the tail. The fin was also of wood covered with ply, and was braced to the tail-plane by a strut on each side; the horn-balanced rudder was of steel tube with a covering of doped fabric. In shape the tail-plane and balanced elevator formed an ellipse; the former was of ply-covered wood, the latter of fabric-covered tubing. The twin floats, of modified pontoon form, had a single step apiece. Twin Spandau guns were provided for the pilot; they were fixed to fire forward on each side of the cylinder heads.

Two more W.4s, Nos. 785 and 786, were supplied in September and December 1916, and a further batch of ten (902–911) were accepted between February and April 1917. The latter machines were slightly modified; their floats were of better streamlined shape, with the steps farther forward. Smaller cockpits were provided and the front float struts were positioned farther aft.

More W.4s were completed between April and December 1917; they bore the serials 948–967, 1107–1116, 1302–1326, 1484–1513 and 1719–1738. No. 1496 for some reason was not delivered. On the later models the side radiators were replaced by a radiator set in the top wing, offset to starboard, and ailerons, connected by light struts, were fitted to both wings.

The type was used at the German seaplane stations on the coast of Flanders. In spite of the handicap of floats, the W.4 had a fair turn of speed (100 m.p.h.) and gave good service. A number of W.4s are believed to have operated in the Aegean; they were probably the seaplanes known to the British as 'Blue Birds', from their blue-grey camouflage markings. One was shot down by Lieutenant H. T. Mellings of No. 2 Wing, R.N.A.S., Mudros, flying N5431, the only Sopwith Triplane to reach that part of the world.

With the coming into service of the Hansa-Brandenburg W.12 two-seater seaplane, the W.4 fell into disfavour. The W.12 was a better proposition from the operational viewpoint, being equally fast, capable of carrying a heavier load and armed with a flexible rear gun to beat off attacks from astern.

1. and 2. The first production Albatros W.4, No. 747, with side radiators. 3. No. 1486 with radiator in top wing and ailerons on both wings. 4 and 5. No. 1512 a late production machine, with a Friedrichshafen FF 49 seaplane in the background.

116

ALBATROS W.4 SEAPLANE

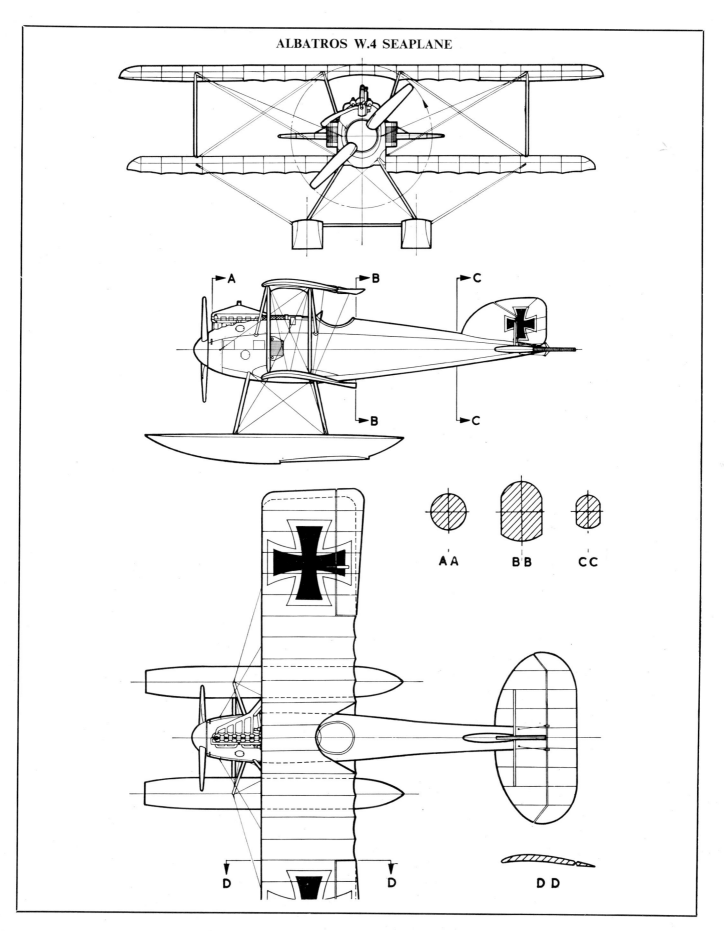

A'A   B'B   C'C

D'D

DORNIER D-I

In addition to its world-famous airship works at Friedrichshafen on Lake Constance, the Zeppelin concern maintained two subsidiary factories for the construction of aeroplanes, at Staaken near Berlin, and at Lindau, to the east of Friedrichshafen. The Staaken works concentrated on the development of *Riesenflugzeuge* or 'Giant aeroplanes', while at Lindau the designer Dornier constructed a series of flying boats, the forerunners of the successful post-war Dornier-Wal machines.

In 1916 the design of landplanes began with the Dornier V.1, an experimental single-seater pusher; then followed the CL-I and CL-II two-seater landplanes and the Cs-I sea-monoplane.

A new single-seater fighter of advanced design, the D-I, flew for the first time on June 4th, 1918. Both the 160 h.p. Mercedes and the 185 B.M.W. engines appear to have been installed at different times; the radiator was of the rectangular car type, mounted above the thrust-line, and the exhaust gases discharged through a short manifold on the starboard side. Ventilation louvres were provided on the port side of the nose.

No interplane struts were fitted; the forward two-thirds of each flat cantilever wing were constructed of duralumin spars and ribs, covered with metal; the rear third consisted of metal ribs attached to the rear spar with a covering of fabric. There was a slight amount of stagger; ailerons were carried on the top wing only. The splayed-out metal centre-section struts were attached to the upper plane by four bolts, and the lower plane was bolted to the lower longerons. Built up of duralumin with a smooth riveted metal skin, the fuselage had flat sides and a rounded top. A plain one-piece elevator was fitted; the small fin and large horn-balanced rudder were mounted above the tail-plane, and the tail-skid was provided with a fairing. The undercarriage was of unusual form, with a single streamlined metal strut to each wheel. Under the fuselage was an egg-shaped fuel tank, which could be jettisoned if the machine caught fire. The standard armament of twin synchronised Spandau guns, fixed in front of the cockpit, fired through the airscrew arc.

The little biplane was viewed with some distrust by both pilots and officials; it was considered to incorporate too many new ideas to be completely safe. A D-I was sent to Adlershof in June 1918 to compete in the third fighter contest. As was by then standard practice, each of the prototypes assembled there was tested by experienced front-line pilots. On July 3rd the Dornier (D2085/18) was taken up by Hauptmann Reinhard, leader of *Jagdgeschwader Nr. 1*, the Richthofen 'Circus'. At a height of 3,000 feet the wings broke away and the remains crashed to earth, fatally injuring Reinhard.

The accident confirmed the opinions of the sceptics, and the D-I never went into production. One example, D1750/18, was given reinforced wings and underwent test late in the war. After the Armistice two Dornier D-Is were taken to the United States. One was evaluated by the Army, one by the Navy. A third machine was preserved in the museum of the Dornier company up to September 1939. During the Second World War it was destroyed.

1. to 5. The unorthodox Zeppelin (Lindau) Dornier D-I. Interesting points are the cantilever wings, absence of interplane struts and external fuel-tank. The part-duralumin, part-fabric covered wings can be seen in the last two photographs.

DORNIER D-I

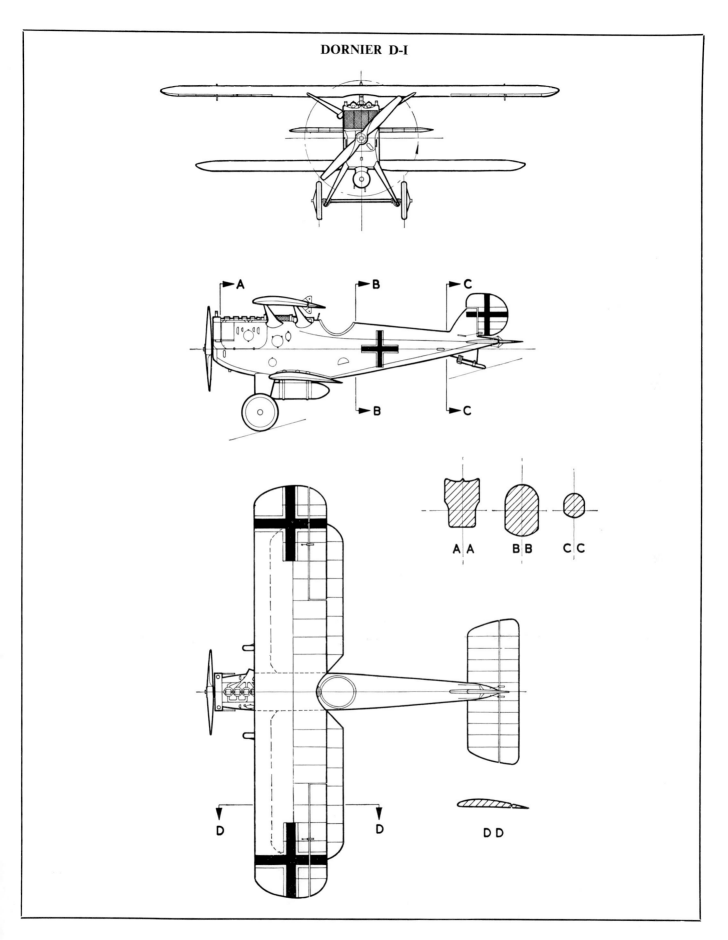

119

FOKKER D-I, D-II, D-III AND D-IV

In late 1915 the Fokker Monoplane was at the height of its career, but the Fokker company was well aware that the type could not be further developed. Design work therefore began on two new biplane types, the M 17 Z and M 18 Z (Military designations D-II and D-I).

The D-II, powered by the 100 h.p. Oberursel rotary, was completed first. Its equal-span two-bay wings had fabric-covered wooden spars and ribs, and were wire-braced internally and externally. The trailing-edges were of wire, which gave a 'scalloped' effect. Wing warping was used for lateral control. The front pair of steel-tube centre-section struts was reinforced by auxiliary struts, forming inverted vees. So narrow was the gap that the centre section had to be raised to permit the mounting of a machine-gun. An aluminium 'horseshoe' cowling housed the engine. The flat-sided fuselage, of wire-braced welded steel tubing, was fabric-covered except for metal panels which curved forward and downward from the cockpit to the leading-edge of the lower wing. The balanced elevator and rudder were typically Fokker. An undercarriage of rather small dimensions was fitted; the front legs were reinforced. A Spandau fired through the airscrew arc.

The D-I was very similar, but had the 120 h.p. Mercedes stationary engine enclosed in an aluminium cowling; its exhaust pipe passed horizontally along the starboard side of the nose. Elongated box-like radiators were fixed on each side of the cowling. The standard undercarriage was of simpler design, with longer vees.

Neither type had a particularly good performance; in some respects they were inferior to the Fokker Monoplanes. The D-I was tested by Oswald Boelcke as possible equipment for the early *Jagdstaffeln*, but it was turned down as being too stable.

The twin-row 160 h.p. Oberursel rotary was fitted to the Fokker D-III (M 19). Although the engine was unreliable, the increase in power gave the D-III an enhanced performance. Its cowling was deeper and had cooling holes and frontal bracing for the heavier engine. N-shaped steel-tube centre-section struts were fitted; there were two guns. Later production models of the D-I, D-II and D-III appear to have had fuselages of hexagonal cross-section.

The fourth Fokker biplane, the D-IV (M.20), had the 160 h.p. Mercedes engine, a hexagonal-sectioned fuselage, and balanced ailerons fitted to the top plane. The D-IV was no great improvement on its predecessors. One modified machine, Fok. D-IV 1640/16, had a streamlined spinner, 'chimney'-type exhaust pipe and extra centre-section struts.

All four types were supplied in small numbers to the *Feldfliegerabteilungen* (reconnaissance units) for escort duty, and to the *Kampfeinsitzerkommandos* (early single-seater fighter units).

When the Albatros Scouts were introduced, the Fokkers were gradually withdrawn to training schools or exported. Late models with ailerons fitted were distinguishable by the suffix 'K', e.g. M 19 K; those with wing warping by the suffix 'F', e.g. M 19 F. At least two D-Is were sent to Austria-Hungary, and batches of D-IIs and D-IIIs were built under licence by MAG of Budapest.

1. First production Fokker D-I 140/16 accepted 11.7.16. 2. Fokker D-II 2387/16 with single gun. 3. Fokker D-III 352/16 with twin guns, flown by Boelcke. 4. Fokker D-IV. 5. D-IV 'Long-wing'. Note the unsymmetrical interplane strutting.

FOKKER D-II

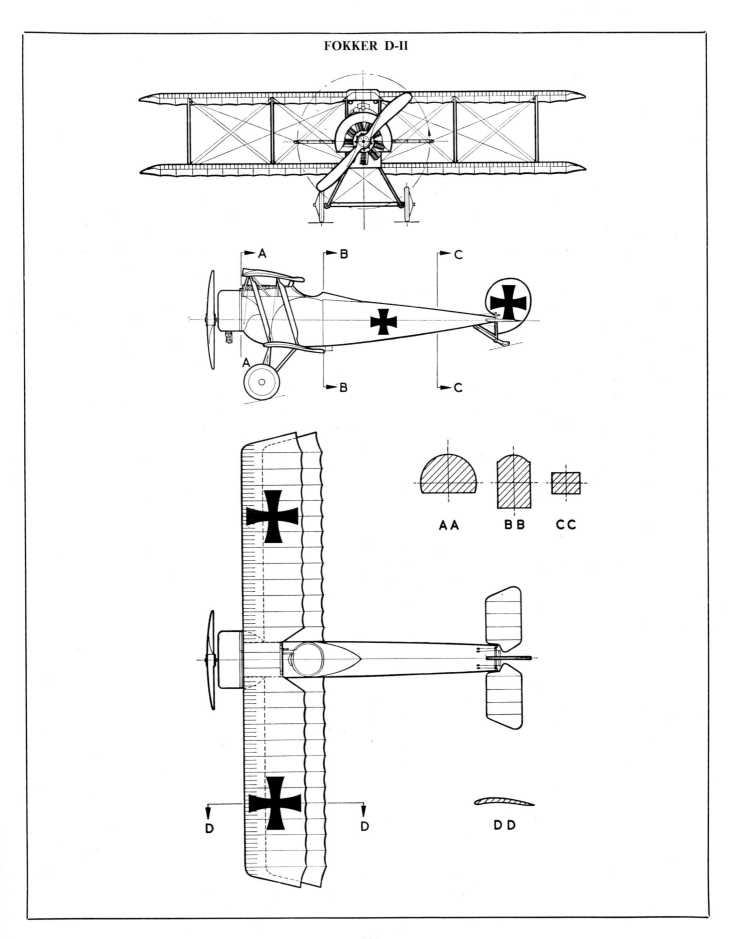

A A   B B   C C

D D

121

FOKKER Dr.-I

Following the sensational début of the Sopwith Triplane in April 1917, many German and Austro-Hungarian firms hastened to design triplane fighters.

The Fokker V.3 (V meant *Verspannungslos* or 'unbraced wing'), designed by Reinhold Platz, was a cantilever triplane with unbalanced ailerons and elevators. *There were no interplane struts*, and on test there was considerable wing vibration. The second Fokker triplane, the V.4, was therefore given interplane struts and balanced control surfaces. The V.4 was the prototype Dr.-I.

Production models had the 110 h.p. Oberursel rotary engine. Many machines used the 110 h.p. Le Rhône rotary, built under licence by the Swedish firm of Thulin and supplied to Germany. The 145 h.p. Oberursel UR III, 160 h.p. Goebel III and 160 h.p. Siemens-Halske III rotaries were experimentally fitted. The standard cowling was frontally enclosed to a point just below the airscrew boss and provided with two cooling holes, but a few machines had 'horseshoe' cowlings. The cantilever wings were unbraced, apart from two cross-wires in the cabane. Each plane had two box spars joined together to form a solid full-span spar. The ribs were of plywood; the leading-edges as far back as the spar were covered with the same material; the remainder was fabric-covered. The trailing-edges were of wire. Balanced ailerons, fitted to the top wing only, were framed in steel tube and fabric-covered. The shape of their inboard ends varied. The middle wing had two cut-outs, and the bottom wings on later models had small ash skids. The interplane struts were thin wooden sections, and the cabane struts were steel-tube inverted vees.

The welded steel-tubing fuselage, braced by diagonal wires, was fabric-covered including triangular plywood fillets from the cowling to just behind the cockpit, and plywood top decking. The tail-plane, balanced elevators and balanced rudder were framed in steel tubing. Two struts braced the tail-plane from below. The undercarriage was of steel tubing; its axle had a large fairing, which provided extra lift.

Twin Spandau guns, which could be fired independently or simultaneously, were synchronised to fire through the airscrew arc.

The first three production aircraft were designated Fok. F-I 101–103/17. F-I 103/17 was supplied to Werner Voss on August 28th, 1917, and F-I 102/17 was flown by Manfred von Richthofen himself from September 1st. All later triplanes were given the military designation 'Dr.-I'.

The Triplane had an excellent rate of climb and could match the Camel for manœuvrability, merits which outweighed its lack of speed at combat height, and for two months the pilots of *Jagdgeschwader Nr. 1*, the Richthofen 'Circus', ably demonstrated its capabilities.

In late October 1917, however Leutnants Gontermann and Pastor were killed when their Dr.-Is broke in the air, and the type was withdrawn from operations. Although it was reissued with strengthened wings in December 1917, it never recovered from this setback and was not supplied to many *Jagdstaffeln*. Some 320 Dr.-Is were built before production finished in May 1918.

1. The V.3 triplane. 2. F-I 101/17 the first production machine, tested at Adlershof, August 7th and 8th, 1917. 3. A typical Dr.-1. 4. Leutnant Gontermann with Dr.-1 115/17, which broke up in flight on October 30th, 1917, and resulted in his death from the injuries sustained.

FOKKER Dr.-I

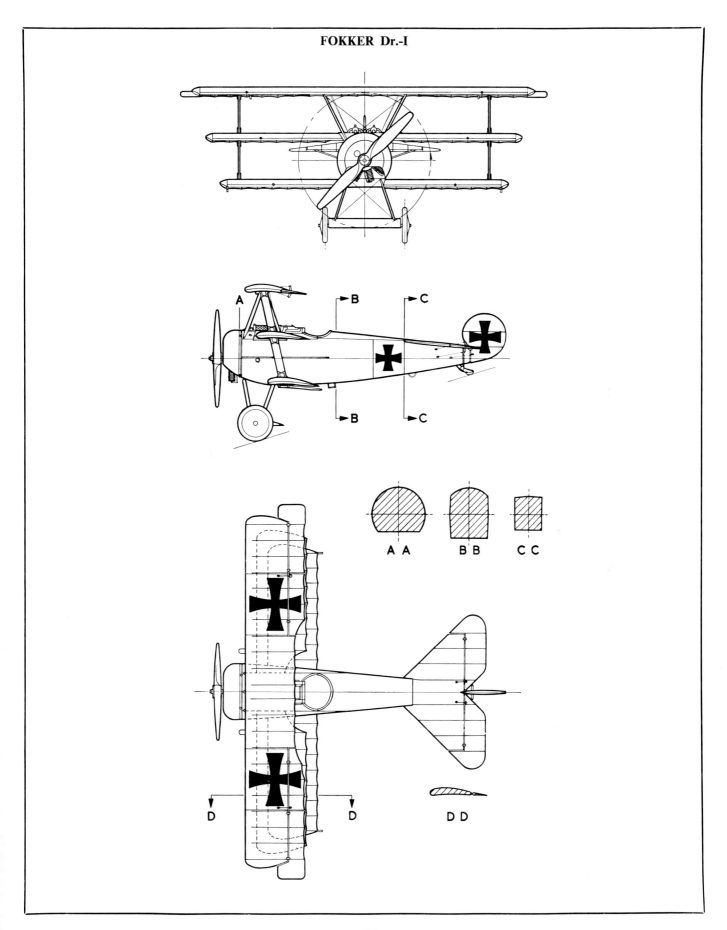

A A   B B   C C

D   D   D D

123

FOKKER D-V AND D-VI

Reinhold Platz's first design was the Fokker D-V (M.22) single-seater, which was brought out in the autumn of 1916. The engine, a 100 h.p. Oberursel rotary, was provided with a circular open-fronted cowling. A large bowl-shaped spinner covered the airscrew hub, so that there was only a small annular opening left for cooling purposes. The single-bay wing cellule was unusual in that the upper plane, which carried horn-balanced ailerons, was swept back. Horizontal stringers were used to give rounded sides to the fuselage; the empennage was of typical Fokker shape. A single synchronised Spandau gun was fitted. Some 250 D-Vs were constructed, but the type was apparently mainly used as an advanced trainer. It gained the reputation of being difficult to fly and was thoroughly unpopular with pilots.

Late in 1917 Platz designed a single-seater cantilever biplane, the V.13, which had a very similar fuselage to that of the Fokker Triplane. There were two versions, the V.13/1 powered by a 110 h.p. Swedish-built Le Rhône rotary, and the V.13/2 which had a Siemens-Halske Sh III.

Although the former type was considered quite promising, the success of its more powerful relative the prototype Fokker D-VII in the fighter competition of January 1918 rather overshadowed its development. Trials of the prototype took place in March 1918, and a small production order was placed for the D-VI, as it was designated, probably as a precaution against the possible failure of the far superior D-VII.

D1631/18, the first production example, was delivered on April 26th, 1918. Like the V.13/1, it had the 110 h.p. Le Rhône rotary; the cowling was enclosed in front to a point just below the airscrew hub and was provided with two cooling apertures. The cantilever wings had two spars; ribs and leading-edges were of ply, while the unequal-span horn-balanced ailerons, fitted to the top plane only, were framed in welded steel tubing. Interplane and centre-section struts were similar in form to those of the D-VII.

The fuselage was of tubular wire-braced construction, tapering to a vertical knife-edge. Immediately behind the cowling, and stretching back to behind the cockpit on each side, were triangular plywood fairings. The rest of the fuselage was fabric-covered, except for a plywood top decking from the cockpit to a point half-way towards the tail.

The empennage was framed in steel tubing and struts braced the tail-plane from below. A steel-tube undercarriage was fitted; the axis had a large fairing, which acted as a lifting surface. The armament consisted of twin synchronised Spandau guns.

From late April to August 1918 a total of 59 D-VIs were delivered (D1631/18 to 1689/18). Most of them had the 110 h.p. Le Rhône engine, but 1637, 1639, 1640, 1643 and 1669–1676 had the Goebel Goe III rotary. Seven examples, 1632, 1633, 1634, 1635, 1641, 1642 and 1644, were supplied to Austro-Hungary in August 1918.

The type equipped or partly equipped some *Jagd-staffeln* during the summer months. When sufficient D-VIIs became available, the remaining machines were relegated to training duty.

1. Production Fokker D-V. 2. The experimental V.13/1 with 110 h.p. Le Rhône engine, the forerunner of the D-VI. 3 and 4. Two views of an early production D-VI with twin synchronised guns. 5. A D-VI without guns, probably at a training unit.

FOKKER D-VI

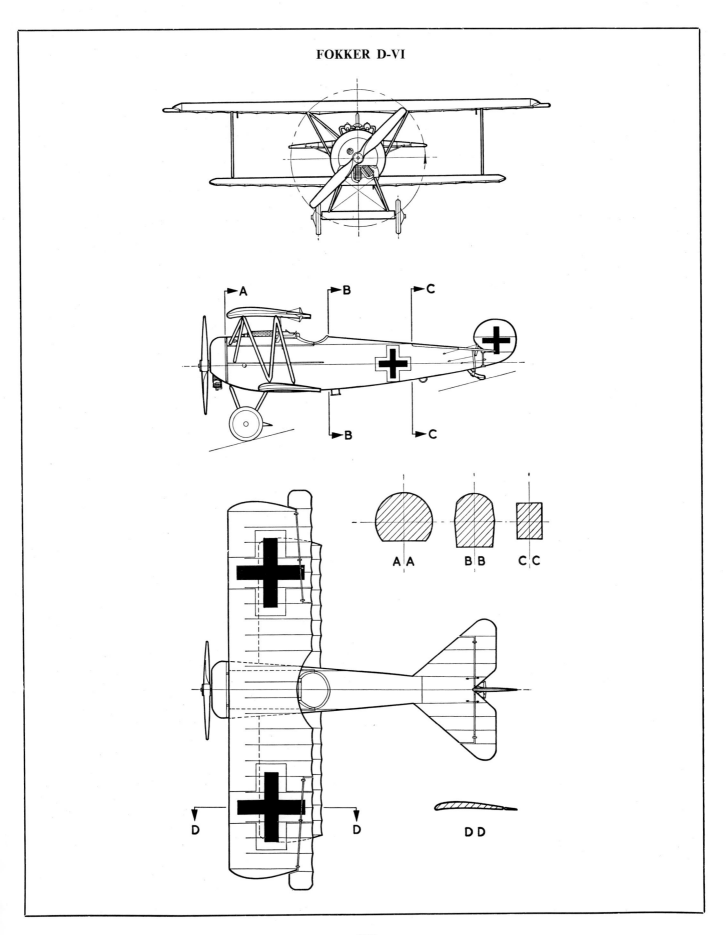

A A   B B   C C

D D

FOKKER D-VII

In January 1918 a competition open to single-seater fighters powered by the 160 h.p. Mercedes engine was held at Johannisthal, near Berlin. It was won outright by an angular little biplane with thick cantilever wings, the Fokker D-VII, designed by Reinhold Platz. Unquestionably the best all-round German fighter of the First World War, it was a development of Platz's experimental V.11, built late in 1917.

Its engine was either the 160/180 h.p. Mercedes or the 185 h.p. B.M.W., neatly cowled and fitted with a frontal radiator. B.M.W. D-VIIs had the better performance and were much sought after. The 200 h.p. Benz was experimentally fitted without great success. The exhaust system was either the usual external horizontal pipe on the starboard side, or separate internal pipes connected to a large main pipe which protruded through the starboard cowling.

D-VII wings had two spars with plywood ribs; the leading-edges were of ply, the rest of the structure fabric-covered. Unequal-chord ailerons framed in steel tubing were fitted to the upper wing only, which had a slight curved cut-out in its trailing-edge. The lower wing was housed in a recess in the fuselage bottom; both planes had wire trailing-edges, giving them a 'scalloped' appearance. Interplane and centre-section struts were of streamlined steel tubing.

The fuselage was constructed of wire-braced welded steel tubing with a three-ply top decking behind the cockpit; the whole being fabric-covered, except for the engine cowlings. Fin, balanced rudder, tail-plane and balanced elevators were also of fabric-covered steel tube. Two struts braced the tail-plane from below. The undercarriage was of streamlined steel tube and its axle was enclosed in a large fairing which gave some extra lift.

Twin Spandau guns were synchronised to fire through the revolving airscrew.

Following its success at Johannisthal, the type was ordered in large quantities; not only was it built by the Fokker concern (Fok. D-VII F), but also by its rivals, the Albatros Werke (Fok. D-VII (Alb.)) and the Ostdeutsche Albatros Werke (Fok. D-VII (O.A.W.)). Mercedes and B.M.W. engines appear to have been distributed impartially to all three companies.

While not especially fast, the D-VII's strong point was its great manœuvrability at high altitudes. It was extremely easy to fly and had no terrors for the beginner. *Jagdgeschwader Nr. 1*, the Richthofen 'Circus', received the first D-VIIs in time for the Second Battle of the Aisne in May 1918, and soon found that the new type gave them a good margin of advantage over their opponents. By the autumn the majority of the *Jastas* had been re-equipped with D-VIIs. So highly did the Allies esteem the machine that their Armistice terms specifically ordered the surrender of all Fokker D-VIIs.

As a safeguard against a possible shortage of steel tubing and competent welders, the Albatros company built a D-VII with a plywood fuselage, but it was not found necessary to produce this variant. When the war ended, production of the type for Austro-Hungary had begun at the Hungarian Engineering Factory, Budapest (MAG).

1. The experimental V.11, predecessor of the Fokker D-VII. 2. D-VII prototype. Note absence of axle fairing at this stage. 3. Production D-VII 597/18 with B.M.W. engine. 4. Fokker D-VII F 461/18, built by the Fokker company. 5. D-VII with decorations.

FOKKER D-VII

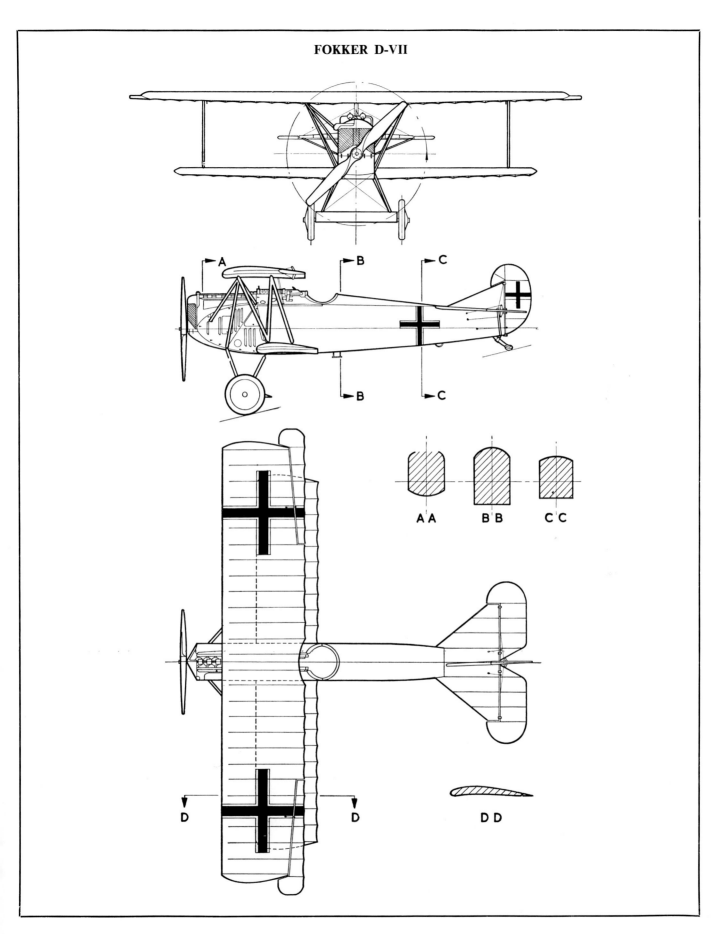

A A   B B   C C

D   D   D D

FOKKER E-V AND D-VIII

The development of the Fokker E-V began when, at the request of Anthony Fokker, the test pilot Kuhlisch successfully flew a Fokker D-VII minus its bottom wing. An experimental parasol monoplane, the V.26, was then constructed to the designs of Reinhold Platz. The E-V, a modified V.26, was entered for the fighter contest in April 1918.

The new type was unanimously declared the winner of the competition; its take-off was rapid, its climb and manœuvrability first class. The decision was made to produce the E-V as a replacement for the Fokker D-VII.

The power unit was the 110 h.p. Le Rhône rotary engine, which was enclosed in a circular aluminium cowling similar to that of the Dr.-I. Two tapering box spars were used in the construction of the cantilever wing; the front spar was swept back towards the wing-tips from the connecting points of the centre-section struts; the rear spar was straight. Wing ribs were of three-ply, and the whole wing surface, including the ailerons, was covered with the same material. There was a large angular cut-out in the trailing-edge, and typical Fokker streamlined steel-tube centre-section struts were fitted.

The fuselage was a welded steel-tube box girder, braced with wire, with a rounded plywood top decking. The circular cowling was streamlined into the flat-sided fuselage by means of fabric-covered three-ply fillets like those used on the Fokker Dr.-I. Fabric covered the whole of the rest of the fuselage. The strut-braced tail surfaces were framed in steel tubing and fabric-covered; the rudder was larger than that of the D-VII but had a much smaller fin. Streamlined steel tubing was also used for the undercarriage struts; as on earlier Fokkers, a large aerofoil covered the axle. The standard armament of twin synchronised Spandau guns was fitted.

In May 1918 loading tests were carried out on the E-V at Adlershof. The authorities demanded that the rear spar be strengthened, to conform with the standard for wire-braced aeroplanes. (No standard existed for cantilever wings.) This modification was therefore carried out, and the first six aircraft were sent to the front in August. Within a few weeks three E-Vs crashed through wing failure, killing their pilots. As a result of these unexplained accidents it was decided not to issue some sixty machines which had been completed, and production was temporarily stopped.

The source of the trouble proved to be the strengthened rear spar; when the front spar flexed under load, the rear spar remained rigid, and the resultant torsion caused the wing to collapse.

Production recommenced, using the original wing, which was found to be perfectly satisfactory; but valuable time had been lost. With the new designation Fokker D-VIII, the type was supplied in small numbers to the *Jagdstaffeln*, where it flew alongside the D-VII. The 'Flying Razor Blade', as it was called by the British, scarcely had a chance to prove itself. It had many advantages over the D-VII and would certainly have replaced it if the war had lasted through the winter of 1918–1919.

While the later production models had the 140 h.p. Oberursel engine, the Goebel Goe III rotary was fitted to E-V 169/18 and D-VIII 692/18; the latter aircraft had a longer cowling.

1. Fokker V.26 cantilever parasol monoplane, forerunner of the E-V. 2. Production Fokker E-V. 3. A rare photograph of a Jasta 6 E-V in service at the front. 4. Production D-VIII. 5. A D-VIII undergoing evaluation tests in the United States.

128

FOKKER D-VIII

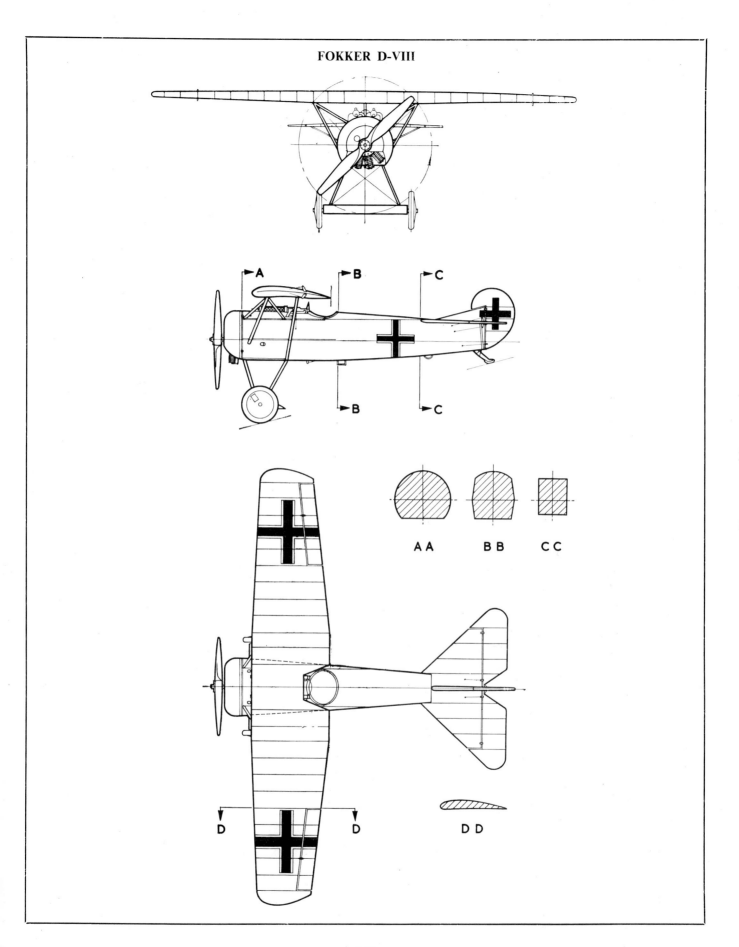

FOKKER E-I, E-II, E-III AND E-IV

During the early months of the war the Fokker Aeroplanbau, directed by the young Dutchman Anthony Fokker, supplied three operational monoplane types to the German Forces. They were the M 8, M 5 L, and M 5 K (military designations A-I, A-II and A-III).

On April 19th, 1915, the well-known French pilot Roland Garros fell into German hands; his Morane was found to have a fixed machine-gun firing forwards through the airscrew arc. There was no synchronising gear; steel wedges fitted to the airscrew deflected any bullets which might have damaged it. Crude though this device was, the German authorities realised its potentialities, and asked Fokker to supply an aeroplane with a similar type of armament.

The result was the interrupter gear rapidly devised and built by Anthony Fokker and Lübbe in July 1915. It was by no means the first of its kind, for interrupter gears had already been patented; in Germany by Franz Schneider, the L.V.G. designer, and in Britain by the Edwards brothers; it was, however, the first gear to be given active Government support.

The aeroplane in which it was installed was the M 5 K, the single-seater monoplane already in service. After being armed and modified, it was designated the M 5 K/MG (MG meant *Maschinengewehr* or machine-gun); its military title was the Fokker E-I.

The E-I had the 80 h.p. Oberursel rotary engine, partially enclosed in an aluminium 'horseshoe' cowling. The fabric-covered wings were of composite construction; twin wooden spars, wooden ribs and steel-tube compression members. The front-wing cables gave rigid bracing; the rear cables controlled the warping of the wing extremities from cranks under the fuselage. The upper control cables ran over a pulley wheel at the apex of the steel-tube fuselage pylon. The fuselage was framed in wire-braced welded steel tubing, fabric-covered except for metal panels from cowling to cockpit. The balanced elevators and typical Fokker comma-shaped balanced rudder were framed in steel tubing. The undercarriage was a complicated arrangement of steel tubes; the elastic shock absorbers were inside the fuselage at the top of the main vertical struts.

At first a Parabellum gun was fitted, but the standard armament was a Spandau gun fixed slightly to starboard.

The E-I was underpowered and soon replaced by the E-II and E-III, (both designated M14) bigger machines with the 100 h.p. Oberursel.

Most of the Fokker monoplanes constructed were of these types; they were not outstanding aeroplanes, but their synchronised guns made them most formidable against the slow, ill-armed Allied machines. The Fokkers were used entirely in a defensive role; one or two being attached to each reconnaissance unit. The new methods of single-seater fighter attack were successfully evolved by such pilots as Immelmann, Boelcke and Wintgens.

The E-IV was a larger machine, powered by the 160 h.p. two-row Oberursel, and armed with two guns. The engine proved to be unreliable and few were built.

About twenty Fokkers (serialled approximately from 03.40 to 03.59) were used by Austro-Hungary.

1. The Fokker M5/MG (E-I) with synchronised Parabellum gun; note the wooden stock. 2. 03.43, an Austro-Hungarian Fokker with synchronised Schwarzlose gun. 3. Fokker E-II. 4. An E-III in British hands. 5. The E-IV with early streamlined top-decking.

FOKKER E-III

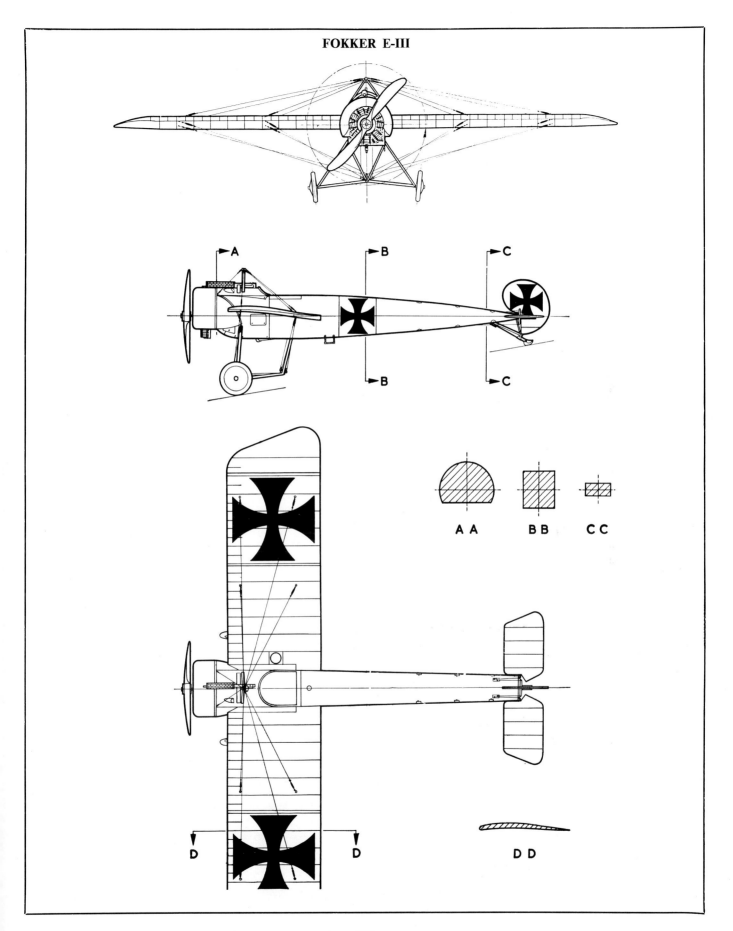

A A   B B   C C

D   D   D D

131

HALBERSTADT CL-II, CL-IIa AND CL-IV

By early 1917 the German 'C' class aeroplane (armed two-seater biplane) had developed into a large machine with a wing span of over forty feet and a horse-power in excess of two hundred. The need was felt for a lighter and handier two-seater capable of defending itself. The new CL (light C) category specified a machine with an engine of 160–180 h.p., provision for wireless and camera, and a total weight of less than 360 kg. (793 lb.).

The first CL type to go into production was the Halberstadt CL-II, a carefully designed aeroplane with the lines of a single-seater. Its power unit was the 160 h.p. Mercedes, installed with a good deal of exposed cylinder block; its exhaust pipe discharged on the starboard side of the nose, which was neatly finished off with a pointed spinner. The radiator was in the top plane, to starboard of the centre section. The staggered wings had built-up wooden spars reinforced by broad webs of plywood running horizontally, with stringers at their edges; the whole being fabric-covered. Balanced ailerons were carried on the top plane only. Each half of the lower wing was given a heavy wash-out at its junction with the fuselage bottom, a Halberstadt characteristic. Interplane and cabane bracing were of wire-braced steel tubing; the rearmost cabane struts forming inverted vees. The fuselage was a flat-sided three-ply shell built up on light wooden formers, tapering to a knife-edge aft. Pilot and observer occupied the same long cockpit, the latter being provided with a raised gun ring of streamlined section; as the upper wing came close to the fuselage top, he had a good field of fire in all upward directions. A guard rail was sometimes fitted to the top plane to prevent him firing into the airscrew. The wooden-framed tail-plane was fixed on the centre line of the fuselage; the large one-piece elevator was fabric-covered, as was the pointed rudder. Steel tubing was used for the undercarriage; because of the shortage of rubber, its axle was sprung with coiled steel springs. The armament consisted of one or two fixed Spandau guns for the pilot, and a Parabellum for the observer; external racks of stick grenades or mortar bombs were carried when attacking targets on the ground.

The type was supplied to the *Schlachtstaffeln* or *Schlastas*, units which carried out the dangerous task of trench fighting. The first mass attack of CL-IIs was on British infantry at Cambrai in November 1917, and thereafter they were used in increasing numbers. Those fitted with the 185 h.p. B.M.W. engine were designated CL-IIas, and could be distinguished from the CL-IIs by their better streamlined noses.

Early in 1918, an improved version, the CL-IV, was brought out. The same Mercedes engine was used; the nose was blunt, there was no spinner and the fuselage was nearly three feet shorter. The front cabane struts instead of the rear were reinforced. The tail-plane was positioned on top of the fuselage, and had a balanced elevator; the fin and rudder had a rounder outline and the tail-skid was given a small fairing. CL-IVs built under licence by L. F. G. Roland were designated Halb. CL-IV (Rol.).

The *Schlachtstaffeln* proved highly successful, and as their numbers increased, they were organised into *Schlachtgruppen* or *Schlachtgeschwaden*.

1. Prototype Halberstadt CL-II with enclosed engine.
2. and 3. Halberstadt CL-II (160 h.p. Mercedes engine).
4. and 5. Halberstadt CL-IV (160 h.p. Mercedes). Note the wash-out given to the lower wing-roots on all three types.

HALBERSTADT CL-II

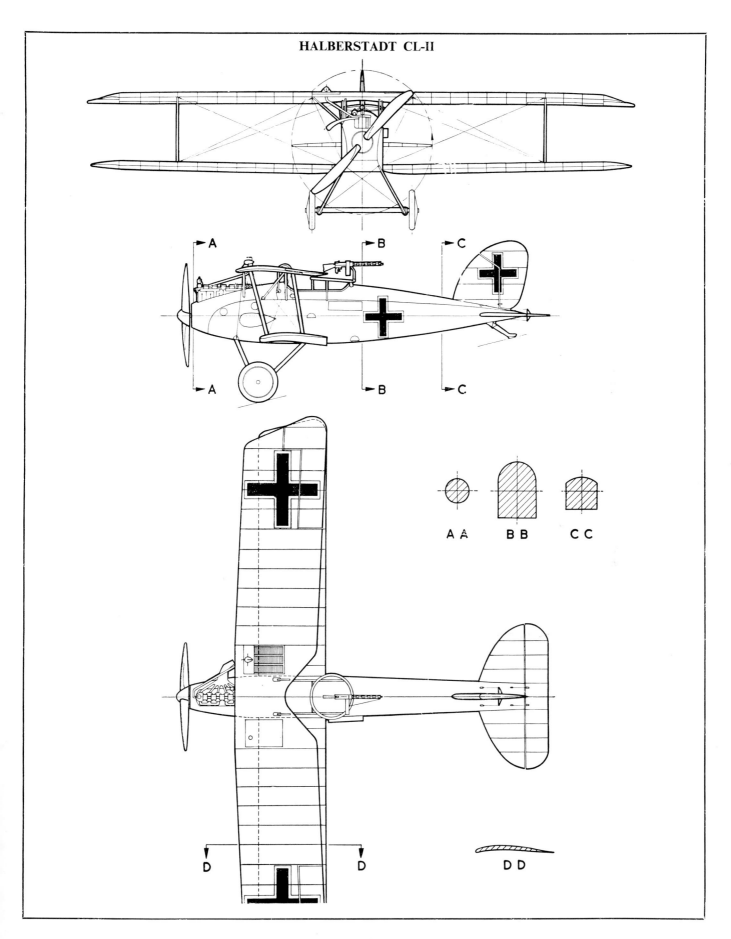

133

HALBERSTADT D-I, D-II, D-III, D-IV AND D-V

The Halberstädter Flugzeugwerke was originally a branch of the British and Colonial Aeroplane Company of Bristol, known as the Deutsche Bristol-Werke, Halberstadt, and the early equipment of the firm's flying school included the Bristol 'Boxkite' and Bristol Coanda monoplanes.

Taube (Dove) monoplanes were the first German designs to be built; then followed in the early months of the war the Halberstadt A-II (the Fokker M.8 constructed under licence) and the B-I and B-II training biplanes.

A single-seater fighting biplane, the D-I made its appearance in 1915. It had a 100 h.p. Mercedes engine, wing radiator and staggered two-bay wings; a modified version with staggered wings, car-type radiator and 'chimney' exhaust pipe was known as the D-Ia.

Early in 1916 the design was further developed and went into production as the Halberstadt D-II. It was powered by the 120 h.p. Mercedes, installed in a rounded metal cowling; the exhaust pipes, of various shapes, discharged on the starboard side. In the top wing, offset to starboard, was situated the radiator. The two-bay staggered wings had fabric-covered wooden spars and ribs; straight wooden members formed the trailing-edges. Equal-chord ailerons were carried on the top wing only, which was of slightly greater span than the lower. There was an angular cut-out in the centre-section trailing-edge. Interplane struts were of wire-braced steel tubing; the cabane was of the trestle type. The fuselage was a wire-braced wooden box girder, tapering to a horizontal knife-edge. Behind the pilot's seat was a curved turtle-back of stringers and formers and the whole structure was fabric-covered except for a plywood top decking in front of the cockpit and a similar covering for the rear bay. The balanced elevator was hinged about its spar; two steel tubes supported the weak-looking balanced rudder. Steel tubing was also used for the plain vee undercarriage. A synchronised Spandau gun on the starboard side of the engine fired through the arc of the airscrew.

The D-II was at first attached to reconnaissance units for escort work and to the *Kampfeinsitzerkommandos*. From the autumn of 1916 it flew alongside the far superior Albatros Scouts in the early *Jagdstaffeln*. It was manœuvrable and very strong. McCudden wrote of a Halberstadt: 'I have never in my experience seen a machine, under control, dive so steeply and so long.'

Soon after the D-II came the D-III, D-IV and D-V. The D-III, and D-IV had balanced ailerons, vertical centre-section struts and circular cut-outs, and were powered by the 120 h.p. Argus and 150 h.p. Benz engines respectively.

The D-V was a more streamlined design, with the 120 h.p. Argus, 'chimney' exhaust, a spinner, a single bay of struts and a modified rudder; it proved inferior to the Albatros. At one period all four types were in service together. Some D-IIs were licence-built by Aviatik and Hannover.

In January 1917, after the wing of his Albatros had cracked in combat, Manfred von Richthofen flew the Halberstadt for a time. The type was used in Macedonia and Palestine after it had disappeared from the Western Front.

According to one source, only eighty-five Halberstadt D types were constructed.

1. Halberstadt D-I. 2. A D-II probably belonging to a Kampfeinsitzerkommando at Vaux, 1916. 3. D-II D.605/16 flown by Boelcke. 4. A captured D-III. 5. Halberstadt D-V. This type was improved and streamlined to compete with the Albatros Scouts of early 1917.

HALBERSTADT D-II

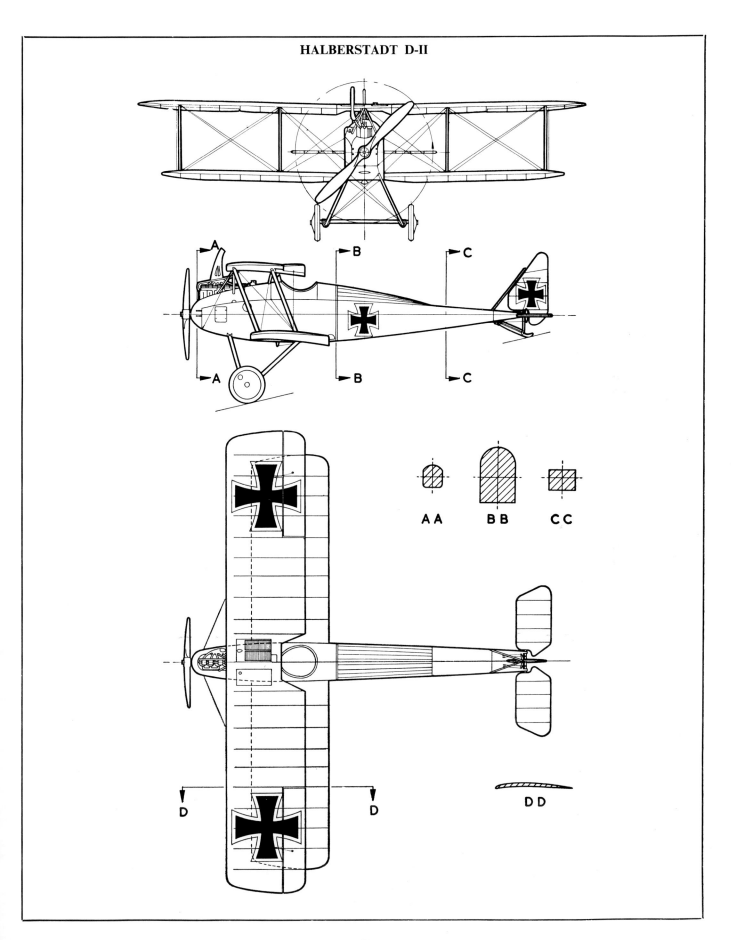

A A   B B   C C

D D

135

HANNOVER CL-II, CL-III AND CL-IIIa

The Hannoversche Waggonfabrik (Hawa) at first constructed Rumpler, Aviatik and Halberstadt types under licence. In mid-1917 the veteran designer Dorner, who was in charge of the factory, developed a new CL (light two-seater) model, the Hannover CL-II, which reached the front in December 1917. The licence-built Aviatik C-I was the first of the Hannover C-types. For some time the Hannover, with its peculiar biplane tail (intended to reduce the 'blind spot') could not be identified by the Allies; not until March was a captured example available for testing and evaluation.

The CL-II had the 180 h.p. Argus As III engine, enclosed in metal cowlings with double exhaust pipes discharging to starboard. In the centre section, offset to starboard, was the radiator; balancing it to port was a fuel tank, slightly raised above the wing surface. The wings, which had uniform dihedral, were formed by two hollow wooden spars with wooden ribs, and were fabric-covered; the trailing-edges were of wire. Ailerons incorporating wash-out, with their cranks at mid-span, were fitted to the top plane only. They were balanced on the prototype, but unbalanced on production aircraft. The lower wing, of narrower chord, had pointed tips; interplane struts were of steel tube, faired with wood and wrapped in fabric, and N-shaped tubular centre-section struts were fitted. The fuselage, a wooden frame covered with plywood, then fabric, came close up under the top wing, to provide the observer with a good field of fire forwards. Pilot and observer sat close together, making communication easy; behind them the fuselage tapered away to a vertical knife-edge, of which the upper and lower fins were integral parts. Both tail-planes had angular tips; the top member was of fabric-covered steel tubing, the bottom was framed in wood and covered in fabric; there were no bracing struts. Rudder and double elevators were of fabric-covered steel tube. The undercarriage had steel-tube vees faired with wood wrapped with tape; its axle was sprung with coiled steel springs—there was a shortage of rubber. A single synchronised Spandau gun was provided for the pilot; the observer had a Parabellum gun on a ring mounting. Racks of stick grenades were carried on ground-attack duty.

Further models appeared during 1918; their distinguishing features may be summarised thus: CL-III: 160 h.p. Mercedes; dihedral not uniform; gravity tank flush with top wing; aileron cranks at the inboard ends of the ailerons, which were balanced and had overhang; rounded tail-planes; short struts from top of fin to upper tail-plane. These struts were augmented on some machines by vertical interplane struts; late production models had internally strengthened tail-planes and no vertical struts; CL-IIIa: CL-III with the 180 h.p. Argus engine; CL-IIa (Rol.): CL-IIIa built by L.F.G. Roland. The CL-IIIb (190 h.p. NAG), CL-IIIc (wider span and two bays of interplane struts), CL-IV and CL-V were only experimental. The Hannover was extensively used during the summer and autumn of 1918. Easy to fly and very manœuvrable, its lack of blind spots made it a dangerous adversary. Four hundred and thirty-nine CL-IIs, eighty CL-IIIs and 537 CL-IIIas are believed to have been built.

1. Hannover CL-II prototype, C.4501/17. 2. and 3. Unpainted Hannover CL-IIa, the version built under licence by the L.F.G. Roland company. 4. A standard production Hannover CL-IIIa. 5. Late model CL-IIIa, with Balkan-type crosses, in French hands.

HANNOVER CL-IIIa

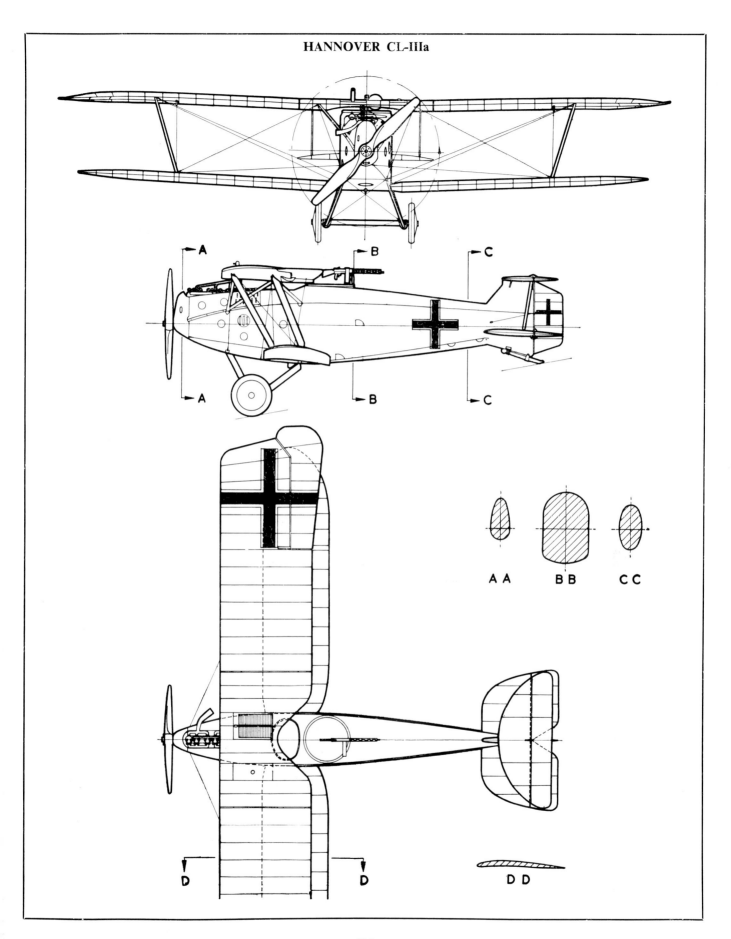

A A   B B   C C

D D

HANSA-BRANDENBURG W.12 AND W.19

In the autumn of 1916 Ernst Heinkel, the Hansa-Brandenburg designer, began work on a two-seater seaplane, the W.12, which was destined to be a thorn in the side of the British R.N.A.S. The prototype was destroyed during tests at Warnemünde in January 1917, but it had proved so promising that a production order was given. No. 1011, the first machine of the first batch (1011–1016), appeared in February 1917. It was powered by a 160 h.p. Mercedes engine with its radiator fixed in front of the leading edge of the top plane.

The single-bay wings, of wood and fabric construction, had blunt tips, and were without dihedral. Unbalanced ailerons were carried on both wings. The cabane struts were of the trestle type, and there was a small circular cut-out in the trailing edge of the top plane. The unusually deep fuselage sloped upwards from the back of the observer's cockpit to the semi-circular tail-plane, which was set flush with the upper longerons. A rectangular rudder with a horn balance on the lower end was hinged to the stern-post. Twin floats of the single-step type were fitted; addition bracing struts were carried out from these to the underside of the lower wings beneath the lower connecting points of the forward interplane struts. A Spandau gun was mounted on the starboard side of the fuselage for the pilot's use; the observer had a Parabellum.

Further batches were built during the next sixteen months; their distinguishing points were as follows: *1178–1187:* Benz 150 h.p. engines with car-type radiators and 'chimney' exhausts; rounded wing-tips; N-shaped cabane struts; longer fuselages; rectangular tail-planes with horn-balanced elevators of unusual shape; rounded trailing-edges to rudders; *1395–1414:* Similar to the second batch, but with stub exhausts, shorter fuselages with high sides to the pilot's cockpit; rounded tailplanes with horn-balanced elevators of the same shape as those of the second batch; shallower rudders with smaller horn balances; *2000–2019:* Similar to the third batch but with longer fuselages, square tail-planes, horn-balanced elevators and shallower rudders; *2023–2052:* Similar to the fourth batch but with connecting struts between the ailerons; *2093–2132 and 2217–2236:* Similar to the fifth batch, but with 160 h.p. Mercedes engines; some had 'chimney' exhaust pipes.

The type was supplied to the seaplane stations of Zeebrugge and Ostend. Aggressively led by the Zeebrugge station commander, Oberleutnant F. Christiansen, W.12s dealt roughly with British seaplanes operating from Dunkirk; so much so, that in July 1917 a Seaplane Defence Flight was formed, equipped first with Pups and then with Camels.

The W.19, a larger and heavier development of the W.12, was brought out in November 1917. Its power unit was the 240 h.p. Maybach engine, with the radiator mounted above the leading edge of the top plane. A small spinner was fitted to the airscrew. Double bays of struts braced the wings, and light struts connected the ailerons. The later seaplanes 2207–2216, 2237, 2259–2278 and 2537 differed from the first three machines 1469–1471 in having additional float bracing and larger rudders. No. 2237 was experimentally armed with a 20 mm. Becker cannon.

1. Hansa-Brandenburg W.12 of the first batch. 2. W.12 of the first batch in service at Zeebrugge. 3. and 4. 2016, a seaplane of the fourth batch, but with aileron struts. 5. The Hansa-Brandenburg W.19, a larger and more powerful version of the W.12.

HANSA-BRANDENBURG W.12 SEAPLANE

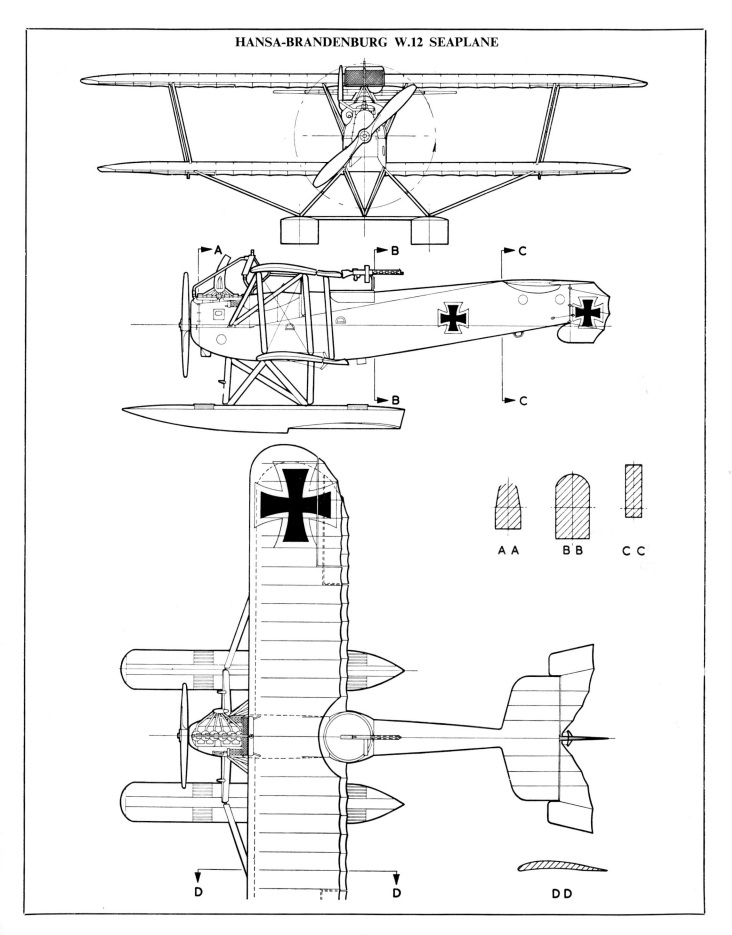

A A　　　B B　　　C C

D　　　　D　　　　D D

HANSA-BRANDENBURG KDW SEAPLANE

In the early part of the war, Ernst Heinkel, the Hansa-Brandenburg designer, developed a variety of seaplanes for the German Navy. They included the successful W and NW two-seaters and the GW twin-engined torpedo plane. The little KDW, which appeared in 1916, was his first single-seater seaplane, and the only one to be built in any quantity. It was the nautical version of the D-I fighter used by Austro-Hungary. The first three machines, Nos. 748, 783 and 784, ordered in June 1916, were completed in September. They were powered by 150 h.p. Benz engines, fitted with car-type radiators. 748's exhaust gases escaped through stubs on the port side of the nose; the other two seaplanes had exhausts of the 'chimney' type. The wings had fabric-covered wooden spars and ribs; they were without dihedral and had square-cut tips. Ailerons with wash-out of incidence were carried on the top plane only. Interplane bracing was of the distinctive 'star' type then favoured by Heinkel; constructed of steel tubing, they were streamlined with laminated wood fairings; no bracing wires were needed. Cabane struts of the trestle type were fitted.

The fuselage, framed in wood and covered in three-ply, tapered to a vertical knife-edge at the rudder-post; the top decking was high and narrow, which partly compensated for the lack of a fin. Two bracing struts on each side supported the low aspect-ratio tail-plane from below; the rectangular rudder had a horn balance and a small triangular lower fin. Single-step floats were fitted; in plan view they were rounded at the front and pointed aft. Twin synchronised Spandau guns were mounted well forward on each side of the nose; they could not be reached by the pilot if stoppages occurred.

The second series (912–921) was completed in February 1917; these KDWs had 160 h.p. Mercedes engines and radiators inset into their top wings to starboard of the centre line; their tail-planes had modified bracing struts. A third series of machines (1067–1076), which appeared in March and April 1917, was generally similar, but reverted to the 150 h.p. Benz power unit and had rudders of smaller area. The last two series (1380–1394 and 1554–1573), brought out in the summer of 1917 and the winter of 1917/18 respectively, had 160 h.p. Maybach engines, shorter floats, long upper fins and plain rudders; a few of these aircraft had additional interplane bracing, an indication that the 'star-strut' arrangement was insufficiently strong.

KDW seaplanes are believed to have served at seaplane stations on the coast of Flanders; a few are said to have operated with German units on the Adriatic. In all, fifty-eight of the type were constructed.

The Hansa-Brandenburg W.11 single-seater seaplane much resembled the KDW; it had, however, the 200 h.p. Benz engine and a larger wing span. Only three examples, Nos. 988–990, were built. Heinkel designed two later single-seater float-planes; the W.16, which had the 160 h.p. Oberursel rotary, and the W.25, with the 150 h.p. Benz. Neither type went into production, for the two-seater Hansa-Brandenburg W.12 and W.19 had proved to be so successful by the beginning of 1918 that they superseded the single-seat seaplanes in the German Navy. Three W.16s (1077–79) and one W.25 (2258) were constructed.

1. and 2. The first KDW, No. 748, with stub exhausts.
3. The second machine, No. 783, with 'chimney' type
exhaust. 4. and 5. A late model KDW with 160 h.p.
Maybach engine, wing radiator, additional wing bracing
and upper fin.

HANSA-BRANDENBURG KDW SEAPLANE

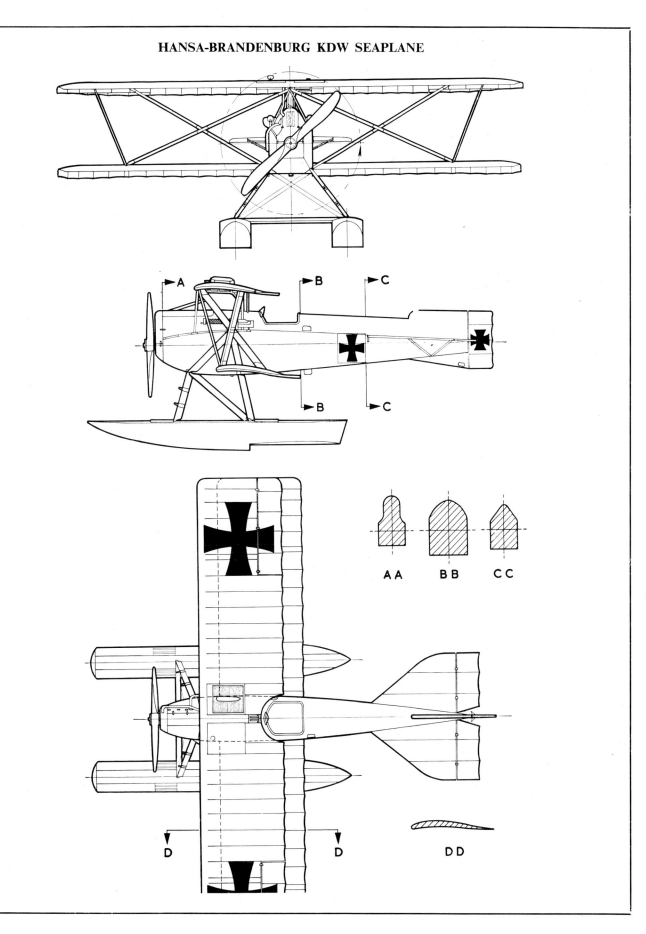

A A   B B   C C

D   D   D D

HANSA-BRANDENBURG W.29 AND W.33

An entirely new type of seaplane was evolved by Heinkel during the last months of 1917; a two-seater low-wing monoplane, the W.29. The first batch, Nos. 2201–2206, were ordered in December and reached the operational units in the following spring and summer; they had 195 h.p. Benz engines with frontal radiators. Six exhaust stubs discharged above and to port of the exposed cylinder heads. Ventilation louvres were provided in the metal side panels which enclosed the bulk of the engine.

The thick, broad-chord wings, of wood and fabric construction, had blunt tips and horn-balanced ailerons, and were rigged with several degrees of dihedral. The fuselage closely resembled that of the W.12, but the tail-plane was neater, with a rounded leading-edge; the elevators were horn-balanced and of unequal chord. Hinged to the vertical knife-edge of the fuselage was the rudder, with a large horn balance on its lower end and a straight trailing-edge; its upper end extended above the top of the tail-plane. Similar floats to those of the W.12 were fitted, and additional N-shaped bracing struts connected them to the under-surface of the wings. The armament consisted of twin synchronised Spandau guns fixed on each side of the curved top decking in front of the pilot's cockpit, and a Parabellum gun on a ring mounting for the observer.

The new monoplane was an immediate success, and the further batches 2287–2300, 2501–2536 and 2564–2583 were ordered in April and May 1918. These aircraft had 150 h.p. Benz engines; the final batch of W.29s, Nos. 2584–2589, had Benz IIIas of 185 h.p.

The Brandenburg monoplanes augmented the W.12s and W.19s already operating from the seaplane bases at Zeebrugge, Ostend, Borkum and Nordeney. Their top speed of 110 m.p.h. and excellent manœuvrability made them dangerous adversaries for the opposing Short seaplanes and Curtiss and Felixstowe flying boats. They also preyed on naval vessels; on July 6th, 1918, the British submarine C25 was surprised on the surface by a formation of Brandenburgs led by Christiansen. In a short time the submarine's motors had been put out of action, and many of the crew, including the C.O., had become casualties. Eventually the C25 was towed into Harwich, leaking 'like a sieve'. The damage was all done by machine-gun fire, for the submarine was old, and the thin plating of its hull was not bullet proof.

An enlarged and more powerful version of the W.29, the W.33, was ordered in April 1918. It had the 260 h.p. Mercedes engine, with six unusually long exhaust stubs, which discharged above and to starboard of the nose. The tail-plane was squarer in shape. Nos. 2538–2563 are known to have been built, and there was certainly at least one later batch, for No. 2670 was surrendered to the British. This aircraft had a 240 h.p. Maybach engine.

The Hansa-Brandenburg monoplanes influenced German seaplane design quite considerably; several copies appeared in 1918, such as the Friedrichshafen FF 63, the Dornier Cs-I, the Junkers J.11, and the L.F.G. Roland ME 8. After the war a version of the W.29 was used by Denmark, while a licence for the manufacture of the W.33 was obtained by Finland.

1. and 2. Hansa-Brandenburg W.29, with 150 h.p. Benz engine. 3. The first production W.33, 2538, with 260 h.p. Mercedes. 4. and 5. Number 2670, a late production type, during evaluation tests by the R.A.F., at Isle of Grain, post-Armistice.

HANSA-BRANDENBURG W.29 SEAPLANE

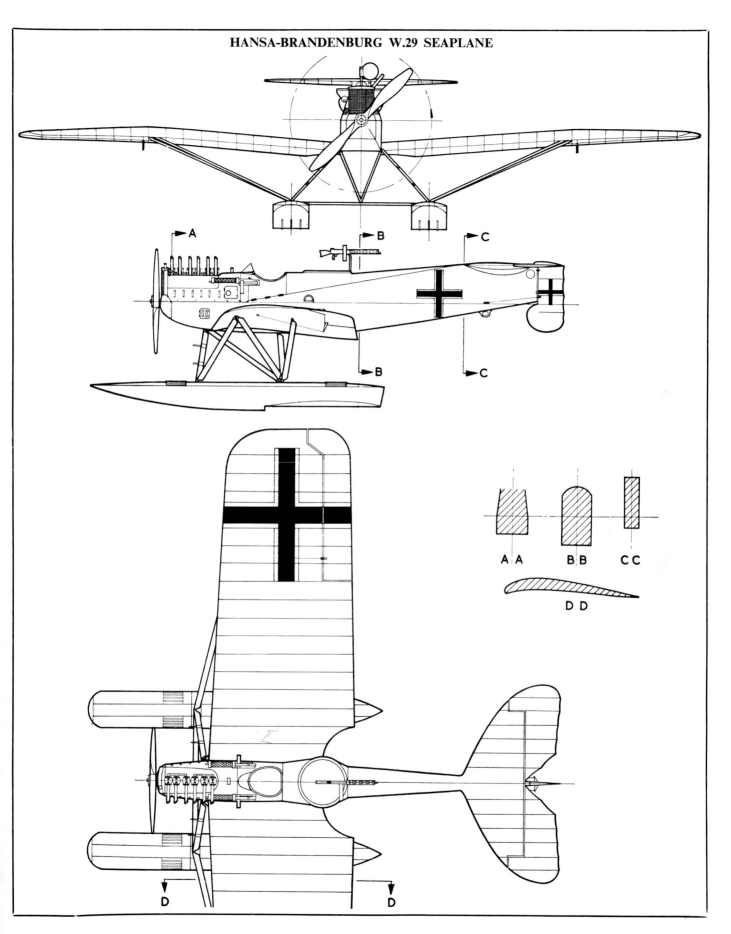

A A   B B   C C

D D

JUNKERS CL-I

A two-seater development of the D-I all-metal fighter monoplane, the Junkers J.10 (military designation CL-I), likewise presented a deceptively simple appearance. Constructionally it was years ahead of its time; its system of internally braced corrugated metal sheeting providing great strength with lightness.

The power unit used was the 160 h.p. Mercedes engine, fitted with a frontal car-type radiator mounted above the thrust-line. In typical German fashion the cylinder heads protruded above the top of the cowling and the exhaust gases were ejected through a curved pipe fixed on the starboard side of the nose. The construction of the thick-sectioned cantilever wing was complicated; seven tubular metal spars, parallel in plan view but staggered in side elevation, were interconnected by metal struts to form Warren trusses. Ribbed aluminium sheeting was used for covering; the wing-tips were at first rounded and long-span ailerons with horn balances were fitted. Production machines had square-cut tips and plain ailerons of shorter span.

Framed in metal with a covering of horizontally ribbed metal strips, the fuselage had flat sides and tapered to a point under the tail-plane. A tubular metal crash pylon of pyramidal shape was provided between the cockpits. To facilitate the movement of the observer's ring-mounted machine-gun, the rear cockpit was built up level with the rounded top decking. The empennage was framed in metal with a corrugated metal covering; the one-piece unbalanced elevator was rectangular; the rudder was balanced and pivoted at a point approximately one-third across its chord. Plain but strong metal undercarriage vee struts were fitted, the axle and spreader bars were enclosed in a streamlined fairing, and the shock absorbers were of the coil-spring type. A pair of Spandau guns were provided for the use of the pilot, while the observer had a Parabellum. Racks for signal cartridges were provided on each side of the fuselage.

Strong, agile and fast, with a good field of fire for the observer, the Junkers CL-I was probably the best of the German 'CL' category, and would have made a name for itself had the war lasted longer. At the Armistice, only forty-seven examples had been delivered; they were issued in ones and twos to various *Schlachtstaffeln* for evaluation.

After the war both the Junkers CL-I and D-I saw service with volunteer units against the Bolsheviks in Finland, Estonia and Lithuania. Flown by the veteran German pilots Jacobs, Sachsenberg and Osterkamp, the Junkers types proved to be useful weapons. A civil version of the CL-I was later constructed, which was equipped with a cabin for passengers.

A seaplane development of the CL-I, the Junkers J.11, was brought out late in the war. It was powered with the 195 h.p. Benz engine, and the vertical tail surfaces underwent some modification. Three machines, numbered 7501–7503 by the German Navy and all differing in detail, were constructed. The type was intended for use as a fighter-reconnaissance aircraft, but did not merit a production order.

The corrugated metal sheet construction continued to be used by the Junkers company until the mid-1930s.

1. Early Junkers CL-I with horn-balanced ailerons. 2. and 3. Junkers CL-I 1802/18 in operational camouflage. 4. CL-I 1803/18 soon after completion. 5. Junkers J.11 7501, the first of the seaplane versions of the CL-1, with triangular fin in front of the rudder.

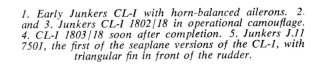

JUNKERS CL-I

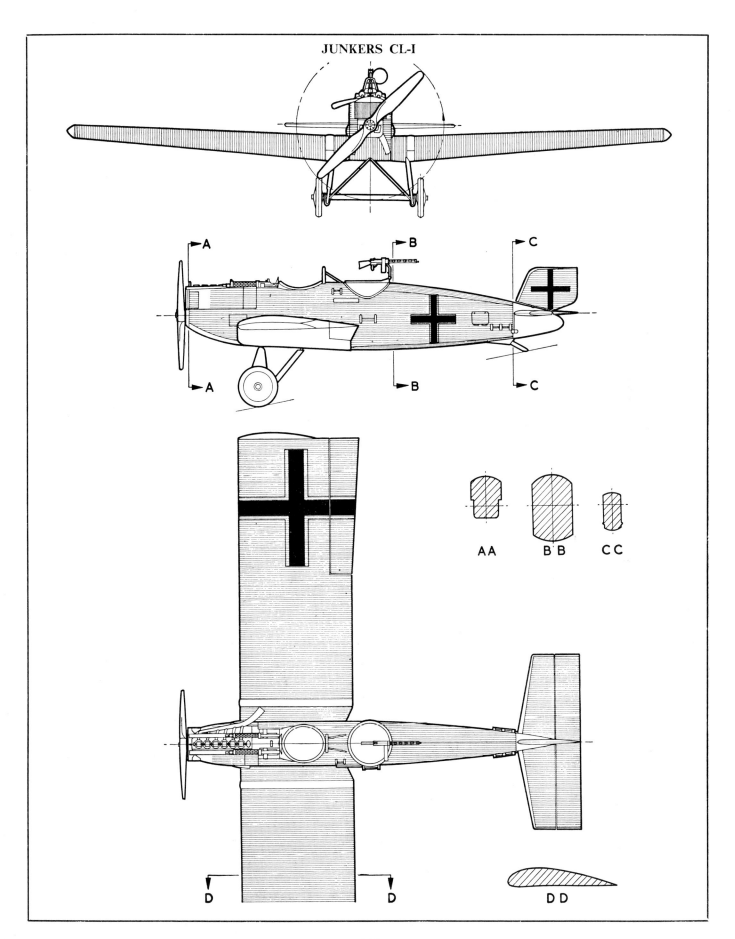

AA   BB   CC

DD

JUNKERS D-I

The world's first all-metal aeroplane, the Junkers J.1, was completed in 1915 under the direction of Professor Hugo Junkers. Its structure consisted of ribbed metal sheeting with internal tubular bracing.

Installed in the pointed nose was a 120 h.p. Mercedes engine, fitted with a 'chimney'-type exhaust pipe, and an interesting innovation—an underslung radiator. The wings were thick in section, with sharply cut tips and ailerons which extended behind the line of the trailing-edge. The fuselage was square in section, the tail and balanced rudder had square edges, and the whole appearance of the aircraft was strong but crude. Nicknamed the 'Blechesel' (Tin Donkey), the J.1 was, quite naturally, regarded with suspicion by the authorities.

In 1916 a development of the J.1, the J.2, was constructed; a single-seater fighter monoplane with remarkably modern lines. A deep underslung radiator was provided for its 160 h.p. Mercedes engine and a crash pylon was fixed behind the cockpit to protect the pilot in the event of the plane turning over. A single Spandau gun was synchronised to fire through the revolving airscrew. The J.2 was given the military designation of E-II, but only six examples, E250–255, were built.

Although Professor Junkers had achieved only partial success with his designs, officialdom was impressed with their strength, and persuaded him to work with Anthony Fokker on the design of a new armoured two-seater biplane intended for army co-operation duty. The new model, the J.4 (military designation J-I), proved to be most useful, but relations between the partners were never happy.

The next Junkers fighter design was the J.7, another all-metal monoplane, which made its appearance in October 1917. In its early form, the nose installation of its 160 h.p. Mercedes engine was fairly well streamlined and the airscrew had a small spinner. A clumsy exhaust pipe stretched down the starboard side of the fuselage. Almost as an afterthought, a radiator was fixed inconveniently above the cylinders. Wing construction consisted of ribbed aluminium, braced internally by seven parallel tubular metal spars, interconnected to form Warren girders. Oddly shaped unequal-chord ailerons replaced the original rotating wing-tips. The fuselage was covered with horizontally corrugated metal strips. Both elevators and rudder were balanced. A high head-rest behind the cockpit acted as a crash pylon. A second J.7 had a neat underslung radiator, modified undercarriage and a blunt nose without a spinner; the head-rest was reduced to skeleton form. A third version, equipped with a car-type radiator, was an excellent aeroplane and would have performed with success at the Adlershof fighter competition in January 1918. Unfortunately, only four weeks before the contest it sustained damage, when flown by Fokker himself.

A further development, the J.9 (military designation D-I), was brought out in March 1918. It was flown with both the 180 h.p. Mercedes and 185 h.p. B.M.W. engines, and carried twin Spandau guns. The D-I was speedy and manoeuvrable, but was more difficult to build than the useful Fokker D-VII, which was already in production. Only forty-one examples reached the front; these were issued in ones and twos to various *Jagdstaffeln*.

1. One of the Junkers J.7 prototypes, with frontal radiator and solid fairing behind the cockpit. 2. Early D-I with crash pylon. 3. Variant with vee-type engine and underslung radiator. 4. and 5. Production Junkers D-Is in operational camouflage.

146

JUNKERS D-I

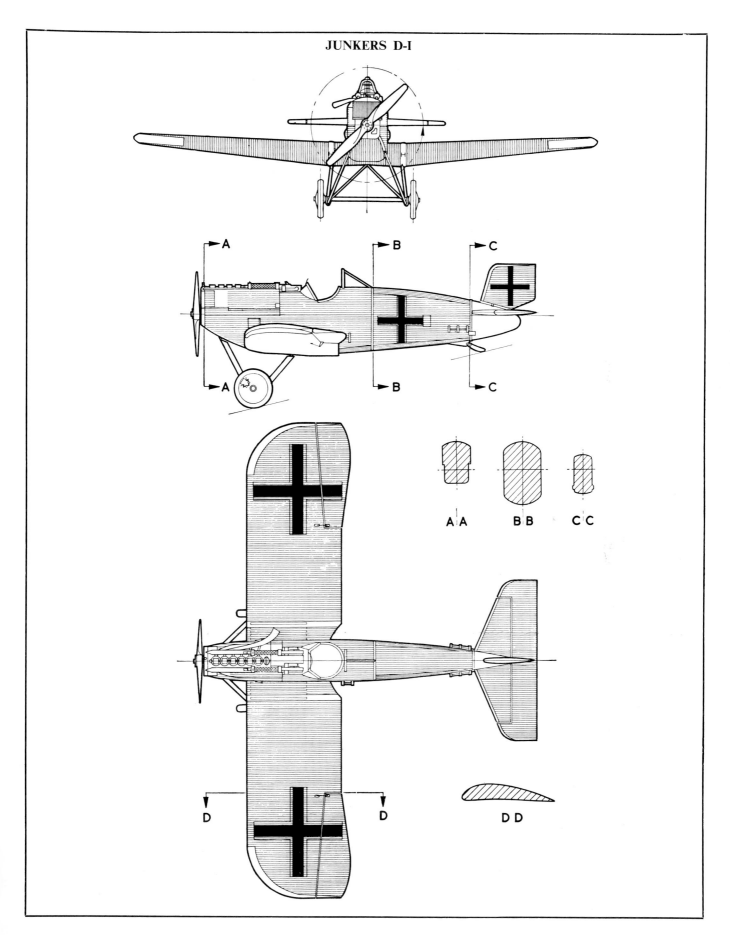

A A   B B   C C

D D

L.F.G. ROLAND C-II

The L.F.G. Company (Luftfahrzeug Gesellschaft) was founded in 1908, and at first built non-rigid airships of the Parseval type. A subsidiary organisation, the Flugmaschine Wright Gesellschaft, constructed Wright biplanes. When this concern failed, L.F.G. turned to the manufacture of aeroplanes, adopting the name 'Roland' to avoid confusion with the L.V.G. firm.

After the outbreak of war three Albatros types were built under licence, the Alb. B-I (Rol.), B-II (Rol.), and B-IIa (Rol.). A new and striking model, the L.F.G. Roland C-II, appeared in October 1915; its construction greatly influenced the trend of German design. In order to provide a good field of fire for the observer, the upper plane was attached to the top of the fuselage, which entirely filled the gap between the wings. A 160 h.p. Mercedes engine was neatly installed in the pointed nose; its exhaust gases passed to starboard through a bulbous manifold before discharging through a 'chimney' exhaust inclined to the rear. A simpler 'chimney' exhaust was later fitted. The airscrew had a bowl-shaped spinner; characteristic Roland ventilation louvres were provided at the front of the engine, and 'ear'-type radiators were fixed on each side of the fuselage.

The broad-chord staggered wings were of wood-and-fabric construction; unequal-chord ailerons were carried on the top wing only, and there were clear-view cut-outs at the roots of both wings. Interplane bracing consisted of a single broad wire-braced 'I' strut on each side. The deep semi-monocoque fuselage was framed in wood and covered in ply; fairings for the lower wing-roots were built in. Two interlocking half-hoops of steel tubing in front of the pilot's cockpit were intended to protect the crew should the machine overturn, and the square windows on each side of the fuselage could be used as escape-hatches if necessary.

The tail-plane, of wood and covered with ply, had raked tips; the unequal-chord elevators were wooden-framed and fabric-covered, and a low-aspect ratio fin and plain rudder were fitted. The observer had a Parabellum gun on a ring mounting; a tubular half-hoop between the cockpits was fitted to some C-IIs to prevent him from depressing the gun too much when firing forwards, and thereby damaging the airscrew. A centrally mounted synchronised Spandau gun was provided for the pilot on later models.

The C-II's fish-like fuselage earned it the name 'Walfisch' (Whale). Nominally a C-type reconnaissance aeroplane, the *Walfisch* was often used as a two-seater fighter. Albert Ball, who had many combats with C-IIs during the summer of 1916, described the type as the 'best German machine now . . . her guns fire backwards and forwards and everywhere except below'. The blind spot below and in front was the great fault of the type, and the pilot had to make what was virtually a 'blind-approach' when landing.

Late production machines had larger rectangular fins braced to the tail-plane by a strut on each side, and lower wings incorporating wash-out. *Walfische* manufactured under licence by Linke-Hofmann of Breslau were designated Rol. C-II (Li) or Li C-II.

The type was in service for a long period; some examples continued to operate on the quieter sectors of the Western Front until the autumn of 1917.

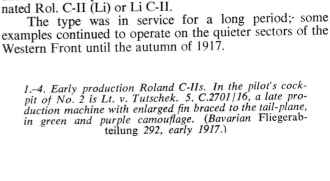

1.–4. Early production Roland C-IIs. In the pilot's cockpit of No. 2 is Lt. v. Tutschek. 5. C.2701/16, a late production machine with enlarged fin braced to the tail-plane, in green and purple camouflage. (Bavarian Fliegerabteilung 292, early 1917.)

148

L.F.G. ROLAND C-II

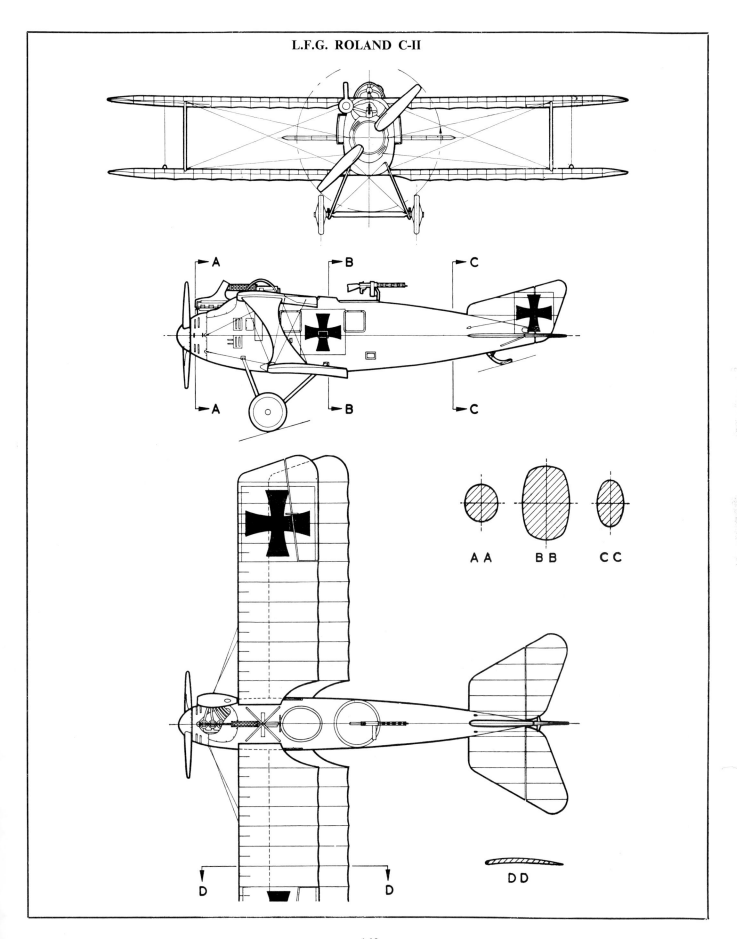

A A   B B   C C

D D

L.F.G. ROLAND D-I, D-II AND D-III

In July 1916 the L.F.G. Roland company tested a new single-seater fighter, developed from the C-II. The D-I, as it was later designated, was carefully streamlined; its 160 h.p. Mercedes engine was neatly installed in a deep fish-like nose with only a small portion of its cylinders protruding. The airscrew had a bowl-shaped spinner and there were the usual Roland ventilation louvres in front of the engine. Side radiators were fitted. The unstaggered wings of wood and fabric construction had one and a half degrees of sweep-back, no dihedral and some wash-out at the tips; the plain equal-chord ailerons were carried on the top plane only. The interplane struts, of steel tubing faired with wood, were wire-braced.

Six layers of plywood formed the shell of the fuselage, which entirely filled the gap between the wings. Below the cockpit on each side was a square window which could be used as an escape hatch; fairings were provided to take the lower wing-roots. The wooden-framed tail-plane was strut-braced from below, and unequal-chord elevators were fitted. A horn-balanced rudder was carried on the plywood fin, which was an integral part of the fuselage. Steel-tube undercarriage vees were fitted.

After the destruction by fire of the Adlershof factory, all L.F.G. land-planes were constructed at the Exhibition Hall, Charlottenburg, Berlin.

The D-I, nicknamed the 'Haifisch' (Shark), went into limited production late in 1916; the type was also built under licence by the Pfalz company. Production machines had upper bracing struts to the empennage and modified tail-skids, but no fuselage windows.

As the view forwards and downwards from the Haifisch's cockpit was particularly poor, modifications were carried out to remedy this defect. The fuselage in front of the cockpit was remodelled so that the top wing was now carried on a long narrow pylon. A wing radiator replaced the side radiators; the cockpit had lower sides, and a new downward-curving exhaust pipe was provided. Twin synchronised Spandau guns were mounted inside the fuselage with only their muzzles protruding. The modified version, designated the D-II, was tested in October 1916, and the first examples reached the front early in 1917. A third model with the 180 h.p. Argus engine, shorter span and longer fuselage, designated the D-IIa, also went into production. Both the D-II and D-IIa were also built by Pfalz.

The Rolands were rather overshadowed by the Albatros Scouts, which in early 1917 were at the height of their fame. Consequently they were used on the less important sectors of the Western Front, on the Eastern Front and in Macedonia.

The design was further modified; the centre pylon was replaced by struts, a longer fin being provided to compensate for the loss. The chord of the lower wing was reduced, necessitating alterations to the interplane strutting. One example was test-flown by Manfred von Richthofen who was not enthusiastic about its capabilities. Only some twenty-five of the new type, designated the D-III, served at the front; the rest of the 150 built presumably were used as advanced trainers.

300 D-IIs and D-IIas were constructed.

1. Production L.F.G. Roland D-I 'Haifisch' (Shark). 2. Roland D-II with modified cabane to provide a better forward view. 3. and 4. Roland D-IIas with lengthened fuselages. 5. Roland D-III outside the Exhibition Hall, Charlottenburg, Berlin. Note enlarged fin.

ROLAND D-II

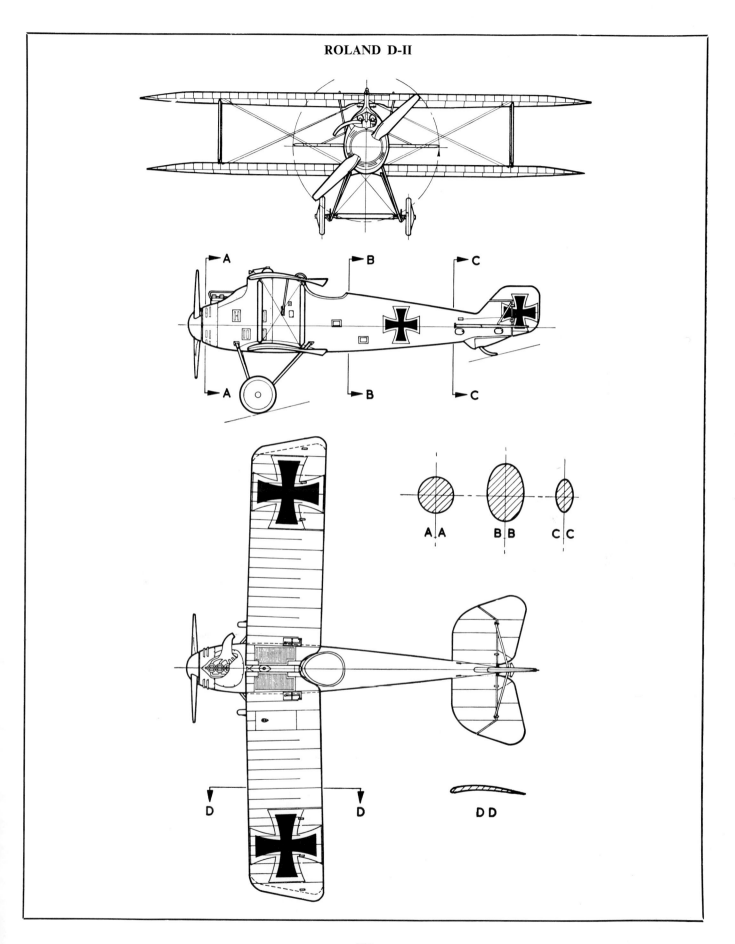

A A B B C C

D D

L.F.G. ROLAND D-VIb

In mid-1917 the L.F.G. Roland company produced the D-IV, an experimental triplane fighter. Although it failed to satisfy operational requirements, it is worthy of note, for it was the first machine to feature a new method of fuselage construction, the so-called *'Klinkerrumpf'* process. This consisted of long tapered strips of wood, fixed longitudinally on a framework of longerons and formers; not a true 'clinker' construction in the nautical sense, for the strips did not overlap each other, as in the case of clinker-built boats. The unsuccessful Roland D-V fighter biplane reverted to the earlier wooden semi-monocoque fuselage, but almost all subsequent Roland fighters incorporated the 'clinker' system.

The next design, the D-VI, underwent many modifications. The prototype, the thousandth L.F.G. aeroplane to be built, did not apparently go into production. Its power unit was the 160 h.p. Mercedes engine installed with characteristic Roland ventilation louvres at the front and detachable metal panels round the cylinder block. A curved exhaust manifold discharged to starboard. The airscrew had a neat pointed spinner; the radiator was situated in the top wing. Wing construction consisted of wooden spars and ribs covered with fabric; plain ailerons were carried; the interplane bracing struts converged slightly in side elevation. A prominent feature of the fuselage was the central 'keel' to which the lower wing-roots were attached. A plain rounded fin and rudder were fitted; the tail-plane, of inverted aerofoil section, had plain steel-tube-framed elevators. Twin synchronised Spandaus were fitted.

In order to improve the pilot's view the gap between the top wing and the fuselage was reduced. Horn-balanced ailerons were fitted, and the modified version was redesignated the D-VIa. Some machines of this type had 180 h.p. Mercedes engines. As supplies of Mercedes power units were unlikely to be available, the firm brought out a third model, which had been altered to take the 200 h.p. Benz engine; this was designated the D-VIb. The D-VIb had modified engine louvres, larger horn-balanced ailerons, and elevators of both the unbalanced and balanced types. A bottom fin was fitted and a variety of balanced and unbalanced rudders.

At the Adlershof competition of January 1918, the D-VI was outclassed by the Fokker D-VII; a small quantity of Rolands were, however, ordered as a precaution against a possible shortage of Fokkers. Both the D-VIa and D-VIb went into production and saw service in small numbers during the summer and autumn of 1918; presumably they were flown by *Jastas* which were unable to obtain Fokker D-VIIs. It was, however, an excellent aeroplane. After the war a D-VIb was test-flown in the U.S.A. It was stated to have similar flying qualities to the Fokker D-VII, with controls which operated more easily. Its manœuvrability was well above that of the average single-seater, and the view from the cockpit was highly commended. On the other hand it was reported that the aeroplane was difficult to control on the ground, owing to its narrow wheel-track, and that the Benz engine was inclined to overheat when fully cowled. Possibly it was not intended to be run at full throttle at low altitudes.

1. L.F.G. Roland D-VI prototype, the 1,000th aircraft built by the firm. 2. Early D-VIb, with 200 h.p. Benz engine, reduced gap and horn-balanced control surfaces. 3. Roland D-VIb on test in the U.S.A. 4. and 5. Production D-VIbs.

L.F.G. ROLAND D-VIb

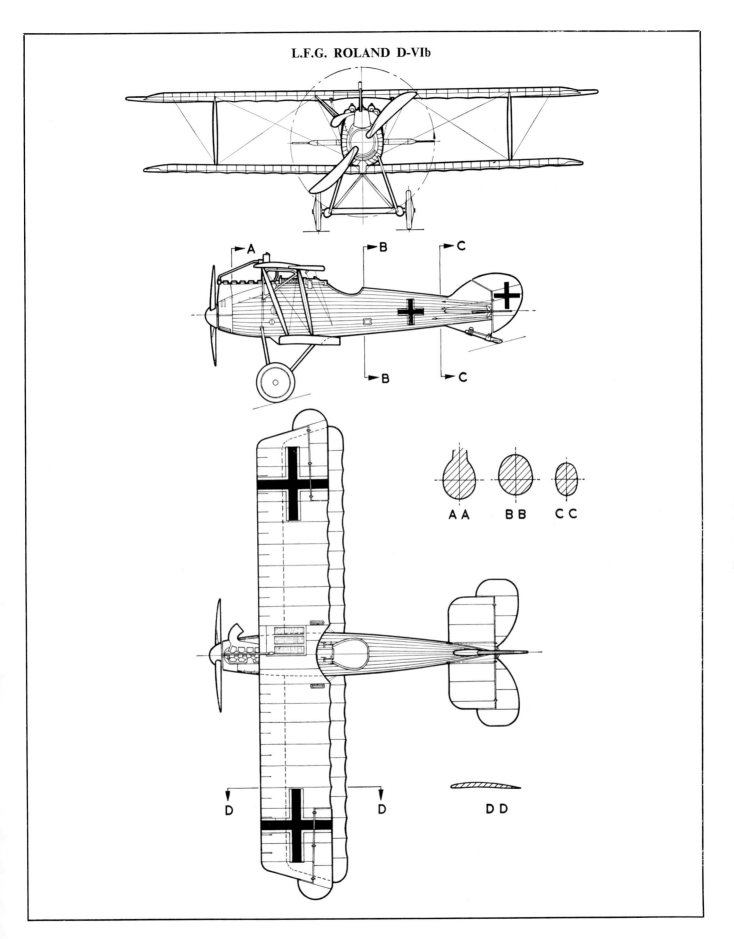

A A   B B   C C

D   D   D D

PFALZ D-III AND D-IIIa

In late 1916 and early 1917 the Pfalz company built under licence the L.F.G. Roland D-I and D-II single-seater biplanes, which were designated the Pfalz D-I and D-II.

The factory's first original D-class design was brought out in the summer of 1917: the D-III, a trim little machine with a finely streamlined fuselage. The power unit was the 160 h.p. Mercedes engine, installed in a rather sharply pointed nose; much of the cylinder block protruded and was enclosed in detachable metal cowlings. The airscrew had a small pointed spinner. A short horizontal exhaust pipe, which appeared in many shapes, discharged on the starboard side. The raked wings, of unequal span and chord, had hollow box spars and plywood ribs interspaced with false ribs of ash. The top wing was flat, the bottom wing had two degrees of dihedral; both structures were fabric-covered. A gravity fuel tank and the radiator balanced each other on the port and starboard sides of the centre section, which had a semicircular cut-out. Balanced equal-chord ailerons were fitted to the upper plane. Splayed wooden interplane struts and wooden centre-section struts of a flattened inverted U shape were fitted.

The monocoque fuselage was constructed of two thin layers of three-ply wood round a wooden frame of longerons and formers, and then covered with fabric, doped and varnished. Fin and tail-planes were of ply-covered wood; the latter was of inverted aerofoil section, a common device of the time to assist recovery from dives. The rudder was framed in steel tubing; both it and the wooden one-piece elevator were fabric covered.

Vees of steel tubing formed the undercarriage, and a small fairing covered the axle and spreader bars. The unusual 'hockey-stick' tail-skid pivoted at the rear end of the fuselage; its forward end was sprung with elastic cord. Twin Spandau guns were fitted to fire through the revolving airscrew; on early models these were mounted inside the fuselage with only their muzzles protruding; later they were placed on top to facilitate maintenance. A special D-III, probably intended for balloon attack, carried three guns.

The first production models reached the front in September 1917; many *Jagdstaffeln* had mixed equipment at this period and it was not unusual for the new D-IIIs to fly in the same formation with Fokker Dr.-Is and Albatros D-Vs. Unfortunately the performance of the Pfalz did not match its sleek appearance. Its manœuvrability and rate of climb were poor, so that it tended to be given to the inferior pilots and the beginners. On the other hand, the D-III's strength in a dive and its excellent forward view recommended it to those who specialised in 'balloon busting'. Its reputation was further damaged in 1918 when crashes were attributed to negligence in construction.

An improved model, the D-IIIa, had the 180 h.p. Mercedes engine, rounded tips to the lower wings and a curved tail-plane of increased area. Early in 1918 Pfalz production was increased, and as availability was then more important than performance, many D-IIIs were sent to the *Jastas*. Largely for want of a better alternative, the Pfalz continued to operate until mid-1918. It was looked upon by the average S.E.5a, Camel and Spad pilot as being 'easy meat'.

1. and 2. Production Pfalz D-IIIs. 3. Pfalz D-IIIa in French markings. Note rounded lower wing-tips and curved leading edge to tail-plane. 4. D-IIIa 6033/17 flown by Baierlein in the first fighter-competition at Aldershof, January, 1918. 5. D-IIIa.

154

PFALZ D-III

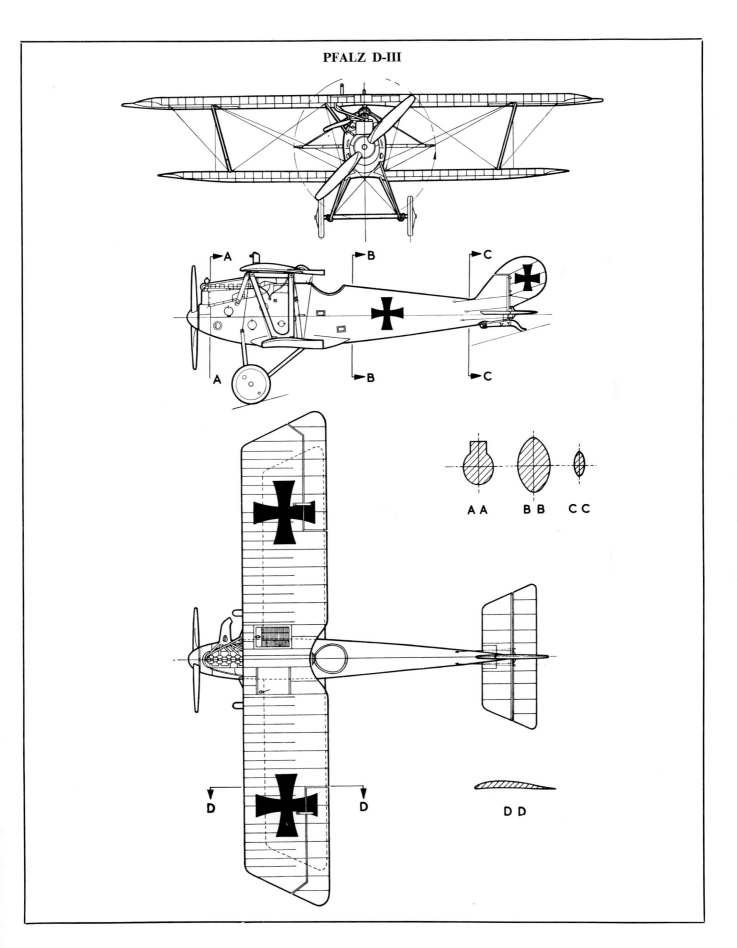

A A   B B   C C

D D

155

PFALZ D-XII

The moderately successful Pfalz D-III was followed by five other fighter designs, none of which was considered worthy of a production order. They were the D-IV, an ugly little biplane version of the E-V monoplane, the D-VI, D-VII and D-VIII rotary-engined biplanes, and the D-XI. The latter machine was virtually a D-III with two-bay wings, horn-balanced control surfaces and a rectangular fin. Unusually for an aeroplane of 1918 vintage, it had box-like side radiators.

Although based on the D-XI, the design of the next Pfalz fighter, the D-XII, was obviously influenced by that of the new and very successful Fokker D-VII; so much so that the type was at first believed by Allied airmen to be a Fokker. It had a 160/180 h.p. Mercedes engine, fitted with a frontal radiator; the exhaust pipe on the early production machines curved outwards and downwards on the starboard side of the nose; later models had horizontal exhausts. Detachable aluminium panels with four adjustable ventilation apertures apiece covered the sides of the cylinder·block. Wing construction consisted of two plywood box spars with steel compression members and tie-rods and three-ply ribs, the whole being braced with wire and fabric-covered. The leading-edges were spruce, the trailing-edges of wire. Only the lower wing had dihedral; horn-balanced ailerons were carried on the top plane only, which had a small semicircular cut-out in the trailing-edge of its centre section.

The two-bay interplane struts and inverted centre-section struts were of tubular steel, braced with wire, forming a structure of great strength. The fuselage, of wood covered with a three-ply skin, tapered gradually to a vertical knife-edge at the tail. Built-in fairings were provided to house the lower wing-roots. The tail-plane and horn-balanced elevators were framed in wood and covered in plywood and fabric respectively. A rectangular fin and horn-balanced rudder were fitted to the first production aircraft, but later a pleasantly rounded fabric-covered steel tube fin and rudder were substituted. Orthodox steel-tube undercarriage vees were fitted; the wheels were sprung by rubber cord or steel coil springs. Twin synchronised Spandau guns were mounted in front of the cockpit.

During the course of the fighter competition of June 1918, two prototypes, one with a Mercedes engine, one with a B.M.W., were tested.

The genuine merits of the design plus the support of the Bavarian Government ensured a production order for the D-XII. In the autumn of 1918 the first machines reached the front, and were issued to *Jastas* which were short of Fokker D-VIIs. They were unpopular both with the pilots, who had expected to be equipped with the more manœuvrable Fokker, and with the ground staff, who disliked the extra work necessitated by the Pfalz's complicated bracing system. Nevertheless the D-XII had an excellent turn of speed and was by no means a bad aeroplane; in particular it was capable of being dived at high speeds with perfect safety.

Further developments were brought out by the Pfalz Flugzeugwerke: the D-XIII and D-XIV, with 185 h:p. Benz engines, and the D-XV with the 185 h.p. B.M.W. None of these types went into production.

1. and 2. Early production D-XIIs. 3. D.2690/18, a standard production machine with rounded fin and rudder. 4. A D-XII in British hands. 5. A well-preserved example —D.7517/18—is to be seen at the Smithsonian Institute, Washington D.C., U.S.A.

PFALZ D-XII

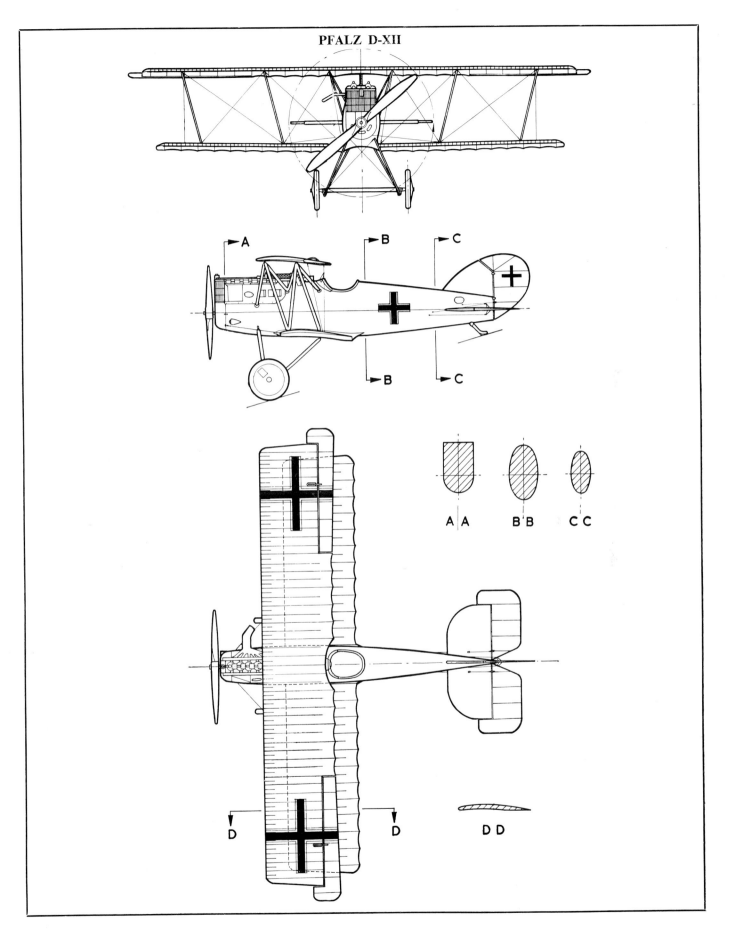

A A   B B   C C

D D

157

PFALZ Dr.-I

A great variety of triplane and quadruplane designs were produced by the German and Austro-Hungarian aircraft factories during 1917, as a consequence of the appearance of the Sopwith Triplane on the Western Front. In Austro-Hungary, in spite of their protests, the designers were ordered to produce experimental triplanes; it was not surprising, therefore, that the resulting models proved operationally unsuitable.

Only two German triplanes were considered satisfactory enough to be put into production; the Fokker and Pfalz Dr.-Is. The latter, a development of the rotary-engined Pfalz D-VII experimental fighter, was entirely designed by Ernst Eversbusch, as his partner brother Walter had been killed in an accident on June 1st, 1916.

The power unit was the eleven-cylinder 160 h.p. Siemens-Halske Sh III geared rotary engine, which was enclosed in a circular aluminium cowling provided with twelve large ventilation holes; in order to remove the complete cowling without taking off the airscrew, the upper quarter was detachable. One at least of the later machines had a redesigned cowling with the lower quarter removed and fewer and smaller vent-holes. The airscrew was of large dimensions and coarse pitch, to make the best use of the slow r.p.m. of the Sh III engine. The wing construction consisted of hollow box spars with three-ply ribs attached, covered with fabric. The three aerofoils varied in span and chord; the top plane was the largest and carried the equal-chord ailerons; the middle plane was the smallest.

The fuselage, a plywood monocoque of thick cross-section, was built up of wooden frames reinforced with ply gussets; the fin was an integral part of the rear portion. Seated high in the fuselage, the pilot had a good view in almost all directions. Fairings for the middle and lower wing-roots were built in. Rudder and elevators were fabric-covered; the three-ply tail-plane was of inverted aerofoil section to assist in recovery from dives. Rather lengthy steel-tube undercarriage vees gave clearance for the large airscrew.

The usual armament of twin synchronised Spandau guns was fitted; they were mounted in front of the cockpit to fire through the revolving blades of the airscrew.

In December 1917 the Pfalz Triplane, with its more powerful engine and better appearance, was suggested to Manfred von Richthofen as a possible replacement for the Fokker Dr.-I. The Pfalz Flugzeugwerke, under the patronage of the Bavarian Government, did not come directly under the control of the *Flugmeisterei* (Directorate of Aircraft Production) and von Richthofen, therefore, made a special visit to Speyer-am-Rhein to flight-test the machine. He was greatly disappointed; its handling qualities were inferior to those of the Fokker, and the Sh III engine did not develop its full rated horse-power. Richthofen therefore found it impossible to recommend the type as being suitable for large-scale manufacture.

Ten Pfalz Dr.-Is were constructed, and it is said that a few were used operationally. Two further Pfalz triplane projects, the Dr.-II (100 h.p. Oberursel) and Dr.-IIa (110 h.p. Siemens-Halske Sh I) were also found to be unsatisfactory and were abandoned.

1. 2. and 3. Early Pfalz Dr.-Is with large cowling apertures. 4. Pfalz Dr.-I 3050/17, which was tested and rejected by Manfred v. Richthofen in December 1917. 5. Late model Dr.-I with re-designed cowling louvres and bottom segment removed.

PFALZ Dr.-I

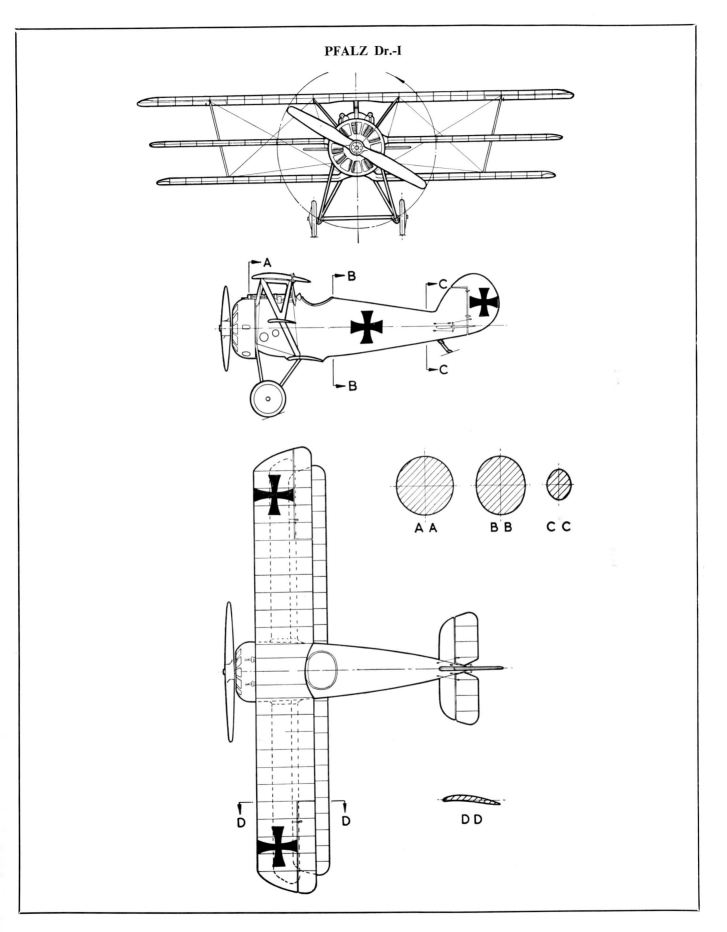

A A   B B   C C

D D

PFALZ E-I, E-II, E-III, E-IV AND E-V

The Bavarian Government, being determined to control the source of its flying equipment, sponsored the establishment of the Pfalz (Palatinate) Flugzeugwerke at Speyer-am-Rhein, the administrative centre of the Rhenish Palatinate, a part of Bavaria. The factory was under the direction of the brothers Ernst and Walter Eversbusch, who designed and flew their own products.

In the early months of the war a version of the Otto pusher was manufactured by the Pfalz company; then the A-I (80 h.p. Oberursel rotary) and the A-II (100 h.p. Oberursel) made their appearances; they were almost identical copies of the Morane-Saulnier L-type Parasol monoplane, even having similar black outlines to their wings, fuselage and tails and similar cowling trade marks! No machine-guns were fitted to these aircraft. In 1915 the success of the armed Fokker monoplane prompted the development of the Pfalz E-I, a mid-wing single-seater. Closely resembling the 1913 Morane-Saulnier H, the E-I was powered by the 80 h.p. Oberursel rotary engine, installed in an open-fronted 'horseshoe' cowling. Wing construction was of the usual wood and fabric type, with a flexible trailing-edge to permit wing-warping. The upper control wires passed over a pulley in the apex of the pylon in front of the cockpit, and the lower wires connected to cranks at the point of the inverted pylon situated behind the undercarriage. The plywood and fabric-covered fuselage was rectangular in section and tapered to a horizontal knife-edge; there were no fixed tail surfaces, the balanced elevator being hinged around its spar. A single synchronised Spandau gun was fixed centrally in front of the pilot, to fire through the airscrew arc. Later models, designated E-IIs, had the 100 h.p. Oberursel rotary.

Both the E-I and E-II were supplied in ones and twos to the two-seater reconnaissance units for the protection of the slower aircraft. A number saw service on the Eastern Front. Inevitably, the Pfalz monoplanes were classed as 'Fokkers' by Allied airmen.

A forward-firing synchronised gun was fitted to the two-seater Pfalz A-II Parasol; as it now came into the 'armed' category it was redesignated the E-III. The Pfalz E-IV was a standard mid-wing monoplane adapted to take the big 160 h.p. Oberursel twin rotary, which was enclosed in a metal cowling fitted with six pear-shaped ventilation holes. The twin-row engine was most unreliable, and the accident rate of the E-IV was particularly high. Yet another engine change was made, the next Pfalz type, the E-V, having the 100 h.p. Mercedes, which lengthened the nose by just over thirteen inches. A square car-type radiator was fitted; the exhaust gases discharged vertically downwards on the starboard side, either through individual pipes which converged to form one main exhaust, or a single thick pipe. Although fairly speedy, the E-V had unpleasant flying characteristics, and was not produced in any quantity.

By the summer of 1916 the German mid-wing monoplanes were outclassed by the Allied Nieuports and D.H.2s, and the Pfalz company by the end of the year had begun to build L.F.G. Roland D-Is under licence, the first of these being D.1680/16.

1. and 2. Unarmed Pfalz E-Is. 3. A Pfalz E-III (the A-II Parasol two-seater with a forward-firing gun). 4. Pfalz E-IV (160 h.p. twin-row Oberursel rotary). 5. The Mercedes-engined E-V. All Pfalz monoplanes bore crosses marked on their elevators.

160

PFALZ E-I

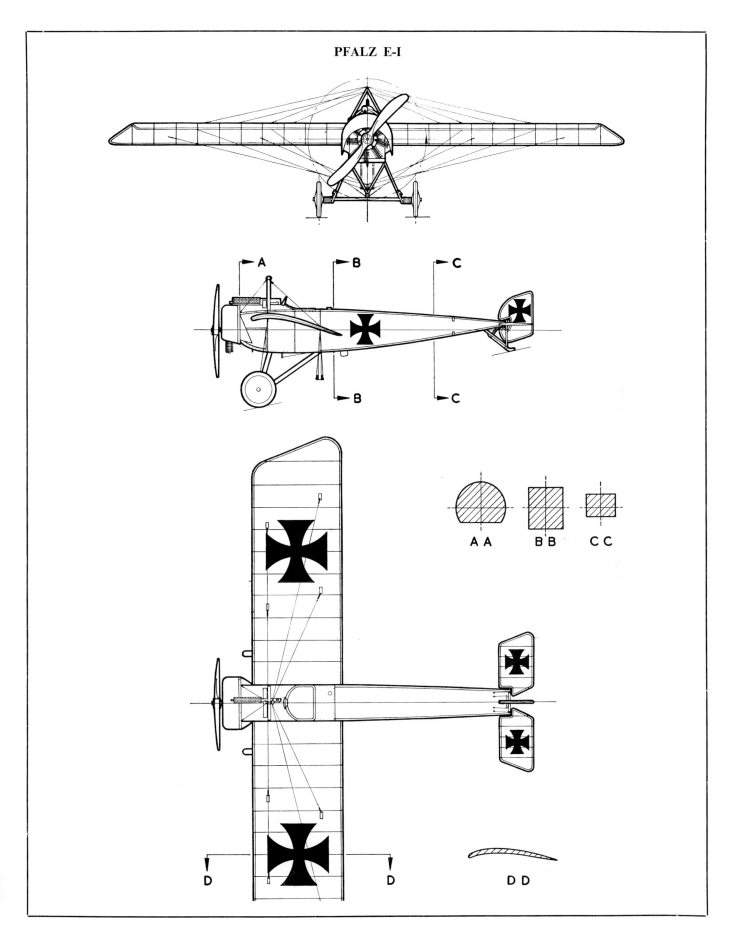

A A   B B   C C

D D

RUMPLER D-I

The 'Taube' or Dove was a bird-like monoplane created by Igo Etrich, an Austrian. Tauben constructed by the E. Rumpler Flugzeugwerke of Johannisthal made a number of record-breaking flights in the years 1913 and 1914.

The first biplane to be designed by Dr. Rumpler made a remarkable non-stop flight in 1914, covering the route Berlin–Budapest–Sofia–Constantinople in eighteen hours. An improved Rumpler biplane, the B-I, was used by the German Army in the first months of the war; the firm then developed a succession of first-class reconnaissance biplanes, the C-I to C-X.

Work began in 1917 on an experimental single-seater, the 7D1, a well-streamlined little machine with a fish-like fuselage which entirely filled the gap between the wings. Its power unit was the 160 h.p. Mercedes engine, completely enclosed and provided with a spinner. The wings had wooden wire-braced spars and ribs, covered with fabric; the upper wing had raked tips and a large centre-section cut-out, and carried equal-chord ailerons; the lower wing was of the 'Libelle' (Dragonfly) type, with a slightly swept-back leading-edge, pointed tips and a curved trailing-edge. Both wings had wash-out of incidence; inverted gull-wing fairings were provided for the lower wing-roots. An 'I' strut on each side braced the wing cellule. The finless balanced rudder was soon replaced by a plain rudder and fin, the modified aircraft being redesignated the 7D2.

Owing to the inaccessibility of the 7D2's engine, the type was unsuitable for production, and a series of modifications were therefore made to facilitate maintenance in the field. The 7D4 had a blunt nose and no spinner; the cylinder heads were exposed and the radiator was mounted in the top wing, which was raised above the fuselage on 'N' struts. The span was reduced and normal bracing struts were fitted. The fuselage was of complicated construction, having fourteen plywood formers and six longerons, covered with a plywood skin except for the middle third, which was of fabric stretched over some fifty stringers. Tail-plane and fin, of plywood, were built into the fuselage; elevators and balanced rudder were wood-framed and fabric-covered. In front elevation the undercarriage had a splayed-out appearance, for its connecting points with the fuselage were close together. Twin synchronised Spandau guns were mounted to fire forward.

To reduce drag, the next development, the 7D7, was fitted with peculiar 'C' struts with single bracing wires, which were later replaced by twin flying wires. Two small radiators replaced the wing radiator. Both balanced and unbalanced rudders were fitted. The 7D8 apparently differed only in having triple flying wires.

The final version, the 8D1 (military designation D-I), was given horn-balanced ailerons and a high triangular fin and rudder; the fuselage was entirely covered with plywood. Some D-Is were powered by the 185 h.p. B.M.W. engine.

Like all Rumpler types, the D-I had a very high 'ceiling'; it could not, however, maintain height when carrying out combat manœuvres, and in addition was a difficult type to mass-produce.

1. The Rumpler 7D2. 2. Practically a new design; the 7D4. 3. The 7D7, with unorthodox interplane struts and side radiators. 4. An intermediate type, probably the 7D8. 5. The final version, the 8D1 (D-I), serial D.1550/18, which appeared on September 9th, 1918.

RUMPLER D-I

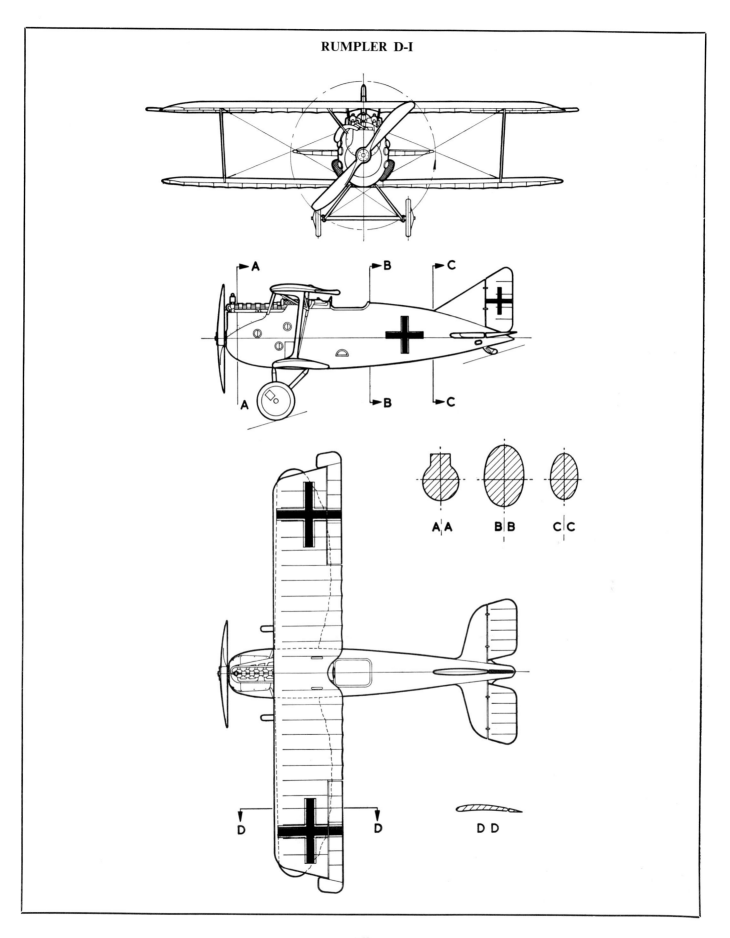

A A   B B   C C

D D

RUMPLER 6B-1 AND 6B-2

During the First World War a variety of single-seater seaplanes were designed for the German Navy by the Albatros, Friedrichshafen, Hansa-Brandenburg, L.F.G. Roland, Luft Torpedo, Rumpler and Sablatnig companies. Only three types, however, went into production; the Albatros W.4, the Hansa-Brandenburg KDW and the Rumpler 6B-1/2.

The Rumpler firm produced seaplane versions of its early designs, and at the outbreak of war Rumpler two-seater seaplanes were in service with the Marine *Fliegerabteilung*.

By 1916 single-seater escort seaplanes were required, and work began on a Rumpler prototype. In order to save valuable time, the 6B-1, as it was designated, was more or less a single-seater version of the well-tried C-I reconnaissance landplane. The same engine, the 160 h.p. Mercedes, was installed, with its radiator mounted under the leading-edge of the cabane. A 'chimney'-type exhaust pipe carried its waste gases over the top wing; the airscrew had a pointed spinner. In contrast to the negatively staggered wings of the C-I, the 6B-1's wings were rigged with a good deal of positive stagger. The tips were raked, the leading-edges were swept back, and unequal-chord ailerons were fitted to the top plane only. The latter had ash spars and plywood ribs, while the lower plane had spruce spars and ply ribs; both were fabric-covered. Two-bay wire-braced interplane struts were provided and the cabane was of the trestle type.

The fuselage longerons were of wood, with steel-tube spacers forward and ash spacers aft; the whole structure was wire-braced and covered with fabric, except for the nose portion. As was the case with the C-I, the pilot sat in front of the rearmost inverted vee of the cabane; the observer's cockpit was, of course, faired over. The triangular low aspect-ratio tail-plane was framed in welded steel tubing and covered with fabric, as was the triangular fin, which carried a plain rudder of larger area than that of the C-I. Twin floats of the double-step type were attached to the fuselage and lower wings by steel-tube struts.

The first two 6B-1s, Nos. 787 and 788, were delivered in July 1916, the prototype, No. 751, in August. Subsequent batches had smaller tail-planes and balanced elevators, the horizontal tail surfaces thus resembling those of the later Rumpler C-types. 890–899 were supplied between November 1916 and February 1917, 1037–1046 in February 1917 and 1047–1061 between February and May 1917, with a belated machine appearing in January 1918.

Although a large aeroplane for a single-seater, the type gave good service at the seaplane stations of Zeebrugge and Ostend. 6B-1s operating over the Black Sea are said to have shot down several Russian flying boats.

An improved version, the 6B-2, based on the Rumpler C-IV landplane, was constructed from January 1917. The power unit was unchanged; the 260 h.p. Mercedes used on the C-IV was not apparently installed. Three batches, Nos. 1062–1066, 1188–1207 and 1434–1458, were supplied between October 1917 and January 1918. No. 1065 was not delivered.

A total of 38 6B-1s and 50 6B-2s was built.

1. to 4. The first production Rumpler 6B-1, No. 751, which was actually the third machine of the type to be supplied to the German Navy. 5. No. 1045, a Rumpler 6B-1 with modified exhaust stack, in operational markings, seen from a machine flying alongside.

RUMPLER 6B-1 SEAPLANE

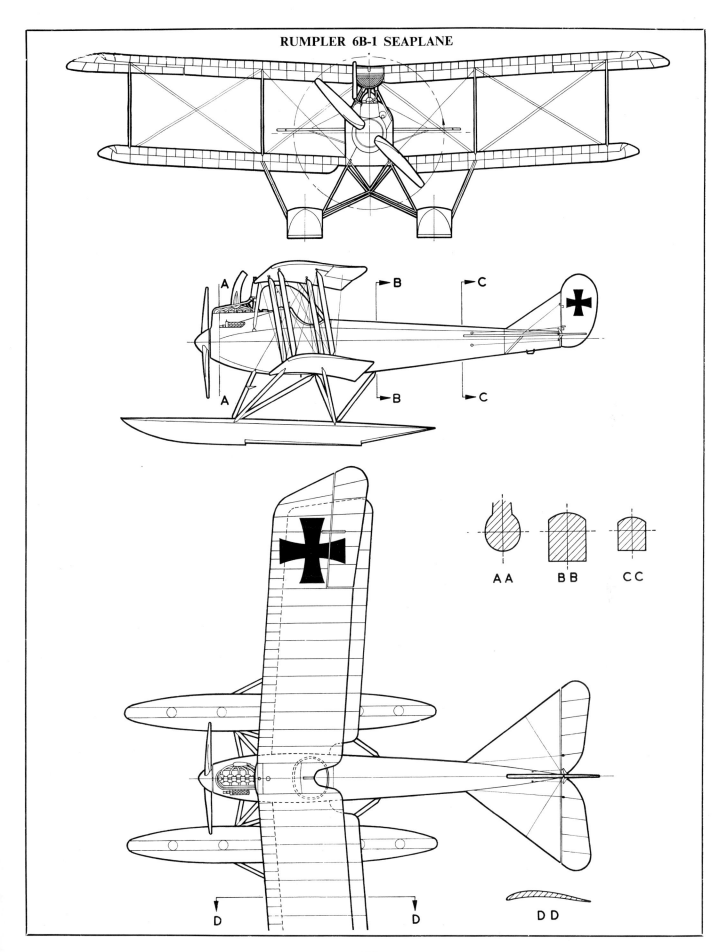

A A   B B   C C

D D

SIEMENS-SCHUCKERT D-I

The world-famous electrical combine of Siemens-Schuckert entered the aeronautical field as early as 1907, with the construction of non-rigid airships. Work on heavier-than-air machines began two years later, but the results were so unpromising that this branch of activity closed down in 1911.

With the outbreak of war the aeroplane department was re-established. Of several types brought out by the designers Forssman and Franz and Bruno Steffen, the most successful were the R series of large bombers (R meant *Riesenflugzeug* or Giant aeroplane).

In autumn 1915, when the Fokker monoplane was supreme on the Western Front, the Steffen-designed SSW E-I made its appearance; a mid-wing monoplane of similar general layout to the Fokker, but with a better streamlined fuselage, stronger undercarriage struts and a fixed tail-plane and fin. Its power unit was the interesting 110 h.p. Siemens-Halske geared rotary; the cylinders revolved in the opposite direction to its airscrew, thereby halving the revolutions per minute of the latter. This reduced the torque and gyroscopic effect common to all rotaries, and permitted a more efficient use of the airscrew. Frontal support for the engine was provided by extending part of the metal cowling. Twenty E-Is were built at the Nürnberg branch; presumably they were sent to the front to augment the Fokker and Pfalz monoplanes. A second SSW monoplane type, the E-II (120 h.p. Argus), crashed on test at Döberitz in June 1916, killing its pilot, Franz Steffen.

Much of the Allied superiority in the air during the summer of 1916 was due to the speedy and manœuvrable Nieuport Scout. The Inspectorate of Flying Troops (*IdFlieg*) dissatisfied with the available Fokker and Halberstadt bi-planes, decided that the best way out of the re-equipment difficulty would be to produce copies of the Nieuport. Accordingly, the Albatros, Euler, Fokker and Siemens-Schuckert companies were provided with captured aircraft as models and ordered to apply themselves to the task.

The SSW copy, designated the D-I, could only be distinguished from the Nieuport 17 by its 110 h.p. Sh I engine with characteristic Siemens cowling and ventilating louvres, and its simplified centre-section bracing. The wing area was slightly less than that of the original. A single Spandau gun was synchronised to fire through the airscrew arc.

One hundred and fifty D-Is were ordered in November 1916, and work began at both Berlin and Nürnberg. An order for a further 100 was placed in the following spring, but by then the superior Albatros Scout was available in numbers, and the crisis had passed.

Many of the SSW D-Is, therefore, were supplied to units on the Russian front, where the opposition was less severe. The later production machines had large stream-lined spinners fitted to their airscrews.

Three modified aircraft, the D-Ia, with a larger wing area, the D-Ib (16) and the D-Ib (19), were constructed, but did not go into production. The two latter machines had wing areas of 16·2 and 19·2 square metres respectively, and were powered by the 130 h.p. Sh Ia engine.

All production ceased in July 1917, after ninety-four D-Is, one D-Ia and two D-Ibs had been delivered.

1. The E-I, of which twenty (E.550–569/15) were ordered 16.11.15. Six similar machines (E.620–625/15) with 100 h.p. Gnôme engines were designated E-IIIs. 2. Prototype D-I with four-bladed airscrew. 3. Early production model. 4. and 5. Late production machines.

SIEMENS-SCHUCKERT D-I

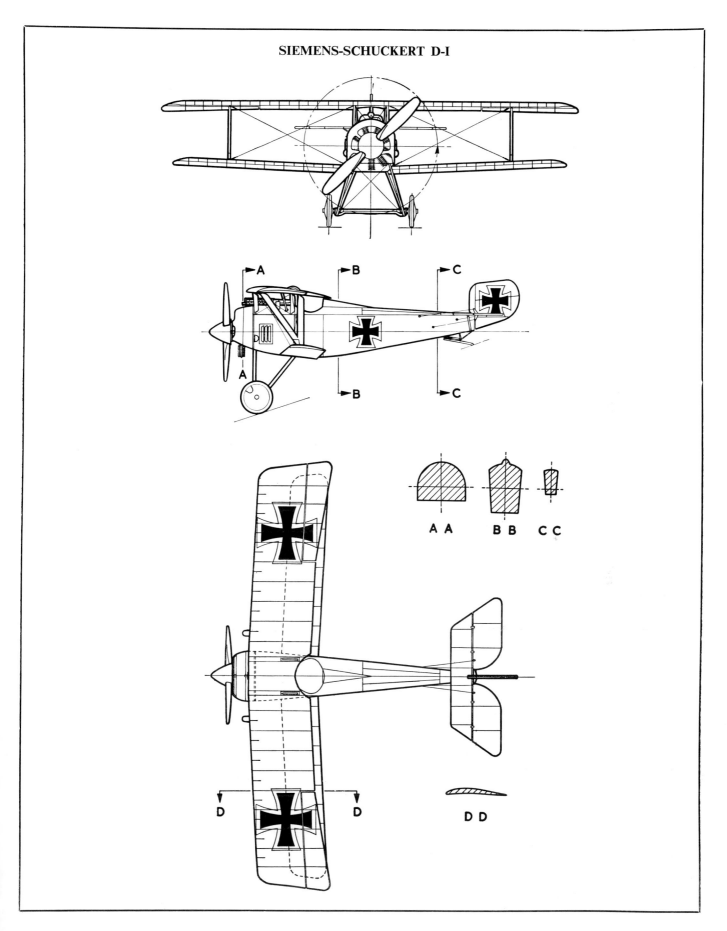

A A   B B   C C

D   D   D D

SIEMENS-SCHUCKERT D-III AND D-IV

Early in 1917 the Siemens-Schuckert Werke at Siemensstadt, Berlin, produced three experimental fighters, the SSW D-II, D-IIa and D-IIb, which were specially designed to utilise the new and promising 160 h.p. Siemens-Halske Sh III eleven-cylinder geared rotary engtne. Flight testing began in June 1917, as soon as the first engines became available, and the experimental machines were found to have phenomenally good rates of climb. After further development work three improved prototypes, the D-IIc shortwing, D-IIc longwing and D-IIe, were completed; one of these, the D-IIc longwing (7551/17), was chosen as the prototype of the new SSW D-III fighter.

Twenty production D-IIIs were ordered by *IdFlieg* in December 1917, while development work was still in progress, and a further order for thirty more followed in February 1918. The early models had four-bladed airscrews with large spinners, large circular aluminium cowlings, balanced ailerons on both wings, stumpy plywood-covered fuselages and balanced elevators and rudders. In April the first D-IIIs were supplied to *Jagdgeschwader II* (Hauptmann Berthold) for operational trials. For security reasons it was forbidden to cross the lines in a D-III, but the fighter's great climbing power made it a useful interceptor. Criticism was, however, levelled at its relatively poor speed in level flight, and trouble was experienced with the Sh III engine, mainly because of poor-quality pistons and inferior oil. A tendency to overheat was rectified by cutting away the lower half of the cowling, a modification which, became standard on all subsequent D-IIIs and D-IVs.

Eventually the first thirty-eight D-IIIs were withdrawn for refitting at the works, and *Jagdgeschwader II* were re-equipped with Fokker D-VIIs. Delivery of the D-III recommenced in July, after the Sh IIIa engine and modified ailerons and rudder had been fitted; this time the type was sent to the *Kampfeinsitzerstaffeln* (home-defence fighter units) Nos. 4a, 4b, 5, 6, and 8, and *Jadgstaffelschule* (Fighter School) No. 1.

Meanwhile the SSW D-IV was undergoing development; it was hoped to combine the excellent rate of climb of the D-III with a fair turn of speed on the level. The D-IV differed only slightly from the later D-IIIs; its spinner had four ventilation holes, and its wings, of smaller span and chord, were fitted with ribs of improved section. As supplies became available, the type was delivered to front-line units, including *Jagdgeschwader II, Jagdstaffeln 14* and *22, Kampfeinsitzerstaffel 2* and the *Marinejagdgeschwader.*

In a number of ways the type was superior to the redoubtable Fokker D-VII, and some pilots claimed that it was the best fighter at the front. Major K. L. Caldwell (twenty-five victories), the New Zealand C.O. of 74 Squadron, R.A.F., in a combat report dated September 24th, 1918, commented thus: 'These E.A. appear to be very handy in manœuvre, but their speed was less than that of an S.E. Their climb seemed much better, but their zoom not so good . . . very handy in dogfighting.'

The teething troubles of their engines and their complicated fuselage construction prevented the D-III and D-IV from being truly successful. 80 D-IIIs and 119 D-IVs were delivered.

1. The D-III prototype D.7551/17. 2. Early production D-III 8341/17. 3. Modified D-III on test, with Fokker Triplanes of Jagdgeschwader II *in background. 4. Production D-IV. 5. D-IV with experimental pitot head and with headrest removed, at Le Bourget.*

SIEMENS-SCHUCKERT D-III

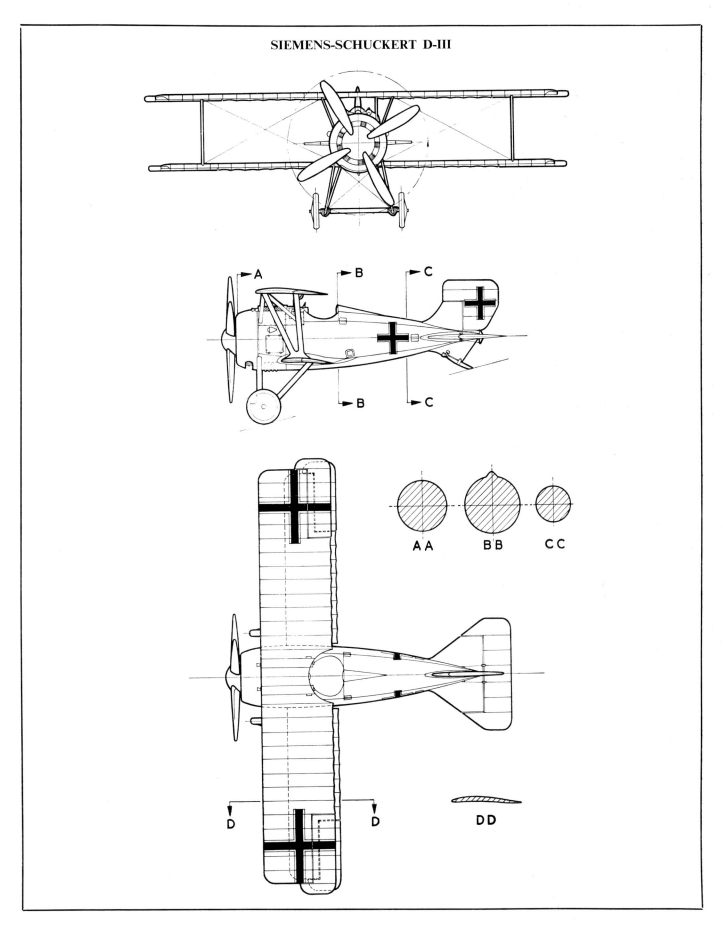

AA   BB   CC

DD

ANSALDO A-1 BALILLA

Throughout the First World War the land-based fighter squadrons of the Aeronautica del Regio Esercito were equipped with single-seaters of French design; the Nieuport 11 and 17, the Spad S.7 and the Hanriot HD-1.

The first attempt to provide an Italian fighter was made in mid-1917, when the Società Ansaldo commenced work on a small biplane, the Ansaldo A-1. The A-1, notable for its very short wing span, was powered by the SPA 6A engine of 220 h.p., equipped with a rectangular frontal radiator. Its exhaust gases discharged to starboard through six stubs. Access to the engine could be obtained by detaching a curved metal cowling which covered the top half of the nose. The wings, of equal span and chord, were constructed of wire-braced wood and fabric; there was neither dihedral nor stagger. Most of the A-1s had rounded wing-tips, but one at least had square-cut tips. Ailerons operated by Nieuport-type vertical rods were fitted to the top-plane only, and there was an angular cut-out in the trailing-edge of the centre section. The tubular interplane struts were cable-braced in the usual manner; the centre-section struts were splayed slightly outwards in front elevation. Care was taken in the design of the wooden plywood-covered fuselage to afford the pilot the best possible view in all strategic directions. The sides tapered gradually both horizontally and vertically from cockpit to tail, the bottom longerons meeting under the leading-edge of the tail-plane. The pilot sat with his eyes just below the level of the top wing; behind him the top decking was high and narrow. Both the tail-plane and the plain elevators were of wood, covered with fabric; the fin resembled that of a Spad, and the rudder had a projecting upper tip and a 'scalloped' trailing-edge. The undercarriage was of the tubular vee type. Twin synchronised Vickers guns were fixed on each side of the fuselage top, and fired through the revolving airscrew.

In November, the aces Baracca, Piccio and Ruffo were invited to Turin to assess the capabilities of the A-1, now named the *'Balilla'* (Hunter). To the disappointment of the engineer Brezzi and all concerned with the design, the machine proved to be unsatisfactory. It had plenty of speed (137·5 m.p.h.) but lacked manœuvrability; possibly the combination of the heavy engine and short wing-span was the cause of the trouble. On the advice of Baracca and his fellow pilots the firm modified the *Balilla*, but it was never suitable for front-line service. The modifications may have included an increase of wing area, for one machine at least had longer wings and two bays of struts.

The improved version of the A-1 was superior only in speed to the standard Italian fighter, the Hanriot HD-1, and was far less agile; it was therefore considered unworthy of a major production order. A limited number of Balillas were constructed during the last year of the war.

In mid-1918 the type was issued to some home defence units, where use could be made of its excellent turn of speed; in particular the A-1 served at S. Nicolò di Lido, Venice. On July 17th, 1918, two machines flew as part of the escort on a mass bombing raid on the Austrian port of Pola, across the Adriatic from Venice. A total of 150 A-1s was constructed.

1.–5. Five views of the Ansaldo A-1 single-seat fighter. Note the painted wing-tips—starboard green, port red, a common Italian aircraft marking, and the relatively short wing-span and large engine, which may have been the cause of the type's lack of manœuvrability.

170

ANSALDO A-1 BALILLA

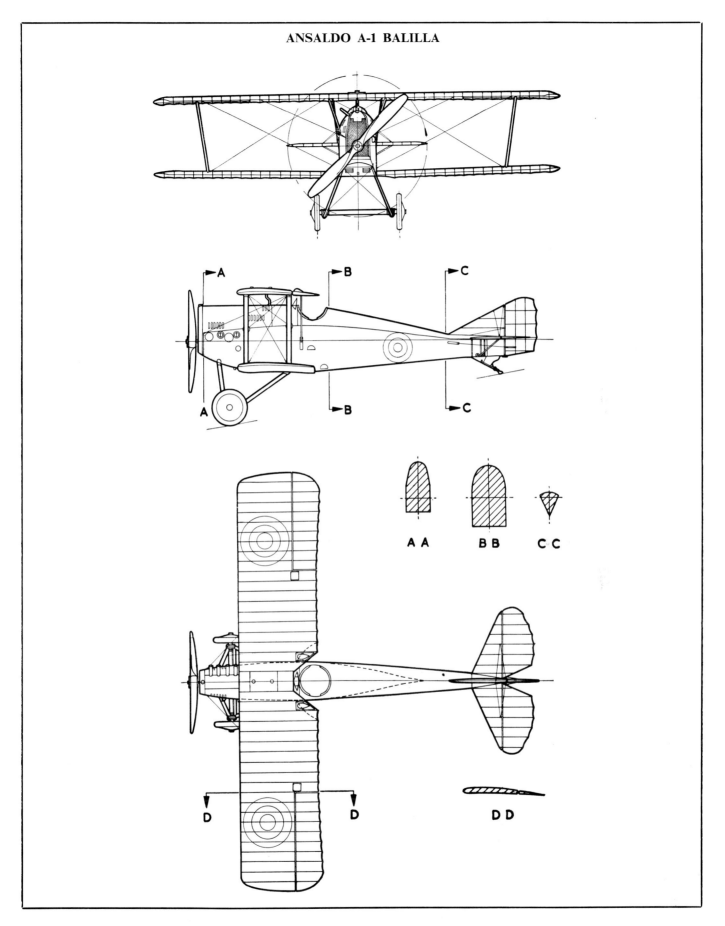

A A   B B   C C

D D

ANSALDO S.V.A.5

The S.V.A. (Savoia Verduzio Ansaldo) aeroplanes were built by the Società Ansaldo of Genoa and Turin. In the summer of 1917 the S.V.A.5 single-seater fighter was designed by Verduzio. Its power unit, the 220 h.p. SPA 6A engine, had a rectangular frontal radiator and six exhaust stubs which discharged on the starboard side of the nose. The wings had the usual wooden spars and ribs, internally wire-braced and covered with fabric; the top wing had no dihedral and carried the ailerons, which were of unequal chord; the lower wing had dihedral and a shorter span. There was no centre section, the cabane struts being of the trestle type. Interplane bracing consisted of tubular struts which formed a Warren truss in front elevation; a system which resembled the bracing arrangements of the ill-fated aeroplanes designed by Professor Knoller for Austro-Hungary No flying or landing wires were necessary.

The plywood-covered fuselage was long in relation to the wing span. Forward of the cockpit it was flat-sided; from cockpit to tail it tapered gradually in both the horizontal and vertical planes, the vertically tapered sides meeting to form a knife-edge to which the tail-skid was attached. The top of the cowling and the fuselage top decking conformed in section to the shape of the pilot's head and shoulders, so that by moving his head slightly he had a good view in most directions. A small tail-plane and plain rounded elevators were fitted; the fin was triangular and the plain rudder had a 'scalloped' trailing-edge. The undercarriage vees were unusually wide. Twin Vickers guns were mounted in the grooves in the top of the cowling, in front of the cockpit; on some machines they were well forward and inaccessible during flight.

The first S.V.A.s were delivered to fighter training schools in autumn 1917. Early in 1918, however, it was decided to use the type as a long-distance strategic reconnaissance aeroplane, and operational flights began in March. The S.V.A.5 was the perfect machine for this role, having plenty of lift to carry heavy fuel loads, and more than enough speed to shake off enemy fighters. The best of the S.V.A. units was the *87a Squadriglia, 'La Serenissima'* —the Venice squadron, whose aircraft carried the Lion of St. Mark painted on their fuselage sides.

Many amazingly long flights were carried out by S.V.A. pilots. On May 21st, 1918, Tenente Locatelli and Ferrarin flew to Friedrichshafen, photographed the airship sheds and returned to their base—a distance of 440 miles.

Locatelli went to Zagreb and back, a distance of 562 miles, on June 24th. The most famous operational trip took place in August, when seven S.V.A.5s escorted a two-seater S.V.A.9 all the way to Vienna, returning unscathed to their point of departure, after a journey of 625 miles. Reconnaissance and bombing raids were also made on Bolzano, Innsbrück and Franzenfeste. All these flights involved dangerous mountain crossings.

Six squadrons and five sub-units were equipped with S.V.A.5s. A seaplane version, the S.V.A. Idro-AM, was supplied to one unit.

After the war, many record-breaking flights were made by S.V.A.s. 1,245 S.V.A.5s and 50 S.V.A. Idro-AMs were built.

1. to 4. Four examples of the highly successful S.V.A. single-seater. The twin synchronised Vickers guns fitted to No. 3 were inaccessible to the pilot during flight. 5. The S.V.A. Idro-AM single-seater seaplane; note the hydrofoils under each float.

ANSALDO S.V.A.5

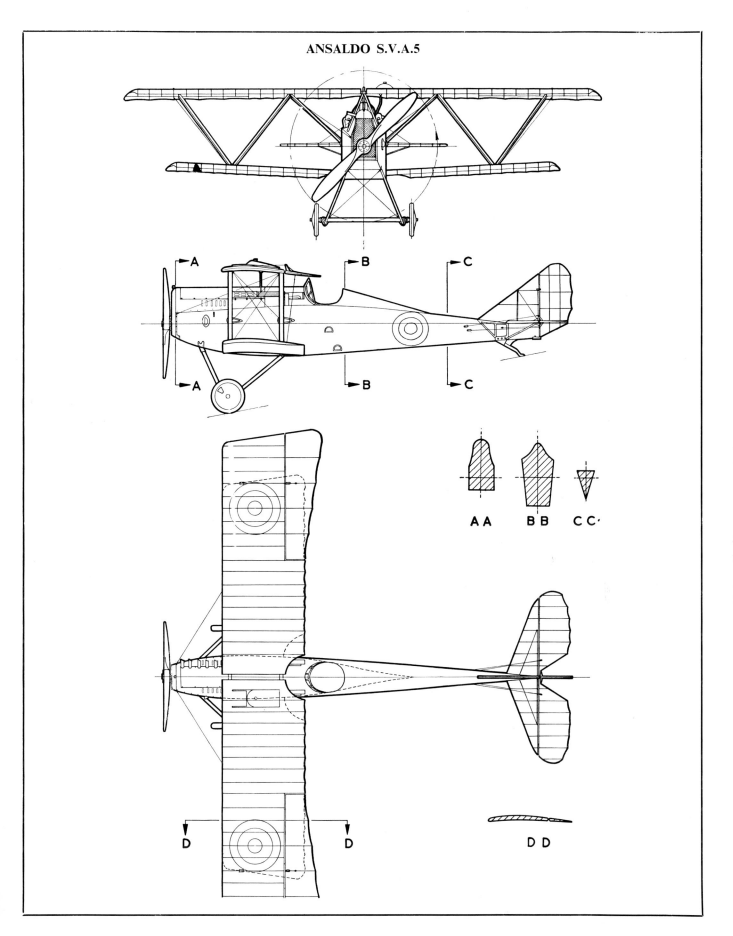

A A   B B   C C'

D D

MACCHI M.5 AND M.7

The Società Anonima Nieuport-Macchi of Varese was a well-known firm of coach-builders which began to manufacture Nieuport monoplanes under licence in 1912. Other types produced in the pre-war years were the Macchi Parasol monoplane and a version of the Maurice Farman pusher biplane. After Italy's entry into the war in 1915, however, the company returned to the building of Nieuports under licence, and later built the Hanriot HD-1.

Nieuport-Macchi was introduced to flying-boat construction entirely by chance. On the night of May 27th, 1915, the Austro-Hungarian Lohner flying-boat L.40 fell almost intact into Italian hands. So impressed were the Italians by their capture that they commissioned the Nieuport-Macchi concern to produce a copy. The resulting machine, the Macchi L.1, was ordered in quantity, and was followed by improved models, such as the L.2, the L.3, the M.3 and the M.4.

The success of the Austro-Hungarian Brandenburg KDW single-seater fighter flying boat during 1916–17 probably inspired the development of the next Macchi design. The M.5, a small single-seater fighter flying boat which displayed many Nieuport characteristics, appeared during the early months of 1918. Its power unit was the 160 h.p. Isotta-Fraschini V4B engine, mounted directly under the centre line of the top plane; it had a frontal radiator and drove a two-bladed pusher propeller. A starting handle was provided below the radiator. Swept-back wings of wood and fabric construction were fitted. The flat upper wing, like that of the early Nieuport Scouts, was of far greater span and chord than the lower, and carried unequal-chord ailerons. The interplane bracing consisted of typical Nieuport tape-bound vee struts, strengthened by additional vees of steel tubing, inclined outwards at angles of forty-five degrees, which supported the overhanging portions of the top wing. The wooden and the tubular vees were braced together by cables, and the usual flying and landing wires were fitted. Wire-braced tubular struts supported the engine. The rear portion of the shapely wooden hull was of rectangular section tapering to a point under the tail. Small floats were fixed under the lower wings below each wooden interplane vee. The pilot sat below the radiator and was provided with twin machine-guns mounted internally to fire forwards. A faired head-rest was fitted behind the cockpit. A number of tubular steel struts carried the tail-plane; these struts were covered with a plywood casing on the later production machines. The fin and plain rudder, braced by wires, were fixed above the tail-plane.

The M.5 was fully aerobatic and with a top speed of 118 m.p.h. was faster than the opposing Phönix land-based fighters. It was issued to five units, the 260a, 261a, 286a Cardiana, 287a and 288a Squadriglia, and did useful work escorting bombers on raids on the Austro-Hungarian naval bases across the Adriatic.

Towards the end of the war an improved M.5, the M.7, was developed. It had the 250 h.p. Isotta-Fraschini V6 engine, a reduced wing-span and a simplified interplane bracing system. It had the remarkable top speed of 131 m.p.h. 344 M.5s and 3 M.7s were built.

1. Macchi L.3 two-seater; the L-type Macchis were copies of the Austro-Hungarian Lohner boats. 2. and 3. Standard production M.5s. 4. A highly decorated operational M.5. 5. The more powerful M.7, which appeared just before the Armistice.

MACCHI M.5

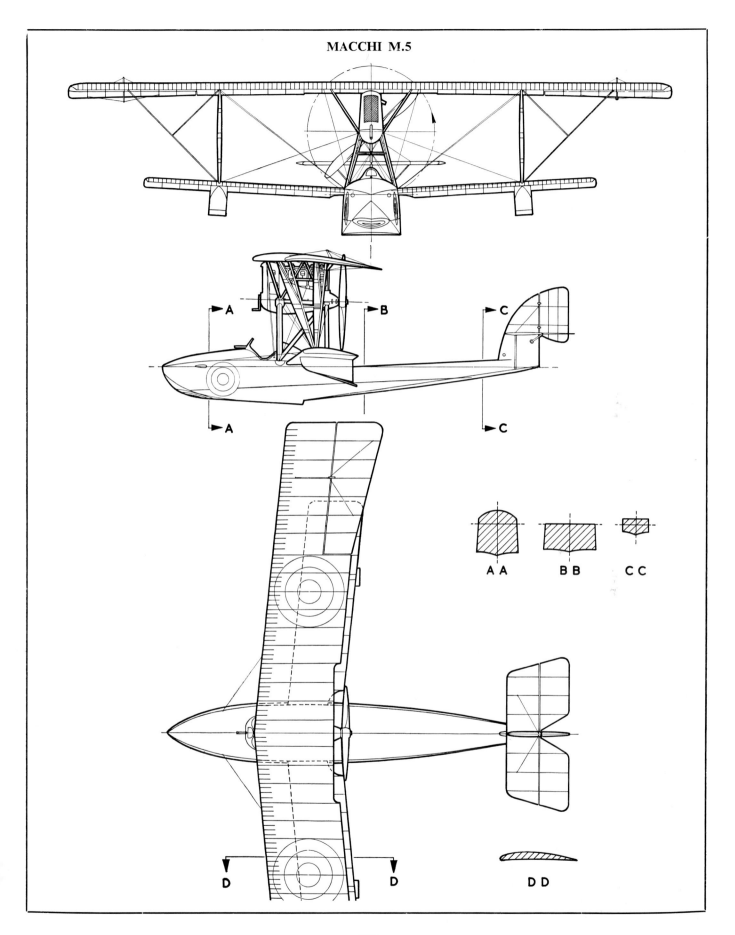

A A   B B   C C

D D

Before the outbreak of the First World War the aeroplane was regarded by senior military ranks as a mere 'substitute for the captive balloon', to use the words of General Bernard, Director of Aeronautics in France. The few enthusiasts who proposed to use armed aeroplanes against airships or ground targets received very little official encouragement.

There is some doubt as to who was the first person to mount a machine-gun on an aeroplane. Among the early experimenters were Euler, the German air pioneer, and Major Brooke-Popham of the Air Battalion, British Royal Engineers, who in 1911 fitted a gun to a Blériot monoplane; he was quickly ordered to remove it!

The first official series of tests appear to have taken place at College Park, Maryland, U.S.A., in April 1912, when a Signal Corps Wright biplane armed with a new air-cooled automatic gun invented by Colonel Isaac Newton Lewis carried out air-to-ground attacks on a white sheet spread on the grass. The new gun did not impress the War Department, which insisted on retaining the standard Benet-Mercié (Hotchkiss) gun. Like other American inventors before him, Lewis left for Europe, and in January 1913 formed a company, 'Armes Automatiques Lewis', at Liège in Belgium. His gun was a new departure in automatic weapons; lighter than its contemporaries, it was fed by detachable forty-seven-round drums, which were convenient to handle and protected the cartridges from dirt and oil.

Similar tests to those carried out in America took place in Belgium in September 1912 and in England in November 1913; on each occasion the Lewis-gunner was Lieutenant Stellingwerf of the Belgian Army.

The first British aeroplane specially designed to carry a machine-gun, the Vickers pusher biplane, made its appearance in 1913. The gunner sat in front of the pilot and operated a belt-fed ·303 inch Maxim gun. The Vickers company had manufactured this gun for the British Government since 1888, so it was the obvious choice; the belt feed, however, was found to interfere with its flexibility. Replacement of the Maxim by the lighter Vickers-Maxim (Vickers) brought no improvement. Meanwhile, the ·303 inch calibre Lewis gun had been tested and accepted by the Royal Flying Corps. It was installed in the Vickers pusher and proved so successful that rather reluctantly the type was ordered by the British Government in July 1914.

Experiments with semi-automatic guns mounted in aeroplanes and a seaplane took place in England late in 1913. Lieutenant Clark-Hall, of the Naval Wing, R.F.C., who initiated the tests, organised a further series of trials in the following year using an aeroplane equipped with a Vickers gun. He believed that 'the function of the machine-gun is not the attack of objects afloat or ashore, but of other aeroplanes'.

In France a number of pushers were armed with the standard army 8 mm. Hotchkiss, which was heavier than the Lewis and had an awkward strip-feed system that was not really suitable for aircraft use.

Top: standard infantry Lewis gun and the Vickers Mk. II Aircraft Gun of 1918. Next: the L.V.G. E-VI and a typical observer's Parabellum gun. Next: Bristol Scouts, with first, an unsynchronised Lewis gun and second, a container of steel darts, released by a lever. Next: the Fokker E-I and an experimental Fokker mock-up, using a 'Spandau'. Lastly: experimental gun mountings on a B.E.2e and on L.V.G. C-1.

AIRCRAFT ARMAMENT 1914-1918

It was fairly easy to fit a forward-firing machine-gun to a pusher aeroplane, and a simple ball-and-socket mounting provided the gunner with a good field of fire. The majority of German machines, however, were of the tractor type, with the airscrew in front; it was perhaps for this reason that the first solution to the problem of firing through a revolving airscrew came from Germany. Franz Schneider, the L.V.G. aircraft designer, who had devised a method of shooting through the hollow airscrew shaft of a tractor aeroplane as early as 1912, patented a practical synchronising system on July 15th, 1913. Others soon followed his example; a simple mechanism was developed in Russia by a Lieutenant Poplavko, who received some support from the authorities. He was more fortunate than the Edwards brothers in England, for their plans were pigeon-holed by the War Office.

Firing trials of a synchronising gear invented by R. Saulnier, of the Morane-Saulnier aircraft firm, took place in 1914. Some of the cartridges of the Hotchkiss gun loaned to him by the French Government 'hung fire' and caused trouble; in order to save time, therefore, he fixed steel plates to the airscrew. These plates deflected any bullets which might otherwise have damaged the blades. Saulnier had to return the gun on the outbreak of hostilities, and the idea was temporarily abandoned.

These developments were almost completely ignored in higher military circles, with the result that when the war began the aeroplanes available to the belligerent Powers were largely unarmed. The main duty of the air services in the early months of the war was that of reconnaissance; it was not long, however, before the first air combats were reported. In the absence of more effective weapons, service pistols, carbines, rifles or *flêchettes* (steel darts) came into use. The more unconventional aviators favoured hand grenades, shotguns, or even grapnels on the end of ropes!

Two German machines were forced down by British aeroplanes on August 25th, 1914, while on October 5th the first confirmed French success was scored by Frantz and Quénault in a Voisin pusher armed with a Hotchkiss gun. For a time the speedy Morane Parasol two-seaters were very effective, although their observers carried only cavalry carbines. Under orders to concentrate on reconnaissance work, the Germans were less aggressive; at this period there was no suitable machine-gun available for use on aircraft, and their chief weapon was a Mauser service rifle.

Towards the end of 1914 Schneider built the L.V.G. E-VI two-seater monoplane, the first aeroplane to be equipped with a synchronised gun for the pilot and a movable gun on a ring mounting for the observer. This very advanced design was not ordered into production, as it deserved to be; the observer's ring mounting, equipped with a 7·92 mm. Parabellum machine-gun, was, however, made a standard fitting on all two-seaters. A light modified Maxim gun, the Parabellum had been developed by Karl Heinemann of the D.W.M. factory. A fretted casing supported the recoil of the barrel, a wooden stock was provided and the ammunition belt was carried on a circular

Top left: British Morane N with deflector plates. Top right: F.E.2b with typical armament. Next: B.E.2c with pilot's Lewis gun on a Strange mounting. Next: synchronised Spandaus on a Pfalz E-IV and on a Fok. E-IV, built for Immelmann. Next: antidotes to the Fokker Monoplane; the Nieuport 11 and the D.H.2, both with forward-firing Lewis guns. Lastly: twin Spandaus on the Albatros D-III and Fokker Triplane.

177

drum. Later in the war a closely fitting barrel casing became standard. The name 'Parabellum', Latin for 'prepare for war', was derived from the classical tag meaning 'if you wish for peace, prepare for war'.

In March 1915 the famous French pre-war pilot, Roland Garros, returned to his unit, *Escadrille M.S.23*, with a Morane-Saulnier N equipped with a fixed forward-firing Hotchkiss gun. Its airscrew was protected by the steel bullet-deflectors invented by Saulnier. Garros shot down a German two-seater on April 1st, 1915, and further successes followed, but on April 19th he came down with engine trouble behind the German lines near Ingelmunster, and did not have time to burn his machine. Perturbed by the discovery of Saulnier's device, the German authorities asked Anthony Fokker to produce a replica. Schneider's patent had been forgotten. Fokker, or perhaps more accurately, his engineers, provided a cam and push-rod mechanism which actuated the gun-trigger from the engine; the rod was hinged so that the pilot could adjust it to control the firing. The aeroplane chosen for the new system was very similar to the Morane, the Fokker M.5K single-seater monoplane; the gun, the Parabellum, mounted on the cowling slightly to starboard. Its wooden stock was retained. A second-rate aeroplane with a rather unreliable armament, the E-I, as it was designated, had an effect on aerial warfare far beyond its merits.

The main reason for this was the feebleness of the Allied opposition. Too stable to manœuvre, the standard British reconnaissance machine, the B.E.2c, was armed with a Lewis gun operated by the observer, but he occupied the front seat, surrounded by struts and bracing wires. In spite of its obvious defects, the type was kept in production, and was still on operations in 1917! The Vickers pusher or 'Gun Bus' had too poor a performance to deal with the Fokker, and the single-seater Bristol Scouts were ill-armed. French reconnaissance types were slow pushers, vulnerable to attack from the 'blind spot' under their tails.

A great variety of makeshift arrangements were made by Allied air crews. Guns were fitted above the wings to fire above the revolving airscrews and slanting forwards and outwards between the wings (the Strange-type mounting). For reasons best known to themselves, Allied armament experts (?) were reluctant to develop a synchronising gear or even to copy that of the Germans. A number of very odd aeroplanes were designed, which it was hoped would do away with the necessity for such a gear; machines in which the observer stood with his head and shoulders through a hole in the top plane to fire his gun, and the 'pulpit' types, with nacelles in front of their tractor airscrews.

Meanwhile the Lewis gun had been considerably modified and lightened; a spade grip had been substituted for the wooden stock, and the radiator enclosing the barrel and gas-cylinder had been removed or replaced by a light aluminium casing. Early in 1916 a double drum containing ninety-seven rounds was introduced. The Hotchkiss gun was no longer in favour in the French air service; it was rapidly being superseded by the Lewis.

On the other side of the lines the Parabellum ·gun

Top left and right: experimental mounting on a B.E.2c.
Top centre: Italian S.A.M.L. biplane with Revelli guns.
Next: synchronised Vickers gun on a Spad S.7. Next: a twin Lewis R.N.A.S. Nieuport 11 and a four-gun B.E.12.
Next: the rearward-firing Lewis on a Martinsyde Elephant, and the Vickers and Lewis on an early 'greenhouse' S.E.5. Lastly: twin guns on a Sopwith Camel and a Pfalz D-III.

ceased to be used as the pilot's weapon. The heavier but more readily available 7·92 mm. 08/15 Maxim gun was modified for aircraft use and became the standard synchronised gun. Its water-jacket, retained to support the recoil of the barrel, was fretted for lightness; some examples had the muzzle attachment and flash eliminator of the infantry model, others were without. As in the case of the Parabellum, the webbing ammunition belt was enclosed to prevent interference by the slipstream. Many of these guns were produced at the arsenal at Spandau, near Berlin, and bore the name 'Spandau', which was mistakenly believed by the Allies to be the official designation of the weapon. Two of these guns were mounted on the later Fokker and Pfalz monoplanes.

During 1916 the Bergmann gun was tried out as an observer's weapon, but it proved less efficient than the Parabellum.

Austro-Hungarian aeroplanes were armed with the belt-fed eight mm. Schwarzlose machine-gun; a bulky, heavy weapon with a slow rate of fire and relatively short range, it operated on the 'spent-case projection' system; the barrel therefore did not recoil and the water-jacket could be entirely removed when used on aircraft. From 1915 the observers of two-seater types were equipped with this gun, fitted on a semicircular mounting. A stripped synchronised version was used on the handful of Fokker monoplanes supplied by Germany; it could only be fired with safety when the engine was running at full revolutions and did not come into general service. The standard forward-firing armament until 1917 was therefore a Schwarzlose mounted above the top plane, enclosed in a streamlined metal casing. In this position it much reduced the performance, and was quite inaccessible during flight.

The 1914 model 6·5 mm. Revelli, manufactured by the Fiat concern, was the first machine-gun adopted by the Italian flying service. Like the Schwarzlose, it operated by the rearward projection of the exploding cartridge, and not by barrel recoil. The infantry model was lightened by the removal of the water-jacket and the use of a barrel with longitudinal ribs. It was not a satisfactory aircraft weapon and was eventually replaced by the Lewis and the Vickers.

In spite of their lack of a synchronising gear, the French and British succeeded in defeating the Fokker monoplane by the early summer of 1916. The credit was due to the superior performance of the Nieuport Scout and the D.H.2 pusher, and not to their armament of a single Lewis gun.

The long-awaited Allied synchronisers now made their appearance in some variety; they were all of the mechanical type; the British Vickers-Challenger, Scarff-Dibovski, Sopwith-Kauper, Ross and Arsiad,* and the French Alkan. They were intended for use with a single ·303 inch Vickers machine-gun. The latter was a lighter, modified version of the Maxim, and as a fixed weapon had several advantages over the Lewis; it was more easily synchronised, had a higher rate of fire, and being belt-fed did not require reloading after every ninety-seven rounds. The water-jacket

* Designed by Major Bettington of the Aeroplane Repair Section, No. 1 Aircraft Depot.

Top: Spad S.13. Next: forward-mounted Schwarzlose on Austrian-Aviatik D-I and an Albatros D-V with captured Villa Perosa. Next: Schwarzlose guns on a Phönix D-I and a Bristol F2A with experimental mounting. Next: Wendell Rogers of Canada in his Nieuport, Bailleul, December 1917, and a Bristol F2B with standard Scarff mounting. Bottom: the pilot's gun on firstly, a Morane P and secondly, a Hansa-Brandenburg W.29.

179

of the basic model was replaced by a light louvred casing, which allowed air to circulate and supported the barrel recoil. It was not entirely trouble-free at first; the rate of fire with the mechanical gears was very slow with the engine throttled back, and it was not unusual to have a 'double feed' caused by the expended end of the webbing belt passing under the gun and re-entering the breech.

More serious was the extreme shortage of the new gears and their lack of uniformity.

Allied defensive armament was much improved by the introduction of the Scarff No. 2 observer's ring mounting, the invention of Warrant Officer F. W. Scarff of the Air Department of the British Admiralty. It replaced the early pillar-and-socket and Nieuport ring mountings. The Scarff ring came into general service with the Allies, and it is a measure of its efficiency that it continued to be used until the mid-1930s.

An improved sliding-rail mounting for wing-mounted Lewis guns was devised by Sergeant Foster of No. 11 Squadron, R.F.C. It enabled the gun to be pulled down so that its breech was conveniently in front of the pilot, thus facilitating reloading and the clearing of stoppages.

In the autumn of 1916 Germany reorganised its fighter branch and brought out the excellent Albatros single-seater, armed with twin machine-guns. The new *Jagdstaffeln* now had the advantage in performance and fire-power. So ill had the Allies understood the importance of armament that they had no available aeroplanes armed with twin guns, and only a handful with a single synchronised gun. Most of the single-seaters with which they had to meet the German challenge were already obsolete, their only weapon a single Lewis. In spite of every effort the command of the air passed for a second time to Germany, and casualties among Allied air crews increased alarmingly. This disastrous situation was not retrieved until May 1917, when new types began to reach the front.

During 1916 a novel type of synchroniser was developed in England by George Constantinesco, a Roumanian designer of rock drills, and Major G. C. Colley. The new system, destined to supersede the earlier British mechanical gears, was of the hydraulic type, the firing impulse being transmitted by oil pressure on a plunger. It did away with the complicated linkage of the mechanical types, and could be readily adapted to every kind of aeroplane. The first machines fitted with it, the D.H.4s of No. 55 Squadron, R.F.C., arrived in France in March 1917, and after some 'teething trouble' the C.C. gear, as it was called, proved superior to all others.

About this time the Fokker gear was redesigned; the drive linkage from the engine, which had required frequent inspection, was abandoned, and the guns were now driven from the camshaft and controlled by a clutch operated by the pilot.

Not until July 1917 did an Allied twin-gun fighter fly over the battlefields. It was the redoubtable Sopwith Camel, in terms of aircraft destroyed the most successful single-seater of the First World War. It had a greater fire-power than its rival, the S.E.5a, which carried a single Vickers and a wing-mounted Lewis. First of the French

Top: twin Parabellum guns. Next: twin Lewis guns, and the unusual gun mountings on the Nieuport 28. Next, left: Avro 504K night fighter with Lewis on Foster-mounting. Right, top: Sopwith Camel. Right, bottom: ground attack 1918—Halberstadt CL-II observer, with improved Parabellum gun, telescopic sight, stick grenades and signal cartridges. Lastly: Pfalz Dr.-I and the first standard multi-gun fighter, the Dolphin.

twin-gun types was the Spad 13, introduced in August 1917. The change-over to double armament was by no means rapid, for British Nieuports with a single wing-mounted Lewis gun continued to serve until early in 1918.

The problem of what to do with the expended portion of webbing machine-gun belts was solved in 1917 by the adoption of the Prideaux disintegrating link. The belt was made up of interlocking metal links, which fell away from the machine as the gun fired. The Aldis gas-filled sight became standard on British aeroplanes in the autumn of the same year; an excellent device against aerial targets, it was liable to mislead pilots on air-to-ground firing duty—they failed to pull out in time.

On both sides the standard aircraft guns, Vickers, Lewis, Spandau, Parabellum and Schwarzlose, underwent frequent modification to increase their rate of fire. A typical development was the muzzle attachment fitted to the Lewis, which speeded up the action. Twin Lewis guns became standard on Allied two-seaters, while the first multi-gun fighter, the Sopwith Dolphin, with two Vickers and two Lewis guns, came into service.

In Italy a dual-mounted aircraft machine-gun, the 9 mm. Villa Perosa, invented by Major Revelli, was introduced. It had the high rate of fire of 3,000 rounds per minute (1,500 per gun) but lacked striking power. Large quantities of this weapon fell into German and Austro-Hungarian hands after the Caporetto disaster of October 1917, and one was experimentally fitted on an Albatros D-V.

Austro-Hungarian single-seaters were by now equipped with twin synchronised Schwarzlose guns. These were either carried on each side of the engine under the cowling, where they were warm but inaccessible to the pilot, or in front of the cockpit, their barrels extended by tubes on each side of the engine, to avoid ignition of petrol fumes. Hollow cone-shaped flash eliminators were often fitted to the forward-mounted weapons.

Production of the ·30 inch Marlin gas-operated aircraft gun was carried on in the United States. A modification of the Colt-Browning, it was intended to replace the Vickers gun then in general use on American machines in France. Aircraft built in the U.S.A., notably the D.H.4, were equipped with these guns; in France their cloth feed belts gave a good deal of trouble in wet weather. At the Armistice, twenty-two squadrons of the A.E.F. were 'partially or fully equipped with Marlin guns, having both hydraulic and mechanised synchronised gears'—to quote an official U.S. report.

The urgent need to deal with Zeppelin and Gotha night-bombing raids spurred on the British to develop the night fighter, and many Home Defence units were formed. From the early days when bombs, grenades, Ranken explosive darts and even duck guns firing chain shot were carried aloft, the armament of the night fighter rapidly improved in efficiency. Twin Vickers guns were surprisingly found to be unsatisfactory, for the glare from their muzzles tended to blind the pilot; it was also dangerous to fire explosive and incendiary bullets through the airscrew. It became usual to carry twin Lewis guns on a double Foster mounting; they could be fired upwards into the undersides

Top: the nose of Captain E. Rickenbacker's Spad S.13; note the slotted bar by which the Vickers guns could be adjusted; and the prototype 2F.1 Camel N.5. Next: twin Spandaus on a Roland D-VIb. Next: the pilot's synchronised Schwarzlose on the experimental Fokker M.16 two-seater, and the downward-firing guns on the T.F.1 Camel. Lastly: Rickenbacker's Nieuport 28, showing Vickers guns offset to port.

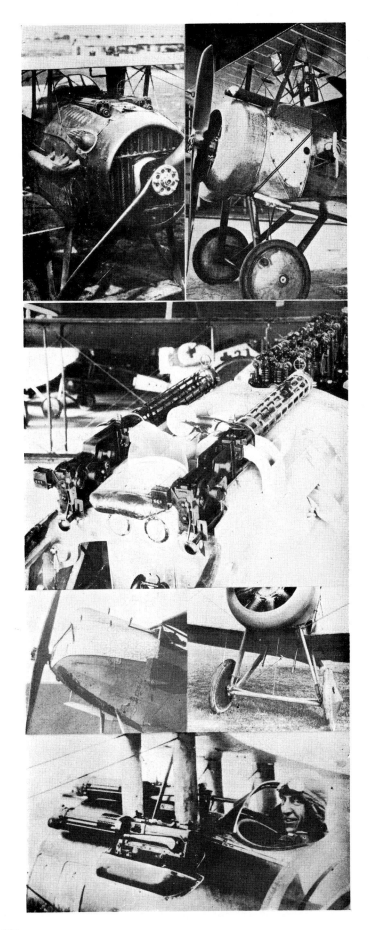

of enemy bombers. Special luminous gun-sights were invented for Home Defence work.

Several experimental aircraft guns were produced in the later stages of the war. The German Gast twin aircraft gun was ingeniously arranged so that the recoil of one barrel reloaded, fired, extracted and ejected the rounds of the other barrel. Efforts were made to introduce this weapon, but only a few saw active service. A new French gun, the Darne, was ordered in large quantities for use in the proposed Allied offensive of Spring 1919; the coming of the Armistice relegated the gun to comparative obscurity. Other aircraft guns which were not used operationally were the French-designed Berthier, forerunner of the Vickers gas-operated gun of the Second World War, the Italian S.I.A. (Socièta Italiana Ansaldo), designed by Giovanni Agnelli, and the American Browning, destined to become famous some twenty years later.

The motor gun, a light multi-barrelled weapon expected to have a high rate of fire, was the subject of a circular directed to aircraft and engine designers by Major Siegert, the Inspector of German Flying Troops, in August 1916. As a result of this circular several types were produced, such as the Siemens, Fokker, Autogen, Szakatz-Gotha and the Austrian Gebauer; luckily for the Allies none of these came into regular use. The Siemens gun was actually fitted to a fighter and shot down an Allied aeroplane. Most of these motor guns bore a resemblance to the nineteenth-century Gatling gun, and had a large number of barrels mounted in a drum-like rotor, which was driven round at high speed by the engine. The rotor was set in motion before opening fire, in order to obtain the maximum rate of fire; in one case this was estimated as being in the region of 7,200 rounds per minute!

In the early days of the war ordinary ball ammunition was found to be quite effective. The tracer bullet, which produced a red bead of light, thereby facilitating sighting, was developed in England before the war, and by 1916 had become standard equipment on both sides of the lines. For use against airships and balloons the incendiary bullet was invented; a common type* contained eight grains of phosphorus in its nose, which was gradually ejected through a side hole as the bullet rotated in flight. Intended for the same purpose, the explosive and explosive-incendiary was eventually used against all kinds of targets, in spite of official discouragement on humanitarian grounds. In the last year of the war a mixture of ammunition was carried, a typical sequence being three ball, one tracer, one armour-piercing and one incendiary, repeated to the end of the belt. In 1918 a 11 mm. bullet fired from a special Vickers gun was introduced by the French for balloon-attack duty. It was used by French and Belgian pilots, in particular by the famous Coppens. Nine hundred 11 mm. Vickers guns were built in the United States, but they were too late for the war.

An aircraft rocket also designed for anti-balloon work invented by Lieutenant Y. P. G. Le Prieur of the French Naval Air Service came into service in 1916. Four of these

* The British Buckingham.

Top: prototype 2F.1 Camel, with rockets. Next: F.E.2b with Vickers 1-pdr. gun, and Spad S.13 with experimental rocket-tubes. Next: the Hispano-Suiza 'moteur-canon'. Next: twin U.S. pattern Lewis guns on a Scarff mounting; the barrels have muzzle-attachments which increased the rate of fire; and twin Marlin guns on an American Spad S.13. Lastly: a German Spandau and a 1917 model of the American Marlin.

projectiles attached to the interplane struts on each side were ignited simultaneously by an electric switch. Rockets were fitted to a large number of Nieuport Scouts, and occasionally proved very effective. Other types sometimes equipped with rockets were the Sopwith Pup and Camel. At least one Spad carried experimental rocket-tubes. The rocket was rendered obsolete by the development of efficient incendiary ammunition.

As early as 1913 firing trials of large-bore semi-automatic guns mounted in aeroplanes were carried out in England; the instigator of the experiments, as has already been related, was Lieutenant Clark-Hall. The weapons were the Vickers 1½-pounder, the Armstrong-Whitworth 1-pounder, and the C.O.W. (Coventry Ordnance Works) 1-pounder. Tests of a 37 mm. Hotchkiss single-shot gun took place in France in the autumn of the same year. As a consequence of this work a Voisin pusher squadron was formed in 1915 for operations against ground and air targets. The rate of fire was too slow to be effective against aeroplanes, and the machines were very vulnerable to attacks by enemy single-seaters. Two F.E.2b pushers supplied to No. 100 Squadron, R.F.C., in the spring of 1917 carried 1-pounder Vickers pom-pom guns, and they made a number of night attacks on ground targets. C.O.W. guns were experimentally installed on Voisin pushers and on one D.H.4.

From America came the Davis-type recoilless gun, which was fitted to some British flying boats and bombers. The recoil of the gun was offset by the simultaneous discharge of a blank round in the opposite direction.

Acting on a suggestion made by Guynémer, the famous French pilot, the Hispano-Suiza designer Marc Birkigt modified a 37 mm. Puteaux shell gun so that it could be loaded with one hand in flight. He placed it between the cylinder blocks of a 220 h.p. geared Hispano-Suiza engine, so that it could fire through the hollow airscrew shaft. The 'moteur-canon' was installed in two specially designed aeroplanes, the Spad 12 and 14. Guynémer and Fonck shot down a number of German machines with their shell-guns, but the muzzle velocity was much too low, the vibration was excessive, and the single-shot rate of fire demanded too high a standard of marksmanship. In Britain the experimental Beardmore W.B.V single-seater was built to take a 37 mm. Puteaux gun. It was most unpopular with pilots and the design was abandoned.

An interesting weapon was devised in 1918, probably by Birkigt. It took the form of a short-barrelled cannon, arranged to fire through the airscrew hub. It was loaded with a cartridge containing thirty-two spherical bullets—a large version of the ordinary shotgun cartridge. Fired at close range, the bullets were certain to destroy an enemy aeroplane. The war finished, however, before the gun could be issued to the squadrons.

Two 20 mm. aircraft guns were developed in Germany, the Becker and the Szakatz. Some examples of the former weapon, installed in various seaplanes and twin-engined aeroplanes, were used on operations. The 20 mm. Hispano gun which equipped British aeroplanes in 1939–1945 was in fact a modified Becker.

Top: searchlight fitted to the experimental Spad S.11 Cn-2, and the twin guns on a Junkers CL-I. Next: experimental mountings on Camel and 1½-Strutter night-fighters. Next: engine and guns, Fokker D-VII. Next: B.E.12b, showing Lewis gun with night-sight (twin electric torches fixed to the barrel.) Lastly: battery of Lewis guns on a B.E.2c in Mesopotamia, and an unusual armament on a night-fighter Camel.

AIRFRAMES

Traditionally, fighter aircraft have been embellished to a greater degree than any other class of aircraft, and it is unlikely that the fighter aircraft colour schemes of the 1914–1918 war will ever be surpassed in brightness and variety. Yet, when that war commenced, only one of the major Powers had envisaged that even such primary markings as national insignia would be necessary. Thus, in the main, aircraft went into their first major war in nondescript varnished fabric, relieved only by a service serial number that served as a mere accounting tag.

Pre-1914, France had led the world both in aeronautics and military aircraft markings. National insignia for aircraft also originated in France. As early as July 26th, 1912, the *Inspection Permanente de l'Aéronautique* decreed that a cockade of tricolour roundels, as an indication of national identity, should be marked under the wings and on the fuselage sides of all military aircraft. The latter position was, however, later changed to the upper surfaces of the wings. The original instruction detailed the proportions and dimensions as 100 : 70 : 40 in centimetres for the outside diameters of red, white and blue respectively.

Not until the autumn of 1914, during the early days of the Great War, when her aircraft were fired upon from the ground by friend and foe alike, did Britain realise the need for an indication of identity and so paint the Union Jack on aircraft. When this marking proved to be indistinguishable from the German cross at moderate heights, the French roundel form was adopted by the Royal Flying Corps, but with the colours reversed. For an interim period, aircraft of the Royal Naval Air Service used a red ring only, but from mid-1915 onwards the now well-known roundel was adopted throughout the British services. Other nations followed suit: Italy, Belgium, Russia, and later the United States for aircraft of the American Expeditionary Force, all adopted a variation of the roundel theme.

The Germans were, of course, loth to follow a Gallic lead, and their adopted marking, a cross, was symbolically the antithesis of the Allied roundels. Not that their choice was conditioned by any such view. The form of cross used was the *Cross Patée*, colloquially known as the 'Iron Cross', derived from the symbol of the old Teutonic Knights; furthermore, it formed part of the German naval ensign and had already appeared on that navy's Zeppelins. Usually it was outlined in white or marked on a white field; this was not merely to contrast the marking, for the white formed an integral part in the display of Prussian colours—black and white. An exception, effective from an order dated in October 1916, was made for night-flying aircraft, where no white markings were permitted.

Whereas other nations adopted the system of striping rudders in national colours, German aircraft displayed the *Cross Patée* on the rudder, or overlapping fin and rudder. Presented in slightly varying forms, it remained essentially a *Cross Patée* until late March 1918 when orders· were issued that it would be superseded by a simple, straight-

National Marking Characteristics. Union Jacks (Bristol Scout 'C' 3015) gave way to roundels and rudder stripes, but the R.N.A.S. had a transitional stage when a red ring (Dyott Experimental Fighter 1598, 50 h.p. Gnôme) was used. German insignia changed from an 'Iron' (Pfalz D-III) to a Greek (Albatros D-II bottom) cross, being outlined heavily (Albatros D-II marked '8') where necessary. ZAK3 meant Zentrale Abnahme Kommission.

edged Greek Cross, to be fully effected by April 15th, 1918. Simple as this new marking was, it was complicated by order and counter-order. On May 31st, 1918, orders were issued that the vertical bar on fuselage sides, and the bars marked from leading to trailing edges of the wings, would be longer than the crossing-bar by one-fifth. This order was rescinded on June 25th, 1918. Unimportant as these minor details may seem, they assist in the dating of photographs, and the facts should settle as well as show the grounds for the persistent argument that the German version of the Greek Cross had arms of unequal length—it had, for a brief period only.

Aircraft of the Austro-Hungarian Empire were at first marked with their national colours in stripes of red, white and red on wing-tips and rudders, but since form is more obvious than colour at a distance, these were often confused with the similar Italian striping in red, white and green. By late 1915 the *Cross Patée* had been generally adopted, but whereas on army aircraft it replaced striping, on naval aircraft it supplemented striping. Positioning of the insignia differed somewhat from German usage, in that the wing crosses were marked farther inboard and that they did not appear on the fuselage sides after early 1917.

It was not only in devising an effectual national emblem that France led in markings; their comprehensive system of registration also originated by an instruction in July 1912. Therein it was specified that each aircraft would bear an indication of the constructor, by a significant letter. These were detailed: A—Antoinette, BL—Blériot, BO—Borel, BR—Breguet, C—Caudron, etc. The letters in 30 cm. characters were to be followed by manufacturers' serial numbers in 15 cm. figures, and to appear on each side of the rudder, or on the outboard sides of twin rudders. Thus, the well-known 'N' and 'S' on Nieuports and Spads was no mere whim of the firms concerned, but a service directive. The system remains similar today.

Britain first introduced a standard serialling system a few months later, in November 1912. It was a simple numerical series with blocks of numbers reserved for R.F.C. and R.N.A.S. aircraft. After 10,000 was reached, the series started again with an alphabetical prefix. The system, restricted to a five-character letter/figure combination, continues, and by 1960 reached up to about XP500.

Germany used a far more revealing system based on the class of aircraft and the number of that class ordered in each year. As a typical example, the captured Fokker D-VII displayed at Biggin Hill early in 1919 can be quoted. This machine was numbered Fok D-VII (Alb) 6786/18 which indicated that it was Fokker's seventh design in the 'D' (single-seater fighter) class, and that it was the 6,786th machine in the 'D' class to be ordered in 1918. The '(Alb)' indicated that it had been built under sub-contract by the Albatros works.

In spite of exhaustive research, so far the serial allocations for French and German aircraft have never been traced, and there has been insufficient material to enable a comprehensive compilation. A more complete record of

A Cavalcade of Camels. Experiments were made to disrupt by optical illusions, the sighting point between the roundels that normally located the most vulnerable point of all—the pilot. However, the standard form as shown by the crashed Camel remained. In the U.K. training aircraft such as the two-seater Camel bore serials under the wings, and sometimes instructors embellished their aircraft to the degree shown in the bottom photograph.

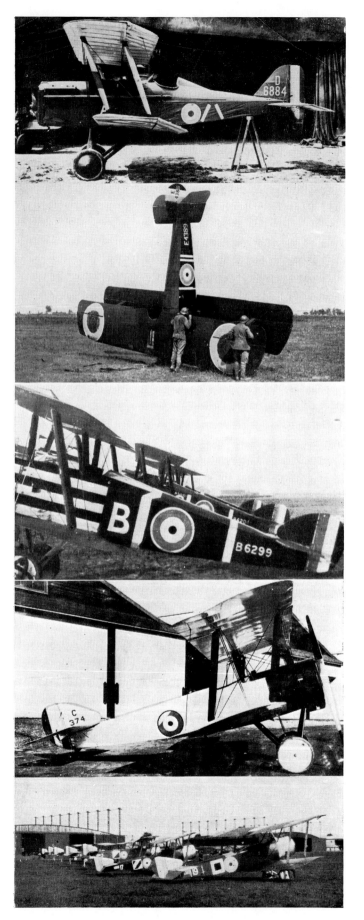

R.F.C./R.N.A.S./R.A.F. serials 1912–1918 has been compiled privately and much of the information appears in *British Aeroplanes 1914–1918* by J. M. Bruce, in *Aircraft Camouflage and Markings 1907–1954* of the 'Harborough' series and other works. But so far, the details of the French fighter and scouting aircraft supplied to Britain have never before been published and they are therefore listed here.

The R.N.A.S. used the following French fighter/scout types: 5 Deperdussin monoplanes, 885 (impressed) and 1376–1379; 15 Breguet de Chasse, 1390–1394, 3209–3213 and 3883–3887; 25 Morane Parasols, 3239–3263; 49 Nieuport 10s, 3163–3186, 3920–3931 and 3962–3974; 106 Nieuport 12s, 8510–8515, 8524–8529, 8708–8713, 8726–8744, 8902–8920, and 9201–9250 built by Beardmore's of which 9213–9232 went to R.F.C.; 9 Nieuport 17s, 8516–8517 and 8745–8751; 23 Nieuport Scouts, 3956–3958 and 3975–3994; 50 Nieuport 24bis, N5860–5909; 2 Nieuport Triplanes, N521 to R.F.C. and N522; 2 Spad S.7s as pattern for British production, 9611–9612.

R.F.C. serial allocations for French fighter/scout aircraft were: 6 Deperdussin monoplanes, 280, 419–421 and 436–437; 40 Nieuport 12s, A3270–3275, A3287–3294 and A5183–5202 ex-R.N.A.S. Additionally, about 1,000 aircraft, mainly fighters, were purchased by G.H.Q., B.E.F., for the R.F.C. in the field and were serialled within blocks of numbers allocated as follows: 5080–5200, A116–315, A6601–6800, B1497–1700, B3451–3650 and B6371–7130. Individual examples are: 5081 Morane Parasol, 5200 Morane M.S.7 biplane, both of No. 3 Squadron, A201 and A211 Nieuport types 17 and 16 respectively of No. 60 Squadron, A6635–6638 Morane Parasols of No. 3 Squadron, B1600 Nieuport 17 of No. 60 Squadron, B3506 Spad S.7 (ex-French No. S1786) and B6737 Spad S.7 of No. 23 Squadron.

Apart from national insignia and registration numbers, aircraft in the first two years of the war were marked with little else; the standard finishing scheme being clear doped fabric. It was the 'Fokker menace' of 1915–1916 that first caused a more colourful appearance, but it was for purely functional purposes. This was the painting of the cowlings of Morane type 'N' monoplanes a bright red in order that they might be distinguished from the Fokker E-type monoplanes of similar configuration. Both the French and the British in early 1916 treated their Moranes in this way, and included the cabane, undercarriage, and wheel covers when fitted, in the coloured area. Examples in British service were A166 with No. 3 Squadron and A122, A171, A176–177 and A186 with No. 60 Squadron. Later that year, aircraft camouflage was introduced generally by all the belligerents, and from then onwards there were the conflicting requirements of bright colours for ease of identification and drab colours for concealment.

Britain adopted a khaki-green colour scheme not only as a camouflage, but because the pigments had proved by experiment to be effectual in excluding the harmful effects of the actinic rays of the sun on the fabric. France approached the problem of concealment in two ways;

Esprit de Corps. *British squadron and unit markings were in general simple and neat in character. Examples from top to bottom are: an S.E.5A of No. 32 Squadron R.F.C., a Camel of No. 209 Squadron R.A.F. (with the white of the roundels screened), Camels of No. 10 (Naval) Squadron R.N.A.S., an immaculate Pup of the Central Flying School and Sopwith 1½ Strutters of the 3rd Naval Wing, Royal Naval Air Service.*

firstly by using a standard two-colour disruptive pattern that proved to be not dissimilar in shade and pattern to modern practice; and an overall aluminium doping, which, pleasing as it was in appearance, was effective for concealment only for high-altitude patrols. German aircraft were given various dappled two-colour schemes; shades of dark green and lilac were officially recommended by German Air Service Headquarters on April 12th, 1917, in a signal to units at the front, following attacks by German airmen on their own aircraft which had been marked in brown. Later printed fabrics were introduced.

It was also in that mid-war year of 1916 that unit markings were generally adopted. In the R.F.C. reconnaissance squadrons were the first to display such markings, using simple geometrical shapes, or bands marked round the fuselage. The British fighters at that time, the Vickers F.B.5, D.H.2, F.E.2b and F.E.8, were all pusher types, allowing little lateral area for the display of markings, but practically all squadrons used a system of letters or figures to identify individual machines. Under the plea of the expediency of recognising individual aircraft of a unit in the air, some squadrons ventured brighter schemes than others. One D.H.2 squadron devised an unusual scheme. Each of the three flights was allotted a colour with which they painted the outer struts and the wheel covers of their six D.H.2s. Within each flight the aircraft were numbered 1 to 6, the figure appearing in the flight colour on the top surface of the upper wing and on the sides of the nacelle. Additionally, the same number of white bands would be marked around the coloured struts. An example was D.H.2 5967 which was No. 4 of 'A' (red) Flight. Later, when Pups and then S.E.5s and Camels came on the scene, the simple shapes of the corps squadrons were generally adopted.

The French and Italian air services devised far more elaborate emblems for their units, and moreover, they were officially recorded devices, and they also set the style for the unit markings used by the American Expeditionary Force. Russia, too, used pictorial emblems, presented in a simple but effective way. For example, No. 3 squadron presented in silhouette form the head of an American Indian with bared teeth, No. 5 Squadron showed an eagle's head and No. 8 Squadron used the ace of hearts. If these markings of the Allies appear to show an imagination that Britain lacked, it should be remembered that simple devices are equally, if not more, functional, and that whereas British aircraft displayed roundels on the fuselage sides, Allied aircraft did not.

The unit schemes of the German *Jagdstaffeln* cannot be considered apart from the bright-coloured overall schemes that 1917 brought. Between the end of 1916 and the 'Bloody April' of 1917 when the R.F.C. suffered such heavy casualties, there was report after report by British pilots, drawing attention to German aircraft bearing mixed colour camouflage schemes or flaunting gay, even bizarre, colour schemes. It was then novel, contrasting with the British schemes of nondescript clear doping which had given way to drab khaki-green.

On February 2nd, 1917, Captain Neale of No. 16 Squadron reported that a red Halberstadt had dived on his

Teutonic Trends. Macabre markings were a feature of some German aircraft and Albatros biplanes (including, second down, the aircraft in which Prince Frederich of Prussia was shot down) show variations on a skull and crossbones theme. Initial letters were a common feature and 'T' here is for Karl Thom (27 victories), in Fokker D-VII (O.A.W.) 2052/18. Some Jasta allowed each pilot an individual scheme, with the result seen at bottom.

187

B.E.2c No. 4592, and who can dispute that this was Manfred von Richthofen himself, making for once an unsuccessful attack. His red Albatros D-III was already known and now it appeared that when he changed his mount, as indeed he did at that time, he kept the colour.

On March 16th, 1917, two officers of No. 43 Squadron in 1½-Strutter A967 were reporting three red Halberstadts together. Richthofen had extended the red colour scheme to his *Jasta 11*, with the reservation that his machine alone would be all-red, while each of the others would have a distinguishing anomaly. Other *Jagdstaffeln* noted the change, and some were influenced into adopting colour schemes, although, of course, red would have been a presumption. It is not suggested that von Richthofen was the first of the German fighter pilots to display bright colours on his aircraft, for Boelcke before him used a blue Halberstadt, but there is no doubt that the example of Richthofen and *Jasta 11* had a profound effect on other German units, who, noting the trend, followed suit.

In the riot of colour that followed, some particular characteristics could be observed: *Jasta 23, 32, 34, 35, 66* and *76*, being Bavarian units, were predominantly in their national colours of blue and white, while *Jasta 21* bore the green and white of Saxony and *Jasta 63* favoured the black and red of Württemberg.

Of German individual markings, these were so varied that no general rule can be expressed, except to remark that the whims of the pilots were indulged to a degree, which illustrations here bear witness, greater than in any other air service. In the R.F.C. it was only at home establishments that bright finishes were attempted, and even then it was regarded by some commanding officers as tantamount to defacing Government property. Some quite original individual markings were used by Russian pilots.

Almost as colourful as the unofficial individual finishing schemes were the officially issued printed fabric that came into general use in 1917 for camouflage purposes on German aircraft. The first mention of this fabric appears in a German order of October 27th, 1916, which called for a return of existing stocks of fabric, pending issue of new fabric. By April 1917 sufficient stocks had accumulated at the Augsburg Cotton Factory to allow a general issue of two types. In theory, the fabric with the lighter shades was for under surfaces and the darker shades for upper surfaces, but this was not always followed in practice, because it was normal to stretch the one piece of fabric over top and bottom surfaces wherever possible. As the final operation, the application of a lacquer produced by the firm of Coln was specified to ensure a non-reflecting matt finish. Struts and all external components, according to official instructions, were to be painted in shades corresponding to the fabric.

When first introduced, the printed fabrics were even used on the plywood-covered fuselages of Pfalz and Albatros types, but this was later stopped as Germany was short of materials. By October 1918 there were even orders about conserving paint, and plywood fuselages, which were weather-proofed by the constructing firm, had to be left unpainted. The wheel had turned full circle.

French Fighter Fashions. The French had a system of escadrille markings of which the stork of N.3 and the greyhound of SPA.81 is typical. Confusing this issue, however, are individual markings and three examples on Nieuports are illustrated. Aircraft used by the A.E.F. for training in France had a formal finish but some instructors ventured decorative schemes such as the fish-scaled Nieuport at the bottom, right.

ENGINES

The cost of a Sopwith Camel airframe was £874 10s. and the cost of a 130 h.p. Clerget engine to power it, £907 10s. That the power unit often cost more than the airframe is not always recognised, and it is evident from books and articles concerning 1914–1918 aircraft, that whereas pains are taken, in general, to ensure correct airframe designations, no such attempt is made to correctly classify aircraft engines. The key to the correct designations is in the marking of the engines and is associated with the engine serial number which appears on a nameplate and/or is stamped on the cylinder block. These markings provide a study in themselves.

In British service 1914–1918 each aircraft engine for the forces bore two serial numbers side by side; one a works serial number and the other an official number prefixed 'W.D.' for 'War Department'. Since W.D. numbers were allotted when contracts were placed, the two series ran consecutively for each production batch. To give an example: Britain's leading ace, Major E. Mannock, V.C., D.S.O., M.C., who was lost flying S.E.5a E1295 powered with Wolseley Viper No. 2603/W.D.33703, was last seen by Second Lieutenant D. C. Inglis in S.E.5a E1294 fitted with a similar engine No. 2646/W.D.33746. From a further example of two Beardmore engines, No. 691/W.D. 7051 (installed in F.E. 2b 6954 of No. 18 Squadron) and No. 757/W.D. 7117 (installed in F.E.2b 5229 of No. 22 Squadron), it is evident that since 757−691=7117−7051, there were engines of the same type with the intermediate numbers 692/W.D. 7052, 693/W.D. 7053 *et seq*, and the same with the S.E.5a engines.

The first production F.E.2d, A1, was powered with Rolls-Royce engine No. 1/250/7/W.D. 6149. Under the revealing numbering system of that famous firm, the numbers indicate that it is the seventh production 250 h.p. Rolls-Royce Mk. 1. F.E.2d A6446 recorded with engine No. 2/275/55/W.D. 13955 reveals, apparently for the first time, for nowhere else does it appear to be mentioned, that F.E.2ds had 275 h.p. Mk. II Rolls-Royce engines. The numbering thus provides the key to Rolls-Royce designations, but a complication is the fact that in 1917 the company introduced their famous 'birds of prey' nomenclature, and all their engine types were redesignated. A conversion table follows:

Pre-November 1917		Actual b.h.p.	Post-November 1917	
250 h.p.	Mk. I	225	Eagle Series	I
250 h.p.	Mk. II	266	Eagle Series	II
250 h.p.	Mk. III	284	Eagle Series	III
250 h.p.	Mk. IV	284	Eagle Series	IV
275 h.p.	Mk. I	322	Eagle Series	V
275 h.p.	Mk. II	322	Eagle Series	VI
275 h.p.	Mk. III	325	Eagle Series	VII
—		350	Eagle Series	VIII
190 h.p.	Mk. I	190	Falcon Series	I
190 h.p.	Mk. II	250	Falcon Series	II
—		280	Falcon Series	III

The Sublime, Ridiculous and Conventional: Italian aircraft show variations from a conventional Hanriot and Nieuport to others with comic characters in place of national insignia! A D.H.5 of No. 68 Squadron A.F.C. displays a leader's streamer (two for a squadron- and one for a flight-commander). An example of a presentation aircraft is represented by a Bristol Fighter bearing the words PRESENTED BY MAHARAJAH BAHADUR SIR RAMESWAR SINGH OF DARBHANGA No. 5.

From the actual brake horse-power listed, it is evident that the designated horse-power was unrealistic and that the system was in need of revision. This change was reflected in the serialling; a late 1918 example bore the number 3/Fal/1651/W.D. 51850 indicating that the 51,850th service engine registered was the 1,651st Falcon Series III engine produced, which, incidentally was fitted to a re-built Bristol Fighter, F6116.

French engines bore constructors numbers, and widely used were Hispano-Suiza engines, particularly in fighter aircraft. The firm was of Spanish origin, but much development work was done in France. Hispano engines were widely built under licence, but each manufacturer had a block of serial numbers allotted as follows:

Hispano-Suiza (Spain)	1– 5,000
Hispano-Suiza (France)*	5,001– 10,000
Aries (France)	10,001– 15,000
Brasier (France)*	15,001– 20,000
La Flaire (France)*	20,001– 25,000
Voisin (France)	25,001– 30,000
De Dion (France)	30,001– 35,000
Fives Lille (France)*	35,001– 40,000
Mayer (France)*	40,001– 50,000
Wolseley (England)	50,001– 60,000
Russian manufacturers	60,001– 70,000
Italian manufacturers	70,001– 80,000
American manufacturers	80,001– 90,000
D.F.P. (France)*	90,001– 95,000
Ballot (France)	95,001–100,000
S.C.A.P. (France)*	100,001–105,000
Hispano-Suiza (France)	105,001–110,000
Chenard (France)*	110,001–115,000
Peugeot (France)*	115,001–120,000
Delaunay Belleville (France)*	120,001–125,000

* These firms supplied engines for British fighters, e.g. Sopwith Dolphin H7245 was fitted with engine 40,369/W.D. 59,035, i.e. 59,035th aircraft engine registered for the British services and the 369th built by Mayer.

German engine markings present the whole system of official aircraft engine designations to which manufacturers were conditioned. Engines were divided into seven classes according to power. Class O=80 h.p., I=100 h.p., II= 110–125 h.p., III=130–195 h.p., IV=200–280 h.p., V= 300+ h.p., VI=500+ h.p. Each engine bore this class number, stamped together with a significant prefix according to the manufacturer as follows: Adler Werke 'Ad', Argus 'As', Basse and Selve 'Bus', Bayerische Motoren Werke 'B.M.W.', Benz 'Bz', Daimler (Mercedes) 'D', Deutsche Motorenbau 'C', Maschinenfabrik 'Man', Maybach 'Mb', Goebel 'Goe', Gasmotoren 'Dz', Motorenfabric Oberürsel 'U', Nationale Automobil Gesellschaft 'Nag', Opel 'O' and Siemens and Halske 'Sh'. Thus, when Benz brought out their famous 150 h.p. engine it was designated Bz III and examples were marked accordingly. When this was followed by a new 185 h.p. model, still in Class III, this became the Bz IIIa, and a subsequent 195 h.p. model, the Bz IIIb.

Formal, Fierce, False and Fanciful: A series of unusual markings: formal Russian roundels on a Spad A2 and Nieuport 17; two fierce-looking canine emblems on Fokker D-VIIs; the striped D-VII used by Josef Mai (30 victories); a captured French Nieuport in German markings—one of several so marked; and the varied forms of markings used within some German units, is shown by two aircraft of a Bavarian Jasta.

190

REBUILT AIRCRAFT

Numbers of British aircraft were built at Aircraft Repair Depots from the salvageable remains of wrecks. These aircraft could be identified as 're-builds' only by their serial numbers which fell outside all the known batches by manufacturers. Fighter aircraft were rebuilt at depots as follows: S.E.5/5a and all Hispano-engined fighters, D.H.5s, Martinsyde types and F.E.2bs at No. 1 (Southern) A.R.D., Farnborough; Pups, Camels, B.E.12s and 1½ Strutters at No. 2 (Northern) A.R.D., Coal Aston; Bristol types, Camels and Snipes at No. 3 (Western) A.R.D., Yate and Vickers types at No. 5 (Eastern) A.R.D., Henlow. (No. 4 A.R.D. at Chelsea did not deal with airframes.) Representative examples are: Bristol Fighters, F5995 (48 Sqn.) and F5997 (80 Sqn.); Camels, F5914 (210 Sqn.) and F6110 (80 Sqn.); Dolphin, F5916 (23 Sqn.); and S.E.5a, F6276 (56 Sqn.).

DETAIL AND COMPONENT MARKINGS

The present interest in aircraft markings now goes beyond a superficial interest in main colour schemes and serialling systems; detail markings now come under the critical eyes of vintage aircraft enthusiasts. These provide studies in themselves. Since mid-1912 it has been a condition that French aircraft should bear an indication of permissible loadings on the rudder and many German aircraft 1914–1918 were similarly marked on the fuselage side near the cockpit. Such rulings did not apply in British service except for certain seaplanes.

Perhaps the most significant detail markings are those which provide an indication of the constructor. This will be seen to be of considerable import when it is appreciated that the vast majority of Sopwith Camels, for example, were built by some ten firms other than Sopwith. Some British firms like Clayton and Shuttleworth and Grahame White stencilled the firm's name and location, in nameplate style, on the fuselage sides of their products, but in mid-1917 instructions were given to R.F.C. units in the field that indication of the constructing firm should be painted out. Indications of construction were invariably given in the French airframe serialling system and often indications of both designing and sub-contracting firms were included in the German serialling. Albatros aircraft usually bore a painted trademark on the top of the rudder and A.E.G. machines the firm's initials marked in a black rectangle.

An interesting facet of detail marking is the many and varied transfers that may be found placed on wooden components, with a veneer, usually of copal varnish, to provide protection. It was in fact usual for British airframe constructors to place their trade mark, by transfer sheet, on the broad outward facing side of wing struts.

Airscrews were normally the product of specialist firms, although some airframe manufacturers produced their own. It was usual for each blade to be marked centrally with a trade emblem, transfers being commonly used. These were in considerable variety, for although there were only two firms in Britain producing propellers in 1914, there were sixty-eight firms by 1918; in Germany there were twenty firms producing propellers by that year.

Further Variations: A striped Albatros of Jasta Boelcke *and the popular 'wound ribbon' marking on Albatros D-Va (O.A.W.) 6553/17; a patriotic marking of the Bavarian Lion chasing the Gallic cock and egotistic markings from a personal initial to a personal overall finish. Unusual is a fighter attached to a bombing unit for escort work and finished in the Bombengeschwader scheme. At bottom, a perfect example of coloured fabric.*

191

Left—Top to Bottom: A.D. Scout 'The Sparrow'. 80 h.p. Gnome, at R.N.A.S. Chingford, 1915.   Alcock A.1. Scout 'The Sopwith Mouse'. 100 h.p. Gnome Monosoupape or 110 h.p. Clerget, 1917. Armstrong-Whitworth F.K.10. 110 h.p. Le Rhone, Production Version of this 2-seater fighter-reconnaissance type, 1916. Armstrong-Whitworth F.K.12. 250 h.p. Rolls-Royce, 2nd version of this multi-seat (3) fighter, 1916. Austin A.F.T.3 'The Osprey'. 230 h.p. Bentley B.R.2, 1917.   Right—Top to Bottom: Armstrong-Whitworth F.M.4 'Armadillo'. 230 h.p. Bentley B.R.2. original form 1918. Austin 'Greyhound'. 320 h.p. A.B.C. Dragonfly I 2-seater. Fighter-reconnaissance 1918. Avro 530. 200 h.p. Hispano-Suizaor 200 h. p. Sunbeam Arab. 2-seater fighter 1917. Avro 531 'Spider'. 110 h.p. Le Rhone 1918. B.A.T. F.K.25 'The Basilisk'. 320 h.p. A.B.C. Dragonfly I, 1918.

BRITISH RARE AND EXPERIMENTAL AIRCRAFT

Left—Top to Bottom: Beadmore 1 W.B.III (S.B.3 D). 80 h.p. Le Rhône or 80 h.p. Clerget, Ship-board fighter, 1917-1918. Beardmore W.B.IV. 200 h.p. Hispano-Suiza Ship-board fi3hter, 1917. Beardmore W.B.V. 200 h.p. Hispano-Suiza 'N-41'. First model with 27 mm. Puteaux Canon, 1917. Blackburn Triplane. 100 h.p. Gnome Monosoupape or 110 h.p. Clerget, 1915-1916. Boultonand Paul P.3 'Bobolink'. 230 h.p. Bentley B.R.2, 1918. Right— Top to Bottom: Bristol Scout 'F'. 200 h.p. Sunbeam Arab, 1917. British Nieuport B.N.1. 23) p.h. Bentley B.R.2, 1918. Mann, Egerton H.1. 200 h.p. Hispano-Suiza, Ship-board fighter with floatation gear, 1917. Nestler Scout. 100 h.p. Gnome Monosoupape, 1916. Port Victoria P.V.7 'Grain Kitten 35 h.p. A.B.C. Gnat, for use off small Naval vessels, 1917.

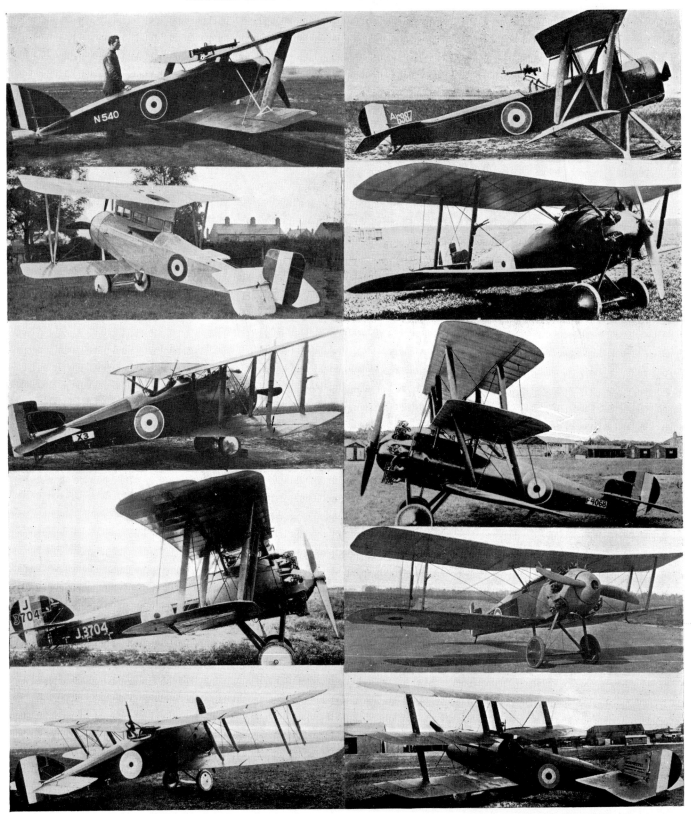

Left—Top to Bottom: Port Victoria P.V.8. 'Eastchurch Kitten'. 35 h.p. A.B.C. Gnat, 1917. Sage Type 2. 100 h.p. Gnome Monosoupape 2-seater fighter, 1916. Sopwith 2 , R.2 Mk. I 'Bulldog'. 200 h.p. Clerget 2nd version of this 2-seater fighter-reconnaissance type, 1917. Sopwith 'Dragon'. 360 h.p. A.B.C. Dragonfly IAe1918. Sopworth 3F2 'Hippo'. 200 h.p. Clerget, 2-seater fighter, 1917-18. Right—Top to Bottom: Sopwith 1½-Strutter 110 h.p. or 130 h.p. Clerget. Experimental version for deck landings, 1917-1918. Sopwith 8 F.1. Mk. I 'Snail'. 270 h.p. A.B.C. Wasp I. Monocoque fuselage, 1918. Sopwith 'Snark'. 360 h.p. A.B.C. Dragonfly IA. 1st prototype, 1918. Sopwith 'Snapper'. 360 h.p. A.B.C. Dragonfly IA, 1918. Sopwith Triplane. 150 h.p. Hispano-Suiza N-509, 1916.

BRITISH RARE AND EXPERIMENTAL AIRCRAFT

Left—Top to Bottom: Pemberton-Billing P.B.23. 80 h.p. Le Rhône. The original 'Push-Proj.' Pemberton-Billing P.B.25. 100 h.p. Gnome Monosoupape, 1915. Supermarine Nighthawk 2 × 100 h.p. Anzani Anti-Airship Fighter, 1915-1916. Vickers E.S.1. 100 h.p. Gnome Monosoupape, 1915. Vickers Fighting Biplane. 100 h.p. Gnome Monosoupape. Forerunner of the 'Gun-Bus', 1914. Right—Top to Bottom: Vickers F.B. 16. 150 h.p. Hart. An early version, 1916. Vickers F.B.26. 200 h.p. Hispano-Suiza with Eman triple gun mounting, 1917. Westland N.1B (Serial N-17). 150 h.p. Bentley B.R.1. Fighter Seaplane, 1917. Its predecessor, N-16, differed in having Sopwith-type main floats and a tail float. Both 1917. Westland Wagtail. 170 h.p. A.B.C. Wasp I. Original version, 1917-1918. Whitehead Scout. 80 h.p. Le Rhône, 1916.

Top left: A.E.G. Dr.-I, 160 h.p. Mercedes, 1917. Next: A.E.G. D-I, 160 h.p. Mercedes, 1917. Next: A.E.G. DJ-I, 195 h.p. Benz, armoured ground-attack fighter, 1918. Next: Albatros D-IV, 160 h.p. Mercedes (geared), 1917. Bottom: Albatros Dr-I, 160 h.p. Mercedes, 1917. Top Right: Albatros D-XII, 160 h.p. Mercedes, 1918. Next: Daimler L-9, 185 h.p. Daimler, 1918. Next: D.F.W. D-I 160 h.p. Mercedes, 1917. Next: D.F.W. Dr.-I, 170 h.p. Körting, 1918. Bottom: D.F.W. D-II, 160 h.p. Mercedes, 1918.

Top Left: Zeppelin Dornier CL-II, 240 h.p. Maybach, 1918. Next: Euler D-I, 100 h.p. Oberursel (a Nieuport copy), 1916. Next: Fokker V.8, 120 h.p. Mercedes, Experimental Quintuplane, 1917. Bottom: Friedrichshafen D-I, 160 h.p. Mercedes, 1917. Top Right: Hansa-Brandenburg W.16, 160 h.p. Oberursel, 1916. Next: Hansa-Brandenburg W.25, 150 h.p. Benz, 1917. Next: Junkers J-I 'Blechesel' (Tin Donkey), 120 h.p. Mercedes, 1915. Next: Junkers E-II, 160 h.p. Mercedes, 1916. Bottom: Kondor D-I, 110 h.p. Oberursel, 1917.

GERMAN RARE AND EXPERIMENTAL AIRCRAFT

Top Left: Kondor D-7, 160 h.p. Mercedes, 1917. Next: L.F.G. Roland D-IV, 160 h.p. Mercedes, 1917. Next: L.F.G. Roland D-XVI, 160 h.p. Siemens or 170 h.p. Goebel, 1918. Bottom: L.F.G. Roland W.1, 160 h.p. Mercedes, 1917. Top Right: Luft Torpedo 5D1, 150 h.p. Benz, 1916–1917. Next: L.V.G. D-II, 160 h.p. Mercedes, 1916. Next: L.V.G. D-IV, 190 h.p. Benz, 1917. Next: L.V.G. D-VI, 190 h.p. Benz, 1918. Bottom: L.V.G. E-VI, 160 h.p. Mercedes, the first two-seater with both fixed and flexible guns, 1915.

GERMAN RARE AND EXPERIMENTAL AIRCRAFT

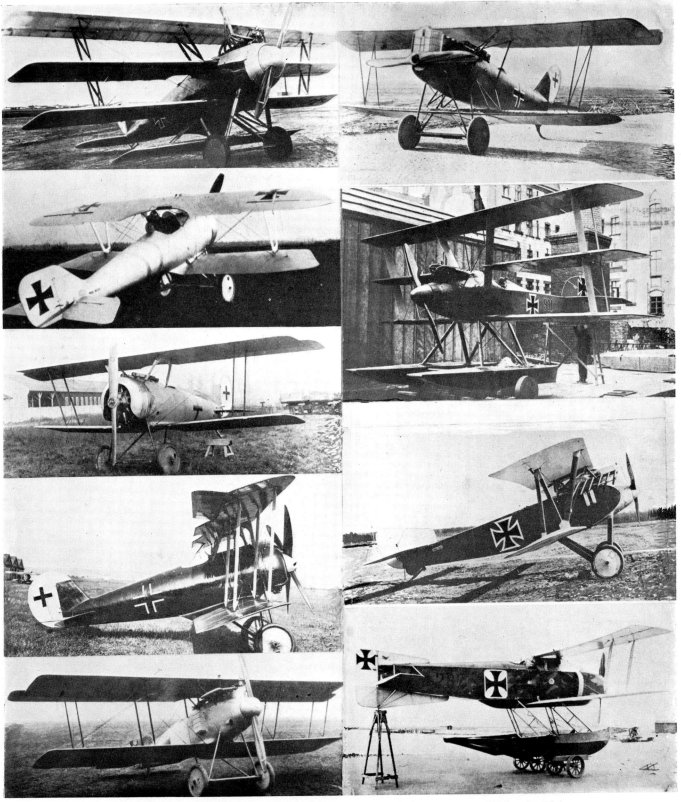

Top Left: Naglo Quadruplane, 160 h.p. Mercedes, 1917. Next: Pfalz D-VI, 110 h.p. Le Rhône, 1917. Next: Pfalz D-VII, 160 h.p. Siemens, 1917. Next: Pfalz D-VIII, 160 h.p. Siemens, 1918. Bottom: Pfalz D-XI, 160 h.p. Mercedes, 1918. Top Right: Pfalz D-XV, 185 h.p. B.M.W., 1918. Next: Sablatnig, S.F.4, 150 h.p. Benz, 1916–1917. Next: Schütte-Lanz D-III, 160 h.p. Mercedes, 1916. Bottom: Ursinus Seaplane, 120 h.p. Daimler, (prototype) 160 h.p. Benz (production). 1916–1917. The floats were retracted during flight.

FRENCH RARE AND EXPERIMENTAL AIRCRAFT

Top Left: All 1918, Breguet 17c2, 450 h.p. Renault. Next: De Marcay C.1, 300 h.p. Hispano-Suiza. Next: Hanriot HD-3c2, 260 h.p. Salmson. Next: Hanriot HD-9, AP-1, 260 h.p. Salmson, Escort fighter. Bottom: Hanriot HD-7c1, 300 h.p. Hispano-Suiza. Top Right: Nieuport Experimental two-seater, 180 h.p. Lorraine-Dietrich, 1915. Next: Nieuport Triplane, 110 h.p. Le Rhône, R.F.C., 1916. Next: Nieuport Triplane, 120 h.p. Le Rhône, R.N.A.S., 1916. Next: Nieuport, 150 h.p. Hispano-Suiza, 1917. Bottom: Nieuport 12, 150 h.p. Hispano-Suiza, 1917.

Left—Top to Bottom: Nieuport 20, 110 h.p. Le Rhône, 1916. Nieuport Monoplane, 170 h.p. Le Rhône, 1918. Nieuport Monocoque (28 variant), 170 h.p. Le Rhône, 1918. Nieuport 28/29, 275 h.p. Lorraine-Dietrich, 1917. Nieuport (28 variant), 200 h.p. Clerget, 1917. Right—Top to Bottom: R.E.P. C-1, 250 h.p. Salmson 9z, 1918. Spad 15, 170 h.p. Le Rhône or 160 h.p. Gnôme-Monosoupape, 1917. Spad 20 C-2, 300 h.p. Hispano-Suiza, 1918. Spad 22, 300 h.p. Hispano-Suiza, 1918. Wibault C-1, 220 h.p. Hispano-Suiza, 1918.

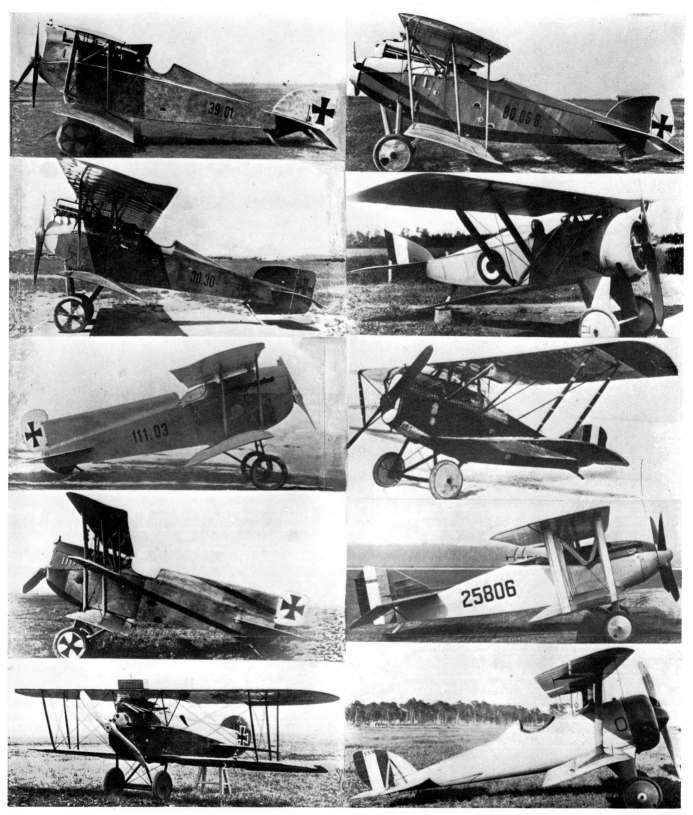

Left, top to bottom: Austrian-Aviatik D-II, 200 h.p. Austro-Daimler, 1918. Austrian-Aviatik D-III, 230 h.p. Hiero, 1918. Lohner D-type, 185 h.p. Austro-Daimler, 1917. Lohner Triplane, 185 h.p. Austro-Daimler, 1917. Phönix D-IIa, 230 h.p. Hiero, 1918. Right, top to bottom: Austrian W.K.F., D-I prototype, 230 h.p. Hiero, 1918. Italian Macchi M-14, 110 h.p. Le Rhône, 1918. Italian Pomilio Scout, 220 h.p. S.P.A., 1918. American Thomas-Morse MB-2 (2-seater), 400 h.p. Liberty, 1918, last, the American Heinrich Scout, 100 h.p. Gnôme of 1917.

"IN STRANGE SURROUNDINGS AND UNUSUAL GARB"

Left—Top to Bottom: A Sopwith Triplane in German hands. A Fokker E-Type experimentally covered with celluloid. Albatros D-V unit on the vacated British airfield of Favreuil. Note the abandoned Sopwith Camel on the right, and the notice in the foreground! An Albatros D-Va captured by the British. Right—Top to Bottom: A captured Sopwith Pup. Rumpler C-IV—the inscription contrasts strangely with the heavy armament! A Pfalz D-IIIa, with British markings. A captured Albatros D-V. 'G-56' is a serial allocated by the British.

Top Left: 80 h.p. Le Rhône (rear view) bore/stroke 105 × 140 mm. Top Right: 110 h.p. Le Rhône bore/stroke 112 × 170 mm. Bottom Left: 130 h.p. Clerget bore/stroke 120 × 172 mm. Bottom Right: 100 h.p. Gnôme-Monosoupape bore/stroke 110 × 150 mm.

ONE RADIAL AND THREE ROTARY NINE-CYLINDER AERO ENGINES

Top Left: 150 h.p. Bentley B.R.1 bore/stroke 120 × 170 mm. Top Right: 200 h.p. Bentley B.R.2 bore/stroke 140 × 180 mm. Bottom Left: 320 h.p. A.B.C. Dragonfly (Radial) bore/stroke 140 × 160 mm. Bottom Right: 110 h.p. Oberursel U.R.II bore/stroke 112 × 170 mm.

FOUR SIX-CYLINDER IN-LINE AERO ENGINES

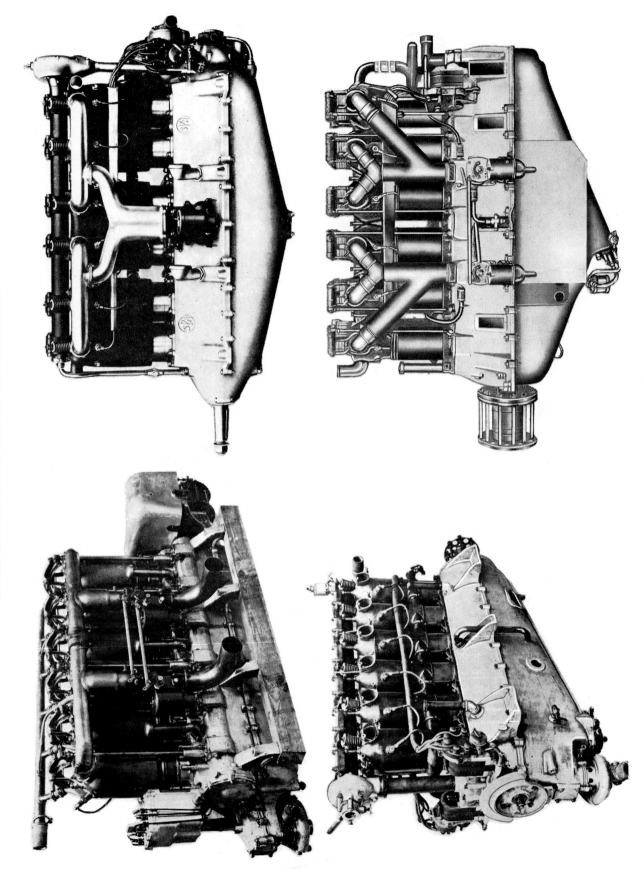

Top Left: 160 h.p. Beardmore bore/stroke 142 × 175 mm. *Top Right*: 210 h.p. S.P.A. bore/stroke 135 × 170 mm. *Bottom Left*: 180 h.p. Mercedes bore/stroke 140 × 160 mm. *Bottom Right*: 195 h.p. Benz bore/stroke 145 × 190 mm.

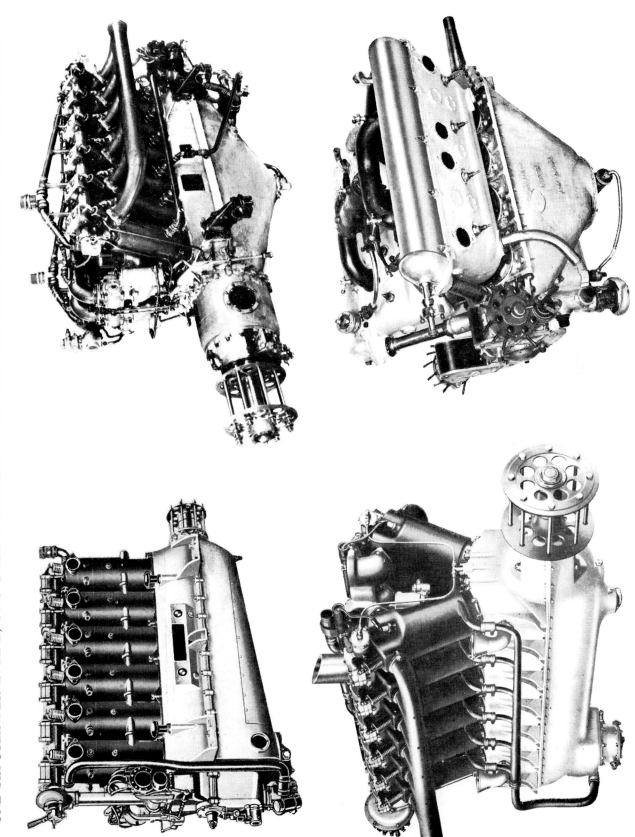

Top Left: 185 h.p. B.M.W. bore/stroke 120 × 150 mm. *Top Right:* 275 h.p. Rolls Royce 'Falcon II' bore/stroke 4" × 5¾". *Bottom Left:* 400 h.p. Liberty bore/stroke 127 × 177·8 mm. *Bottom Right:* 200 h.p. Wolseley 'Viper' 4·72" × 5·12".

207

Top left: 100 h.p. Oberursel rotary on a Fokker E-II. Right: 160 h.p. double-row Oberursel fitted to Fokker E-IV 189/6, built for Immelmann. Next: 110 h.p. Le Rhône rotary of a Nieuport 12; a modified Fokker D-IV and a Viper-engined S.E.5a. Bottom: Bristol F2B; Fokker D-VII (O.A.W.) 4635/18 in the Smithsonian Institute, U.S.A. (flown by Leutnant Heinz von Beaulieu-Marconnay, brother of the German ace) and a B.R.2 powered Snipe.

Top left: Hansa-Brandenburg D-I. Centre: Observer's cockpit on a F.E.2b; note additional gun mountings in front of pilot's cockpit. Right: S.V.A. Next: Fokker B-II (Austrian) and French-built 300 h.p. Dolphin Mark II. Bottom left: S.E.5a, as used by No. 1 Sqdn., R.F.C.; its long exhaust pipes have been replaced by short stubs. Note the Vickers gun and Aldis sight. Bottom right: Fokker D-VII. The left-hand gun has been temporarily removed.

SOME EXAMPLES OF FUSELAGE CONSTRUCTION

Left: American—Thomas Morse Scouts—wood. German—Fokker D-VII—metal. French—Nieuport 12, two-seater—wood. German—Pfalz D-IIIa—wood. Right: British—S.E.5s at the Wolseley factory—wood. German—The experimental Fokker V-37 monoplane with armoured Mercedes engine and cockpit—metal. German—Fokker Monoplane—metal. German—Fokker D-VII—metal. (Note Stapenhorst's chequered triplane behind the D-VII.)

Top left: Sopwith Pup on H.M.S. 'Furious', one of the earliest aircraft-carriers. In foreground is
take-off trolley for floatplanes. Centre: Swinging the propeller of a D.H.2. Right: R.N.A.S.
1½ Strutter showing air-brake. Next: Two views of the Nieuport 12; on the left Lieutenant
Tinne of 46 Squadron, R.F.C., with aerial camera. Lastly: Guynemer in his Spad S.7, and
Leutnant Plüschow in Fokker D-II 2387/16.

H.P.   = Horse-power
Engines: R.-R. = Rolls-Royce; H.-Suiza = Hispano-Suiza;
          Mono = Monosoupape; A-D = Austro-Daimler
Span(T) = Top Wing Span in feet and inches
Span(B) = Bottom Wing Span in feet and inches
Chord   = Distance from leading to trailing edges in feet
          and inches
Gap   = Vertical Distance between leading edges top and
          bottom wings in feet and inches

DIMENSIONS AND PERFORMANCE

Speeds = Miles per hour (M.p.h.) at quoted altitude in feet
         (Ht.) (Example 86·5/10000 = 86·5 M.p.h. at
         10,000 feet height)
Climb = Time in minutes and seconds to quoted height in
         feet. (Example 2.05/2000 = 2 minutes and 5
         seconds to 2,000 feet height)

| PARENT FIRM TYPE AND MODEL | ENGINE | | DIMENSIONS | | | | | | | | | | | WEIGHTS | | SP | |
	H.P.	Type	Span (T) ft. ins.	Span (B) ft. ins.	Chord (T) ft. ins.	Chord (B) ft. ins.	Gap ft. ins.	Length ft. ins.	Height ft. ins.			Empty	Gross	M.p.h./Ht.	M.p.h./Ht
															AM
LE PÈRE														THE PACKARD MOTO	
Lusac C-11	400	Liberty 12A	41 7	41 7	5 6	5 6	5 1	25 6	9 6	2466	3746	132/2000	130·4/5000		
	400	Liberty 12A	39 0	39 0	5 6	5 6	5 1	25 5	9 7	–	–	–	–		
STANDARD														THE STANDARD AIRCRAF	
E-1	80	Le Rhône	24 0	24 0	3 6	3 6	4 0	18 10	7 10	828	1144	100/G.L.	94/6500		
	100	Gnôme	24 0	24 0	3 6	3 6	4 0	18 10	7 10	890	1275	105/G.L.	–		
THOMAS-MORSE														THE THOMAS-MORSE AI	
S4B	100	Gnôme Mono	27 0	26 0	5 6	4 3	4 6	20 3	8 6	890	1325	95/G.L.	–		
S4C	100	Gnôme Mono	26 6	25 6	5 6	4 3	4 6	19 10	8 1	961	1354	100/G.L.	–		
	80	Le Rhône	26 6	25 6	5 6	4 3	4 6	18 6	8 1	963	1373	95/G.L.	–		
S.5	100	Gnôme Mono	As S4B but fitted with twin Floats												
															AUSTRO
AVIATIK														OESTERREICHISCHE-UNGARISCH	
Berg D-I	185	Austro-Daimler	26 3	26 3	4 9	4 9	4 8	22 7	8 3	1342	1815	113/G.L.	–		
	200	Austro-Daimler	26 3	26 3	4 9	4 9	4 8	22 7	8 3	1475	1945	115/G.L.	–		
	225	Austro-Daimler	26 3	26 3	4 9	4 9	4 8	22 7	8 3	1404	1906	115·5/G.L.	–		
PHÖNIX														PHÖNIX-FLUGZEUGWERK	
D-I & II	200	Hiero	32 5	29 7	5 7	4 0	4 11	21 9	9 2	1441	1771	112·5/G.L.	–		
D-III	230	Hiero	32 5	30 0	5 8	4 0	5 4	21 9	9 5	1501	1831	125/G.L.	–		
															BRIT
AUSTIN-BALL														THE AUSTIN MOTOR CO. LTD.	
A.F.B.1	200	H.-Suiza	30 0	30 0	5 0	5 0	4 9	21 6	9 3	1525	2077	138/G.L.	126·5/10000		
AVRO														A. V. ROE AND CO. LTD	
504K (N/F)	110	Le Rhône	36 0	36 0	4 10	4 10	5 6	29 5	10 5	1231	1660	95/G.L.	87/8000		
B.A.T.														THE BRITISH AERIAL TRANS	
F.K.23 Bantam Mk. I	170	ABC Wasp I	25 0	25 0	3 11	3 11	3 3	18 5	6 9	833	1321	138 max.	128/6500		
F.K.22 Bantam Mk. II	100	Gnôme Mono	24 8	24 8	4 11	4 11	4 3	20 8	7 5	866	1260	–	–		
BRISTOL														THE BRITISH AND COLONIAl	
Scout B	80	Gnôme	24 7	24 7	4 6	4 6	4 3	20 8	8 6			Weights and Performanc			
Scout C	80	Le Rhône	24 7	24 7	4 6	4 6	4 3	20 8	8 6	757	1195	92·7/G.L.	91/3000		
Scout D	80	Le Rhône	24 7	24 7	4 6	4 6	4 3	20 8	8 6	760	1250	100/G.L.	94/5000		
F.2A	190	R.-R. Falcon I	39 3	39 3	5 6	5 6	5 4	25 9	9 4	1727	2667	110/G.L.	106/5000		
F.2B	275	R.-R. Falcon III	39 3	39 3	5 6	5 6	5 4	25 10	9 9	1934	2779	121·5/5000	113/10000		
M.1C.	110	Le Rhône	30 9	–	5 11	–	–	20 5	7 9½	896	1348	130/G.L.	127/5000		

OF 1914-1918 FIGHTER AIRCRAFT

Ceiling = Maximum height attainable in feet
Weights = Pounds. Empty and gross
Fuel, End., Range = (1) Fuel capacity in gallons
= (2) Flight endurance in hours
= (3) Range in miles
I.A.F. = Independent Air Force

G.L. = Ground Level
S.L. = Sea Level
Armament = (Armt.). In this column the following abbreviations for various Machine Guns (M.G.) occur, thus: V = Vickers Gun; L = Lewis Gun; Sp = Spandau; Schw = Schwarzlose; P = Parabellum; H = Hotchkiss; S^{TE} = St. Etienne; M = Marlin. S.A. = Small Arms (i.e. Revolvers, Carbines, etc.)

…DS		RATE OF CLIMB					Fuel/ End/ Range	ARM'T	REMARKS
M.p.h./Ht.	M.p.h./Ht.	Time/Ht.	Time/Ht.	Time/Ht.	Time/Ht.	Ceiling			

…RICA

…CAR COMPANY, DETROIT.

127·6/10000	122·5/15000	1.35/2000	4.24/5000	9.48/10000	17.30/15000	20000	73.5gal.	2 M., 2 L.	"Le Père U.S. Army Combat".
–	–	–	–	–	–	–	–	2 M., 2 L.	42128.

…CORPORATION, ELIZABETH.

85/10000	–	10.0/5000	11.12/6500	22.20/10000	–	14800	19 gal.	–	Provision made for 1 Marlin M.G. and/or Camera Gun.
–	–	–	–	10.0/9500	–	–	27 gal.	–	

…CRAFT CORPORATION, ITHACA.

–	–	–	–	12.0/10000	–	15000	30 gal.	–	Provision made for Marlin M.G's and/or Camera Gun.
–	–	–	–	13.0/10000	–	15000	27 gal.	–	
–	–	–	–	22.0/10000	54.0/15000	15000	27 gal.	–	
Reduced Performance.	–	–	–	–	–	–	30 gal.	–	Float Plane

HUNGARY

…FLUGZEUGFABRIK AVIATIK, VIENNA.

–	–	3.12/3280	12.57/10000	18.38/13120	32.49/16400	20000	22 gal.	1 or 2 Schw	
–	–	2.14/3280	7.25/10000	11.17/13120	32.12/20400	20400	–	2 Schw.	
–	–	2.45/3280	–	–	–	20000	18 gal.	2 Schw.	

…A.G., VIENNA-STADLAU.

–	–	3.0/3280	7.0/6500	12.0/10000	–	–	3 hr.	2 Schw.	D-II Balanced Elevators.
–	–	2.30/3280	–	–	–	–	29 gal.	2 Schw.	

…AIN

…NORTHFIELD, BIRMINGHAM.

120·5/15000	114·5/19000	.40/1000	4.45/6000	14.30/14000	29.55/20000	22000	32 gal.	2 L.	

…MANCHESTER AND HAMBLE.

85/10000	–	5.0/3500	10.0/8000	16.0/10000	–	18000	25½ gal.	1 Lewis	Night Fighter Version.

…ORT CO. LTD., WILLESDEN.

125·5/10000	118·0/15000	–	5.10/65000	9.0/10000	17.05/15000	20000	22 gal.	2 V.	
100/10000	–	–	9.05/65000	16.50/10000	43.0/15000	14500	17 gal.	Nil	

…AEROPLANE CO. LTD., BRISTOL.

…pproximately as Type 'C'.				–	–	–	–	S.A.	
88/7000	86·5/10000	2.05/2000	7.00/5000	21.20/10000	50.00/15000	15500	16 gal.	1 L.	Also 80 and 110 Clerget
86/10000	–	–	–	–	18.30/0000	–	–	1 L. or 1V.	Also 100 Monosoupape.
102/9000	96/15000	1.55/2000	7.30/5000	14.30/10000	31/15000	16000	50 gal.	1 V./1-2 L.	
…05/15000	102/16500	1.45/2000	4.50/5000	11.15/10000	24.10/16000	20000	45 gal.	1 V./1-2 L.	Also 220 R.-R. Falcon II, & 200 Sunbeam Arab.
…11·5/10000	104/15000	5.10/6000	10.25/10000	19.50/15000	41.35/20000	20000	18 gal.	1 V.	

PARENT FIRM / TYPE AND MODEL	H.P.	Type	Span (T)		Span (B)		Chord (T)		Chord (B)		Gap		Length		Height		Empty	Gross	M.p.h./Ht.	M.p.h./Ht.
			ft.	ins.	ft.	ins.	ft.	ins.	ft.	ins.	ft.	ins.	ft.	ins.	ft.	ins.				
DE HAVILLAND																			THE AIRCRAFT MANUFAC	
D.H.2	100	Gnôme Mono	28	3	28	3	4	9	4	9	4	9	25	2	9	6	943	1441	93/G.L.	90/5000
	110	Le Rhône	28	3	28	3	4	9	4	9	4	9	25	2	9	6	1004	1547	92/G.L.	85/5000
D.H.5	110	Le Rhône	25	8	25	8	4	6	4	6	5	0	22	0	9	1	1010	1492		102/10000
MARTINSYDE																			MARTINSYDE LTI	
S.1	80	Gnôme	27	8	27	8	4	9	4	9	4	6	21	0	8	2	–	–	87/G.L.	–
G.100	120	Beardmore	38	0	38	0	6	0	6	0	5	8	26	6	10	2	1759	2424	–	95/6500
G.102	160	Beardmore	38	0	38	0	6	0	6	0	5	8	27	0	10	2	1793	2458	103/G.L.	103·7/3000
F.4 Buzzard Mk. I	300	H.-Suiza	32	9	31	2	6	0	5	6	5	3	25	6	10	4	1811	2398	140 max.	138/10000
NIEUPORT																			THE NIEUPORT & GENERAL AIR	
Nighthawk	320	ABC Dragonfly I	27	9	27	9	5	3	5	3	4	6	18	9	9	6	1500	2218	151/G.L.	140/6500
R.A.F.																			ROYAL AIRCRAFT FAC	
B.E.12	150	R.A.F. 4a	37	0	37	0	5	6	5	6	6	3	27	3	11	1	1635	2352	102/G.L.	97/6500
12A	150	R.A.F. 4a	40	9	30	6	5	6	5	6	6	3	27	3	12	0	1610	2327	99·5/3100	95·5/5100
12B	200	H-Suiza	37	0	37	0	5	6	5	6	6	3	–		11	1	–	–		Speed a
F.E.2b	120	Beardmore	47	9	47	9	5	6	5	6	6	3	32	3	12	7	1993	2967	80·5/G.L.	74·5/4000
2b	160	Beardmore	47	9	47	9	5	6	5	6	6	3	32	3	12	7	2061	3037	91·5/G.L.	81/6500
2d	250	R.R. Eagle I	47	9	47	9	5	6	5	6	6	3	32	3	12	7	2401	3549	92/G.L.	–
8	100	Gnôme Mono	31	6	31	6	4	0	4	0	4	6	23	8	9	2	895	1346	94/G.L.	–
S.E.2a	80	Gnôme	27	6	27	6	3	9	3	9	4	10	20	6	8	10	–	1200	96/G.L.	–
5	150	H.-Suiza	28	0	28	0	5	0	5	0	4	7	21	4	9	5	1399	1930	–	119/6500
5 Short Span			26	7	26	7	5	0	5	0	4	7	21	4	9	5	–	–	–	–
5a	200	H.-Suiza	26	7	26	7	5	0	5	0	4	7	20	11	9	6	1400	1953	–	–
5a	200	Wolseley Viper	26	7	26	7	5	0	5	0	4	7	20	11	9	6	–	1940	137·8/G.L.	–
SOPWITH																			THE SOPWITH AVIATION CO	
Tabloid	80	Gnôme	25	6	25	6	5	1	5	1	4	6	20	4	8	5	730	1120	93/G.L.	–
Baby	110	Clerget	25	8	25	8	5	2	5	2	4	6	22	10	10	0	–	1580	92/G.L.	–
Baby	130	Clerget	25	8	25	8	5	2	5	2	4	6	23	0	10	0	1226	1715	100/S.L.	–
1½ Strutter	110	Clerget	33	6	33	6	5	6	5	6	5	5	25	3	10	3	1259	2149	106/G.L.	101/6000
1½ Strutter	130	Clerget	33	6	33	6	5	6	5	6	5	5	25	3	10	3	1305	2150	–	100/6500
1½ Strutter	110	Le Rhône	33	6	33	6	5	6	5	6	5	5	25	3	10	3	1281	2205	–	–
1½ Strutter (N/F)	130	Clerget	33	6	33	6	5	6	5	6	5	5	25	3	10	3	1316	2342	–	102/6500
Pup	80	Le Rhône	26	6	26	6	5	1	5	1	4	5	19	4	9	5	787	1225	111·5/G.L.	103/7000
Pup	100	Gnôme Mono	26	6	26	6	5	1	5	1	4	5	19	4	9	5	856	1297	110/G.L.	107/6500
Triplane	130	Clerget	26	6	(all)		3	3	(all)		3	0 (all)		19	4	10	6	1101	1541	117/5000	112/7000
Triplane	150	H.-Suiza	28	6	(all)		4	3	(all)		3	6 (all)		23	2	–		–	–	120 max.	–
F.1. Camel	130	Clerget	28	0	28	0	4	6	4	6	5	0	18	9	8	6	929	1453	–	115/6500
F.1. Camel	110	Le Rhône	28	0	28	0	4	6	4	6	5	0	18	8	8	6	889	1422	122/G.L.	–
F.1. Camel	100	Gnôme Mono	28	0	28	0	4	6	4	6	5	0	19	0	8	9	882	1387	–	–
F.1. Camel	150	B.R.1	28	0	28	0	4	6	4	6	5	0	18	6	8	6	939	1470	–	–
2F.1. Camel	130	Clerget	26	11	26	11	4	6	4	6	4	11	18	6	9	1	956	1523	–	–
2F.1. Camel	150	B.R.1	26	11	26	11	4	6	4	6	4	11	18	8	9	1	1036	1530	–	124/6500
F. 1/1	130	Clerget	28	0	28	0	4	6	4	6	4	9	18	10	8	3	950	1482	–	–
TF.1	130	Clerget	28	0	28	0	4	6	4	6	5	0	18	9	8	6	–	–	–	–
F.1 (2 Str.)	130	Clerget	28	0	28	0	4	6	4	6	5	0	18	9	8	6	–	–	–	–
5F.1 Dolphin Mk. I	200	H.-Suiza	32	6	32	6	4	6	4	6	4	3	22	3	8	6	1406	1911		

214

		RATE OF CLIMB					Fuel/ End/ Range	ARM'T.	REMARKS
M.p.h./Ht.	M.p.h./Ht.	Time/Ht.	Time/Ht.	Time/Ht.	Time/Ht.	Ceiling			
...RING CO. LTD., HENDON.									
88/9000	73·5/11000	2.30/2000	8.25/5000	20.30/9000	31.30/11000	14000	26.3 gal.	} 1 L.	
82·5/9000	72/11000	4.35/3000	12/6000	23.30/9000	31.0/10000	–	33.0 gal.		
94·5/13000	89/15000	–	6.55/6500	12.25/10000	27.30/15000	16000	26 gal.	1 V.	
...ROOKLANDS.									
–	–	–	–	–	–	–	–	1 L.	
87/10000	–	–	10/6500	19/10000	–	14000	5½ hr.	2 L.	
99·5/10000	93·5/14000	3.30/3000	8.05/6000	15.55/10000	40.45/16000	16000	4½ hr.	2 L.	
132·5/15000	–	–	4.40/6500	7.55/10000	14.0/15000	24000	38 gal.	2 V.	
...AFT CO. LTD., CRICKLEWOOD.									
138·5/10000	134/15000	4.10/6500	7.10/10000	12.40/15000	20/20000	24500	40 gal.	2 V.	
...RY, FARNBOROUGH.									
94/8000	91/10000	5.50/3000	14/6000	27/9000	47.30/12000	12500	57 gal.	2 L. or 1 L., 1 V.	
83·5/8500	72/12000	5.0/3000	11.20/6000	19.30/9000	44/12000	–	57 gal.	1 V.	
...limb greatly improved on BE.12 figures.				–	–	–	57 gal.	1 or 2 L.	
72/8000	–	3.00/1000	9.50/3000	22.45/6000	42.15/9000	9000	51 gal.	2 L.	
	76/10000	2.10/1000	7.24/3000	16.38/6000	39.44/10000	11000	50 gal.	2 L.	
88/8000	–	2.00/1000	6.00/3000	14.30/6000	32.30/10000	–	62 gal.	3-4 L.	
–	–	–	7.30/5000	11/6500	17.30/10000	14500	29 gal.	1 L.	
–	–	–	–	–	–	–	–	2 Rifles or 1 Revolver	
114/10000	98/15000	–	8.00/6500	14.10/10000	29.30/15000	17000	35 gal.	1 V., 1 L.	
–	–	–	–	–	–	–	35 gal.	1 V., 1 L.	
–	121/15000	–	6.0/6500	10.20/10000	18.50/15000	22000	35 gal.	1 V., 1 L.	
126/10000	123/15000	–	4.55/5000	11/10000	19.55/15000	–	35 gal.	1 V., 1 L.	
...TD., KINGSTON-ON-THAMES.									
–	–	1.0/1200	–	–	–	–	3½ hr.	1 L.	
–	–	–	–	–	–	–	25 gal.	1 L.	Also 100 Gnôme Mono.
–	–	–	–	35.0/10000	–	–	25 gal.	1 L.	
96·5/10000	86/14000	1.20/1000	7.45/5000	20.25/10000	35.0/13000	–	40 gal.	1 V., 1 L.	
97·5/10000	–	–	9.10/6500	17.50/10000	41.55/15000	15500	40 gal.	1 V., 1 L.	
103/10000	–	–	10.30/6500	18.55/10000	41.30/15000	16000	40 gal.	1 V., 1 L.	French built.
98·5/10000	–	–	12.40/6500	24.35/10000	–	13000	40 gal.	2 L.	Single Seater.
101/11000	85/15000	2.0/2000	5.20/5000	14/10000	29.10/15000	17500	19¼ gal.	1 V. or 1 L.	
104/10000	100/15000	–	5.40/5000	12.25/10000	23.25/15000	18500	19¼ gal.	1 V.	
107/10000	98/15000	1.45/2000	4.35/5000	11.50/10000	26.30/16400	20500	20 gal.	1 or 2 V.	Originally 110 Clerget.
				9/10000				1V.	Also 200 H.-Suiza.
113/10000	106·5/15000	–	6.0/6500	10.35/10000	20.40/15000	19000	37 gal.	2 V.	
118·5/1000	111·5/15000	–	5.10/6500	9.10/10000	16.50/15000	24000	37 gal.	2 V.	N/F version, 2 Lewis.
110·5/10000	102·5/15000	–	6.50/6500	11.50/10000	23.20/15000	18500	37 gal.	2 V.	Training.
121/10000	114·5/15000	–	4.35/6500	8.10/10000	15.55/15000	22000	37 gal.	2 V.	
114/10000	104/15000	–	6.25/6500	11.40/10000	23.40/15000	19000	37 gal.	1 V., 1 L.	} Detachable fuselage.
122/10000	117/15000	–	6.0/6500	11.30/10000	25.0/15000	17300	37 gal.	1 V., 1 L.	
112·5/10000	106/15000	–	6.0/6500	10.36/10000	21.06/15000	19000	37 gal.	2 V.	Taper wing and 'I' struts.
–						–	37 gal.	3 L.	Gnd. attack. Armoured.
–	–	–	–	–	–	–	–	Nil	Dual control—trainer.
127·5/10000	119/15000	–	6.05/6500	10.30/10000	19.30/15000	21000	27 gal.	2 V., 2 L.	Geared H.-Suiza.

PARENT FIRM TYPE AND MODEL	H.P.	ENGINE Type	Span (T) ft. ins.	Span (B) ft. ins.	Chord (T) ft. ins.	Chord (B) ft. ins.	Gap ft. ins.	Length ft. ins.	Height ft. ins.	Empty	Gross	M.p.h./Ht.	M.p.h./Ht.
SOPWITH													
5F.1 Dolphin Mk. II	300	H.-Suiza	32 6	32 6	4 6	4 6	4 3	22 3	8 6	1566	2358	–	–
5F.1 Dolphin Mk. III	200	H.-Suiza	32 6	32 6	4 6	4 6	4 3	22 3	8 6	1466	2000	–	–
TF.2 Salamander	230	B.R.2	31 3	30 1	5 0	5 0	4 3	19 6	9 4	1844	2512	125/500	123·5/6500
7F.1 Snipe Mk. I	230	B.R.2	30 0	30 0	5 0	5 0	4 3	19 10	9 6	1312	2020	–	–
7F.1 Snipe Mk. I	230	B.R.2	31 1	30 0	5 0	5 0	4 3	19 10	9 6	1312	2020	–	–
7F.1a Snipe Mk.Ia	230	B.R.2	31 1	30 0	5 0	5 0	4 3	19 10	9 6	1329	2271	–	–
VICKERS											VICKERS LTD. (AVIATION DEPARTMENT),		
F.B.5	100	Gnôme Mono	36 6	36 6	5 6	5 6	6 0	27 2	11 6	1220	2050	–	70/5000
F.B.9	100	Gnôme Mono	33 9	33 9	5 6	5 6	6 0	28 5	11 6	1029	1892	82·6/G.L.	80/5000
F.B.12	100	Gnôme Mono	26 0	24 0	5 0	4 0	4 1	21 6	8 7	885	1400	–	93/5000
F.B.12c	110	Le Rhône	29 9	26 9	5 0	4 0	4 1	21 10	8 7	927	1447	–	87/6500
F.B.19 Mk. I	100	Gnôme Mono	24 0	24 0	5 0	5 0	4 0	18 2	8 3	900	1485	–	–
F.B.19 Mk. II	110	Clerget	24 0	24 0	5 0	5 0	4 0	18 2	8 3	890	1475	–	–
F.B.19 Mk. II	110	Le Rhône	24 0	24 0	5 0	5 0	4 0	18 2	8 3	892	1478	109 max.	–
												FRA	
HANRIOT											AVIONS R. HANRIOT,		
HD-1	130	Le Rhône	28 6	24 3	4 1	3 9	3 10	19 2	9 8	898	1350	116/G.L.	–
	110	Le Rhône	28 6	24 3	4 1	3 9	3 10	19 2	9 8	869	1265	113/G.L.	109·1/6500
MORANE											AÉROPLANES MORANE-SA		
AI	160	Gnôme Mono	27 10	–	5 3	–	–	18 6	7 11	924	1425	129/6500	126/10000
	120	Le Rhône	28 7	–	5 3	–	–	18 8½	7 11	891	1155	–	120/10000
L	80	Gnôme	33 9	–	6 6	–	–	20 9	10 3½	869	1496	71·5/max.	–
N	110	Le Rhône	27 3	–	5 5	–	–	22 0	8 3	735	1122	–	102·4/6500
NIEUPORT											SOCIÉTÉ ANONYME DES ÉTABLISSEMI		
10	80	Gnôme Mono	25 11	–	5 3	2 11	–	22 11	8 10	902	1452	87·5 max	–
11	80	Gnôme Mono	24 6	22 5	4 9	2 5	4 3	19 0	8 0	759	1210	97/G.L.	–
11	80	Le Rhône	24 9	22 6	4 9	2 5	4 3	18 8	7 10	774	1133	97 max.	–
12	110	Clerget	29 7	24 2	5 10	3 0	4 6½	23 6	8 11	1155	1815	98 max.	–
16	110	Le Rhône	24 6	22 5	4 9	2 5	4 3	19 0	8 0	781	1133	103.0/6500	–
17	110	Le Rhône	26 10	25 4	3 11½	2 4½	4 1	18 11	8 0	825	1233	107·0/6500	101/10000
21	80	Le Rhône	26 10	25 4	3 11	2 4½	4 1	18 11	8 0	770	1177	93 max.	–
23	120	Le Rhône	26 10	25 4	3 11½	2 4½	4 1	18 11	8 0	825	1256	110 max.	100/6500
24 bis.	130	Le Rhône	26 10	26 0	4 7	2 5	4 1	19 3½	8 0	782	1200	116 max.	106/6500
27	120	Le Rhône	26 10	26 0	4 7	2 5	4 1	19 3½	8 0			Performance a	
28	160	Gnôme Mono	26 9	25 3	4 3	3 3¼	4 3	21 0	8 1¾	960	1540	128 max.	123/6500
29	300	H.-Suiza	32 0	32 0	4 11	4 11	4 7	21 5	9 1½	1672	2420	147·5 max.	–
SPAD											SOCIÉTÉ ANONYME POUR L'AVIA		
A2	80	Le Rhône	31 4	30 10	4 11	4 6½	4 10	23 11	8 6½	935	1562		
A4	110	Le Rhône	31 4	30 10	4 11	4 6½	4 10	23 11	8 6½	–	–	100 max.	
S.7	180	H.-Suiza	25 6	24 10	4 7¼	4 2	3 7½	20 1	7 8½	1100	1550	119·5/6500	111·5/9800
S.12	220	H.-Suiza	26 2	25 8	4 11½	4 6½	3 10	20 11	8 4	1320	1958	–	125/6500
S.13	200	H.-Suiza	26 11	26 5	4 11½	4 6½	3 10	20 8	7 11½	1255	1815	130/6500	128/9800
S.14	220	H.-Suiza	32 2		–	–	–	24 3	13 1	1692	2332	128 max.	–
S.17	300	H.-Suiza	26 11	26 5	4 11½	4 6½	3 10	20 8	7 11½	1408	1980	125 max.	–

M.p.h./Ht.	M.p.h./Ht.	Time/Ht.	Time/Ht.	Time/Ht.	Time/Ht.	Ceiling	End/ Fuel/ Range	ARM'T.	REMARKS
40/10000	133/16400	–	5.10/6500	8.20/10000	12.10/16400	24600	27 gal.	2 V., 2 L.	Direct drive H.-Suiza.
17/10000	110/15000	–	6.20/6500	11.20/10000	21.50/15000	19000	27 gal.	2 V., 2 L.	Direct drive H.-Suiza.
17/10000	–	–	9.5/6500	17.5/10000	–	13000	29 gal.	2 V.	Armour 650 lb.
21/10000	113/15000	–	5.10/6500	9.25/10000	18.50/15000	19500	38½ gal.	2 V.	Unbalanced ailerons.
21/10000	113/15000	–	5.10/6500	9.25/10000	18.50/15000	19500	38½ gal.	2 V.	Balanced ailerons.
14/10000	103/15000	–	7.0/6500	13.25/10000	32.05/15000	15000	56 gal.	2 V.	Long range for I.A.F.
NIGHTSBRIDGE, LONDON AND CRAYFORD.									
–	–	–	16.0/5000	25.0/8000	–	9000	50 gal.	1 L.	
79/6500	75/10000	2.30/1000	10.30/4000	19.0/6500	51.0/10000	11000	50 gal.	1 L.	
–	–	–	7.40/5000	21.05/10000	–	14000	19 gal.	1 L.	Also 80 Le Rhône.
31/10000	–	–	6.55/5000	18.30/10000	48.20/15000	14500	26 gal.	1 L.	Also 100 Anzani.
02/10000	–	–	5.20/5000	14.00/10000	–	16000	2¾ hr.	1 V.	Unstaggered wings.
98/10000	–	–	5.30/5000	14.30/10000	–	14500	3 hr.	1 V. }	Staggered wings.
98/10000	90/15000	–	7.50/6500	14.50/10000	37.10/15000	15000	3¼ hr.	1 V.	
CE									
ARRIÈRES SUR SEINE.									
–	–	5.31/6500	9.17/10000	14.08/13120	20.50/16400	23600	30 gal.	1 V.	
–	–	2.10/3280	5.10/6500	8.30/10000	13.10/13120	21000	25 gal.	1 V.	
NIER, VILLACOUBLAY.									
21/13120	–	4.55/6500	8.05/10000	12.20/13120	–	23000	28 gal.	1-2 V.	M.S.27, 29 C-1.
–	–	5.20/6500	–	–	45.0/10000	18400	300 mls.	1 V.	M.S. 30 E-1.
–	–	3.0/1000	–	–	–	12000	280 mls.	1 H. or 1L.	M.S. 3: also 80 Le Rhône.
6·0/10000	–	–	6.30/6500	12.0/10000	–	13000	1½ hr.	1 H. or 1 StE.	M.S. 5: also 80 Gnôme & 80 Le Rhône.
S, NIEUPORT, ISSY-LES-MOULINAUX.									
–	–	–	16.0/6500	–	–	–	155 mls.	1 or 2 L.	Also 80 Le Rhône.
–	–	5.0/3280	11.0/6500	18.0/9800	41.0/15000	15000	20 gal.	1 L.	Also 110 Le Rhône.
–	–	5.0/3280	11.8/6500	18.37/9800	27.40/13100	18000	2½ hr.	1 L.	Macchi-built.
–	–	–	15.0/6500	–	–	–	312 mls.	1 V. / 1 or 2 L. }	Also 130 Clerget.
Improved performance on Type 11			–	–	–			1 L. / 8 Rockets	
–	–	3.0/3280	5.30/6500	9.0/10000	19.30/13100	17400	2 hr.	1 or 2 L. / 1 V. }	Also 130 Clerget (17 bis).
–	–	–	8.45/6500	–	–	–	150 mls.	1 L.	Also 110 Le Rhône (Russian)
–	–	–	–	–	–	–	150 mls.	1 L., 1 V.	Also 80 Le Rhône (Trainer).
04·5/9800	103/13100	5.40/6500	9.25/9800	14.40/13100	21.30/16400	18200	20 gal.	1 L., 1 V.	
pe 24 and 24 b:s		–	–	–	–	18200	20 gal.	1 L., 1 V.	
1·5/9800	119/13100	5.30/6500	9.0/9800	14.0/13100	21.15/16400	20000	33 gal.	2 V.	
–	–	4.11/6500	–	–	–	27000	360 mls.	2 V.	Also 180 Le Rhône (29 G).
ON ET SES DÉRIVÉS (SPAD), PARIS.									
–	–	–	–	–	–	–	– }	1 Free Gun	Dual control.
8/13100	–	6.40/6500	11.30/9800	19.30/13100	–	18000	2¼ hr.	1 V.	
–	–	–	–	–	–	18000	1¼ hr.	1 V. / 1 Cannon	
5/13100	118/16400	5.17/6500	8.45/9800	13.5/13100	20/16400	22300	2 hr.	2 V.	Also 235 h.p. H.-Suiza.
–	–	7.30/6500	–	–	–	16400	– }	1 V. / 1 Cannon	Seaplane.
Improved performance on S-13								2 V.	

TYPE AND MODEL	H.P.	Type	Span (T)	Span (B)	Chord (T)	Chord (B)	Gap	Length	Height	Empty	Gross	M.p.h./Ht.	M.p.h./H
ALBATROS													ALBATROS-FLUGZEUGWERKE, J
D-I	160	Mercedes	28 4	26 5	5 4	5 4	5 0	24 4	9 8	1488	1976	109 max.	–
D-II	160	Mercedes	27 11	26 2½	5 3	5 3	4 5½	24 0	9 0	1488	1976	109 max.	–
D-III	160	Mercedes	29 7	28 7	4 10½	3 7	4 10½	24 0	9 9½	1454	1949	109/3280	–
D-III	185	Austro-Daimler	29 7	28 7	4 10½	3 7	4 10½	24 0	9 9½	1452	1947	115·5 max.	–
D-V/VA	180	Mercedes	29 7	28 7	4 10½	3 7	4 7	24 0	9 4	1496	2013	117/3280	–
D-XI	160	Siemens-Halske	26 3	21 7	5 0	3 6½	4 8½	18 3½	9 5	1087	1591	118·5/G.L.	–
W-4	160	Mercedes	31 1	30 1½	6 0	6 0	5 9	27 6½	11 6	1705	2255	100 max.	–
DORNIER													ZEPPELIN-WERKE, FLU
D-I	185	B.M.W.	25 8	21 0	4 7½	4 7½	4 7	20 1	8 3½	1518	1914	125 max.	–
FOKKER													FOKKER AEROPLANBA
D-I	120	Mercedes	29 8	29 8	4 11	4 11	4 3	18 10	7 5	1019	1476	93 max.	–
D-II	100	Oberursel	28 8	28 8	3 10½	3 10½	4 5	20 11	8 3½	845	1267	93 max.	–
D-III	160	Oberursel	29 8	29 8	4 11	4 11	4 3	20 8	7 6	994	1562	100 max.	–
D-IV	160	Mercedes	31 10	31 10	4 11	4 11	4 3	20 8	8 0	1333	1850	100 max.	–
D-V	100	Oberursel	28 3	28 3	5 0	5 0	–	22 6	7 6	799	1245	107 max.	–
D-VI	110	Le Rhône	25 1½	19 1	5 4½	4 0	4 9	20 4	8 0	865	1283	125 max.	122/328
D-VII	180	Mercedes	29 3½	23 0	5 3	4 0	4 2	22 9	9 2	1540	1936	116·6/3280	109·7/980
D-VII	185	B.M.W.	29 3½	23 0	5 3	4 0	4 2	22 9	9 2	1513	1993	124/G.L.	–
D-VII	210	Austro-Daimler	29 3½	23 0	5 3	4 0	4 2	22 9	9 2	1514	1993	122 max.	–
D-VIII/E-V	110	Le Rhône	27 3	–	4 11	–	–	19 5	9 4	891	1331	125/G.L.	–
Dr-I	110	Oberursel	23 7	18 6	3 10	3 2½	2 11	19 0	9 9	893	1289	115/G.L.	–
E-I	80	Oberursel	28 0	–	5 11	–	–	22 2	9 6	788	1239	82 max.	–
E-II	100	Oberursel	32 8	–	5 11	–	–	23 2	7 10	880	1340	86·8 max.	–
E-III	100	Oberursel	32 8	–	5 11	–	–	23 6½	7 10	878	1342	87·5 max.	–
E-IV	160	Oberursel	32 1	–	5 11	–	–	24 8	9 1	1025	1593	100 max.	–
B-II (Austrian)	80	Oberursel	25 0	25 0	4 0	4 0	4 1	21 0	7 4	–	–	82/G.L.	–
HALBERTSTADT													HARLBERSTÄDTER FLU
D-II	120	Mercedes	28 11	25 11	5 0	5 0	4 3	23 11	8 9	1144	1606	90/G.L.	–
D-III	120	Argus	As D-II							1155	1617	90/G.L.	–
D-IV	150	Benz	AsD-III							–	–	Performan
C-V	120	Argus	28 11	25 11	5 0	5 0	4 3	21 10	8 9	1040	1460	115·5 max.	–
CL-II	160	Mercedes	35 4	34 11	5 3	4 3	4 6	24 3	9 0	1751	2532	109 max.	–
													–
CL-IV	160	Mercedes	35 4	34 11	5 3	4 3	4 6	20 11	9 0	1550	2288	105 max.	–
HANNOVER													HANNOVERSCHE WAG
CL-II	180	Argus	39 4	36 8	5 11	4 3	5 3	25 5	9 2	1650	2442	–	103·0/2000
CL-III	160	Mercedes	38 4	36 2	5 10½	4 3	5 1½	24 9	9 2	1615	2365	–	103·0/2000
CL-IIIa	180	Argus	As CL-III									Performanc
HANSA-BRANDENBURG													HANSA UND BRANDENBURGISCH
'CC'	150	Benz	30 6	28 10½	5 3	4 11	7 3	25 1	10 6	378	2994	109 max.	
D-I (KD)	160	Austro-Daimler	27 11	27 2	4 11	4 11	5 3	20 10	9 2	1478	2024	116·5/G.L.	–
D-I (KD)	185	Austro-Daimler	27 11	27 2	4 11	4 11	5 3	20 10	9 2	1500	2046	–	–
KDW	150	Benz	30 3	30 3	5 5	5 5	5 2	26 3	10 10	1690	2306	107 max.	–
W12	160	Mercedes	36 8	34 5	6 0	6 0	5 7	31 8	11 6	2200	3219	100 max.	–
W19	240	Maybach	45 3	45 3	7 4½	7 4½	6 1	34 10	12 0	3080	4462	97 max.	–
29	185	Benz	44 4	–	8 9	–	–	30 8½	9 11	2200	3285	103 max.	–
33	260	Mercedes	52 0	–	10 5	–	–	36 4	11 1	3124	4510	108 max.	–

M.p.h./Ht.	M.p.h./Ht.	RATE OF CLIMB				Ceiling	Fuel/End/Range	ARM'T.	REMARKS
l.p.h./Ht.	M.p.h./Ht.	Time/Ht.	Time/Ht.	Time/Ht.	Time/Ht.	Ceiling			

NY

NNISTHAL AND SCHNEIDEMÜHL.

–	–	9.1/6500	15.25/9800	26.0/13100	37.15/16400	17000	26 gal.	2 Sp.	Also 150 Benz.
–	–	5.30/3280	9.30/6500	13.30/9800	19.30/13100	17000	26 gal.	2 Sp.	
96/6500	93/13100	3.20/3280	12.01/9800	18.45/13100	28.48/16400	18000	24 gal.	2 Sp.	
–	–	7.0/6500	12.0/9800	18.0/13100	28.0/16400	18000	22 gal.	2 Schw.	Oeffag-built.
–	96/13100	8.08/6500	17.08/9800	22.10/13100	35.0/16400	20500	2 hr.	2 Sp.	D-VA Gap 1½ ins. less.
–	–	4.30/6500	7.0/9800	10.30/13100	18.0/16400	26000	20 gal.	2 Sp.	
–	–	4.30/3280	23.0/9800	–	–	9840	32 gal.	1 or 2 Sp.	

UGBAU-WERFT, LINDAU.

–	–	–	–	–	–	26500	–	2 Sp.	Also 160 Mercedes

HWERIN-I-MECKLENBURG.

–	–	5.0/3280	11.0/6500	16.0/9800	28.0/13100	13100	1½ hr.	1 Sp.	M. 18z.
–	–	4.0/3280	8.0/6500	15.0/9800	24.0/13100	13100	1½ hr.	1 Sp.	M. 17z.
–	–	3.0/3280	7.0/6500	12.0/9800	20.0/13100	15500	1½ hr.	2 Sp.	M. 19z.
–	–	3.0/3280	5.0/6500	12.0/9800	20.0/13100	16400	1½ hr.	2 Sp.	M. 20.
–	–	–	–	19.0/9800	–	13000	1½ hr.	2 Sp.	M. 22.
–	–	2.30/3280	5.30/6500	9.0/9800	19.0/16400	19500	1½ hr.	2 Sp.	V. 13/1. Also 160 Goebel.
3·5/13100	94·9/16400	6.48/6500	12.0/9800	18.30/13100	31.30/16400	19600	20 gal.	2 Sp.	
–	–	8.30/9800	11.42/13100	16.0/16400	21.15/19600	22900	20 gal.	2 Sp.	
–	–	7.0/9800	10.20/13100	14.0/16400	18.34/19600	22000	2 hr.	2 Schw.	M.A.G.-built.
–	–	2.0/3280	7.30/9800	10.45/13100	19.30/19600	21000	1½ hr.	2 Sp.	Also 140 Oberursel.
03/13100	80/18000	3.45/6500	6.30/9800	10.0/13100	14.30/16400	19600	16½ gal.	2 Sp.	Mid span 20 ft. 5 ins.
–	–	7.0/3280	20.0/6500	40.0/9800	–	10000	1½ hr.	1 P. or Sp.	M5K/MG.
–	–	5.0/3280	15.0/6500	30.0/9800	–	12000	1½ hr.	1 Sp.	M. 14.
Performance approximately as E-II.				–	–	12000	1½ hr.	2 Sp.	M. 14.
–	–	3.0/3280	8.0/6500	15.0/9800	25.0/13100	13500	1½ hr.	2 or 3 Sp.	M. 15.
–	–	7.0/3280	–	–	–	8500	1½ hr.	1 Schw.	

UGWERKE, HALBERSTADT.

–	–	4.0/3280	9.0/6500	15.0/9800	–	–	18½ gal.	1 or 2 Sp.	
–	–	4.0/3280	9.0/6500	15.0/9800	–	–	22 gal.	1 or 2 Sp.	
perior to D-III.	–	–	–	–	–	–	22 gal.	1 or 2 Sp.	
–	–	Climb superior to D-III		–	–	–	22 gal.	1 or 2 Sp.	
7·0/10000	–	9.25/5000	24.30/10000	–	51.55/14000	13500	35 gal.	1 Sp., 1 P.	Heating, radio and camera equipment.
–	–	4.5/6500	8.8/9800	12.8/13100	16.5/16400	16500	35 gal.	1 Sp., 1 P.	

NFABRIK, HANNOVER.

6·0/10000	–	6.1/3280	13.8/6500	23.9/9800	–	24600	34 gal.	1 Sp., 1 P.	Heading, radio and camera equipment.
39·0/13000	–	6.1/3280	13.8/6500	23.9/9800	–	24600	37 gal.	1 Sp., 1 P.	
perior to CL-III.	–	–	–	–	–	–	37 gal.	1 Sp., 1 P.	

UGZEUGWERKE, BRANDENBURG/HAVEL.

–	–	5.0/3280	11.2/6500	–	–	–	3½ hr.	1 Sp.	Flying Boat. Also 220 Hiero and 185 A-D.
–	–	3.0/3280	–	–	–	–	–	1 Schw.	(Phönix) Series '28'.
–	–	–	–	–	–	–	–	1 Schw.	(Ufag) Series '65'.
–	–	4.30/3280	11.0/6500	21.30/9800	–	–	3 hr.	1 or 2 Sp.	Also 160 Mercedes and 160 Maybach.
–	–	8.0/3280	13.0/5000	20.0/6500	38.0/9800	–	3½ hr.	2 Sp., 1 P.	Also 150 Benz.
–	–	8.4/3280	13.8/5000	18.9/6500	28.7/9800	–	97 gal.	1 Sp., 1 P.	{ Possibly a 2 cm. Becker Cannon on No. 2237
–	–	6.0/3280	9.5/5000	13.0/6500	23.0/9800	–	4 hr.	2 Sp., 1 P.	Also 195 Benz.
–	–	5.4/3280	12.8/6500	22.3/9800	42.4/13100	–	4 hr.	2 Sp., 1 P.	Also 240 Maybach.

PARENT FIRM / TYPE AND MODEL	H.P.	Type	Span (T) ft. ins.	Span (B) ft. ins.	Chord (T) ft. ins.	Chord (B) ft. ins.	Gap ft. ins.	Length ft. ins.	Height ft. ins.	Empty	Gross	M.p.h./Ht.	M.p.h./Ht
JUNKERS													**JUNKERS-FOKK**
CL-I	160	Mercedes	40 0	–	7 2½	–	–	25 11	8 9	1617	2541	105 max.	–
D-I	180	Mercedes	29 2	–	6 0	–	–	22 0	8 8½	1439	1841	115·5 max.	–
L.F.G./ROLAND													**LUFTFAHRZEUG-GESE**
C-II	160	Mercedes	33 8	33 8	5 1½	5 1½	4 6½	25 2	9 7	1681	2825	103 max.	–
D-II	160	Mercedes	29 3	28 3	4 10	4 10	4 5	22 8	9 3	1441	1749	105/G.L.	–
D-IIa	180	Argus	29 2	28 3	4 10	4 10	4 5	22 9	9 3	1573	2099		Performan
D-III	160	Mercedes	Slightly larger than D-IIa.							1577	2114		Performan
D-VIb	200	Benz	30 10	27 11	4 7	4 0	4 10	20 10	9 3	1523	1987	114/G.L.	111·5/650
PFALZ													**PFALZ-FLUGZEU**
D-III	160	Mercedes	30 8	26 7	5 5	4 0	4 7½	22 9	9 6½	1390	2050	–	105·0/980
D-IIIa	180	Mercedes	30 8	26 7	5 5	4 0	4 7½	24 10	9 6½	1577	2057	112·5/2000	102·5/100
D-XII	180	Mercedes	29 6	26 2	4 10	4 7½	4 9	20 11	8 10½	1566	1962	120/G.L.	115·0/980
DR-I	160	Siemens Halske	28 0	25 8	3 8	2 4	2 7	18 0	8 10	1122	1551	125 max.	–
E-I	80	Oberursel	36 8	–	5 9½	–	–	22 6	8 2	–	–		
E-II	100	Oberursel								–	–		
E-III	100	Oberursel	Dimensions for all these types generally as for E-I							1705	2277		Maximum spee
E-IV	160	Oberursel											accordi
E-V	100	Mercedes	E-V 13 ins. longer than E-IV.					23 6	–	–	–		
RUMPLER													**RUMPLER FLUGZEUGWERK**
6B1	160	Mercedes	39 6	35 2	5 5	5 5	5 10½	30 10	11 9	1738	2508	95 max.	–
6B2	160	Mercedes	41 6	36 5	5 9	4 4	6 3	32 5	11 7	2288	3564		Performan
D-I	160	Mercedes	27 7	25 6	4 4	3 7	4 9	18 9	8 4½	1298	1771	124/G.L.	112·5/1640
SIEMENS-SCHUCKERT													**SIEMENS-SCHUCKERT-WERK**
D-I	110	Siemens Halske	Approximately as Nieuport 17 of which it was a copy							977	1439		
D-III	160	Siemens Halske	27 7¾	27 3½	4 6¾	3 3	4 4	18 8	8 6½	1155	1584	112 max.	–
D-IV	200	Siemens Halske	27 4¾	27 4¾	3 3	3 3	4 4	18 8	8 2	1190	1620	118 max.	–
													IT
ANSALDO													**GIO. ANSALDO & CO., BORZOL**
Ansaldo A.1	220	S.P.A.	26 1	26 1	5 2½	5 0	4 10	22 5	8 8½	1823	2367	137·5/G.L.	134/6500
S.V.A.5	220	S.P.A.	31 0	25 5	6 4	5 4	5 2	26 8	9 8	1507	2090	143·5/G.L.	–
S.V.A.5	220	S.P.A.	Escort Fighter—data as standard aircraft							1529	2340	136/G.L.	–
S.V.A.-AM	220	S.P.A.	30 6	Otherwise as Landplane						1870	2420	125/S.L.	
MACCHI													**AERONAUTICA MACCH**
M-5	160	Isotta-Fraschini	39 0	29 3	5 0	3 6	6 6	26 2	9 6½	1672	2266	118/S.L.	–
M-7	250	Isotta-Fraschini	32 3	–	5 5	4 4	6 4	26 6	9 7	1705	2376	131/S.L.	–
M-14	110	Le Rhône	26 7	–	4 0½	3 11¼	3 9¼	18 8	7 6½	891	1408	113·5/G.L.	–
	80	Le Rhône	26 7	–	4 0½	3 11¼	3 9¼	18 9	7 6½	830	1235	100/G.L.	–

DS		RATE OF CLIMB					Fuel/ End/ Range	ARM'T.	REMARKS
M.p.h./Ht.	M.p.h./Ht.	Time/Ht.	Time/Ht.	Time/Ht.	Time/Ht.	Ceiling			
G. (JFA) DESSAU.									
–	–	–	–	14.0/9800	–	–	2 hr.	1-2 Sp., 1 P.	
–	–	5.8/6500	9.8/9800	14.8/13100	22.17/16400	19680	1½ hr.	2 Sp.	Also 185 BMW.
HAFT, BERLIN.									
–	–	6.0/3280	12.0/6500	25.0/9800	45.0/13100	13100	5 hr.	1 Sp., 1 P.	
–	–	–	–	–	23.0/16400	–	2 hr.	2 Sp.	
erior to D-II.	–	–	–	–	20.0/16400	–	2 hr.	2 Sp.	
prox. as D-II.	–	–	–	–	–	–	2 hr.	2 Sp.	Also 180 Argus.
08·0/10000	90/17400	6.30/6500	11.30/10000	24.0/15000	38.20/17400	19000	22½ gal.	2 Sp.	
ERKE, SPEYER/RHEIN.									
–	–	–	17.0/9800	–	–	–	–	–	
1·5/15000	–	–	7.0/5000	17.30/10000	41.20/15000	17000	21½ gal.	2 Sp.	
–	–	7.7/6500	12.15/9800	20.18/13100	36.23/16400	18500	18¾ gal.	2 Sp.	
–	–	3.42/6500	6.12/9800	13.30/16400	20.0/19680	–	1½ hr.	2 Sp.	Mid span 26 ft. 7 ins.
		–	–	–	–	–	–	–	
ween 90–105 m.p.h.		–	–	–	–	10000	1½	1 or	Parasol-type.
engine installed.		–	–	–	–	to	to	2 Sp.	
		–	–	–	–	13000	2 hr.		
ERLIN-JOHANNISTHAL.									
–	–	–	25.0/9800	–	–	16400	52 gal.	1 Sp.	Length over floats.
rior to 6B1.	–	–	25.0/9800	–	–	16400	52 gal.	1 Sp.	
–	–	5.6/6500	10.7/9800	16.11/13100	28.14/16400	26200	60 gal.	2 Sp.	Also 185 BMW.
G., BERLIN AND NÜRNBERG.									
formance similar to Nieuport 16 or 17.						–	–	1 Sp.	
–	–	6.11/9800	9.14/13100	14.17/1640	24.17/197000	26500	2 hr.	2 Sp.	200 Siemens Halske
–	–	3.7/6500	–	–	16.30/19700	21100	2 hr.	2 Sp.	
Y									
OLZANETA, GENOA AND TURIN.									
–	–	5.30/6500	8.0/10000	16.0/16000		26000	1½ hr.	2 V.	"Balilla."
–	–	1.40/3280	4.30/6500	8.10/10000	25.0/20000	22000	40 gal.	2 V.	"Primo."
–	–	2.30/3280	7.30/6500	12.0/10000	28.0/20000	20000	75 gal.	2 V.	
Performance inferior to landplane version						–	40 gal.	2 V.	Float Plane.
EUPORT, VARESE.									
–	–	3.30/3280	7.30/6500	12.30/10000	20.0/13120	15000	3 hr.	1 L. or V.	
–	–	3.30/3280	7.30/6500	10.3/10000	23.0/16400	17000	4 hr.	1 L. or V.	
–	–	2.15/3280	5.30/6500	14.15/13100	21.0/16400	17000	5 hr.	1-2 V.	
·	-	4.0/3280	7.30/6500	16.0/9800	–	-	–	Nil.	

Engines

Armament

Camouflage and Markings